2195

MORE ROMAN THAN ROME

Frontispiece to Richardson's Missal for the Laity 1845

More Roman than Rome: English Catholicism in the Nineteenth Century

J. Derek Holmes

Burns & Oates · London
Patmos Press · Shepherdstown

First published in Great Britain in 1978 by
Burns & Oates Limited, 2-10 Jerdan Place,
London SW6 5PT.

ISBN (UK) 0 86012 060 0

ISBN (USA) 0-915762-05-6
Library of Congress Catalog Card Number 77-92886

Printed and bound in Great Britain by Billing &
Sons Ltd of Guildford, London and Worcester
for Search Press Limited and Patmos Press

Downright, masculine, and decided Catholics
— more Roman than Rome, and more
ultramontane than the Pope himself — may
enter English society and be treated with
goodwill and respect everywhere, if only
they hold their own with self-respect and a
delicate consideration of what is due to others.[1]

Have we any right to take it strange, if, in
this English land, the spring-time of the
Church should turn out to be an English
spring, an uncertain, anxious time of hope
and fear, of joy and suffering, — of bright
promise and budding hopes, yet withal,
of keen blasts, and cold showers, and
sudden storms?[2]

Contents

		Page
List of illustrations		11
Introduction		13
Chapter I	The emancipation of English Catholics	19
Chapter II	Wiseman and the Roman restoration	55
Chapter III	Newman and the failure of Liberal Catholicism	111
Chapter IV	Manning and the establishment of Ultramontanism	155
Chapter V	Vaughan and the rise of Triumphalism	199
Conclusion	Prospect and retrospect: An English Spring?	249
Bibliography		259
Index		271

List of illustrations

Page

Frontispiece to Richardson's *Missal for
    the Laity* 1845   iv
John Henry Newman   12
William Ullathorne, as Bishop of Birmingham   18
Cardinal Wiseman   32
Pope Pius IX   54
"No Popery!"   80
Augustus Pugin   110
Interior of St George's Roman Catholic
    Cathedral as originally proposed by Pugin   138
Cardinal Manning   154
William Ward   166
Cardinal Vaughan   198
Cardinal Newman   228
Lord Acton   248

Acknowledgments

The author and publishers wish to thank the following for
permission to reproduce illustrations: National Portrait Gallery,
London (pages 110 and 154); Radio Times Hulton Picture
Library (pages 18 and 198); Mansell Collection (pages 12, 80,
166, 228 and 248).

John Henry Newman

Introduction

On the feast of the Immaculate Conception, 1869, some five years after the publication of the *Syllabus of Errors*, the first Vatican Council began. These three events reflected the success of the movement known as Ultramontanism and their significance, so obvious to later generations, was also recognised by some English contemporaries, Catholic and non-Catholic alike. The famous statesman, W.E. Gladstone, made a typically perceptive, if somewhat hostile and even alarmist comment:

> Between 1788 and 1829 the English Roman Catholics had slid all the way from rejection of Papal Infallibility to alleging merely that they were not bound to believe it. Between 1829 and 1874 the large majority of their laity have gone over, I fear, to what was in 1829 mainly a clerical belief among them. Unless some action is taken on behalf of conscience, another half century will reduce the whole to a dead level of Manningism.[3]

In Gladstone's opinion, the strength of Roman Catholicism in England at the time was 'wholly factitious and unnatural' since it had been caused by the reception of a remarkable body of converts who had brought the English Roman Catholics into contact with contemporary thought and culture. Nevertheless, the Catholic Church was still completely alienated from the life of the nation and the nineteenth-century converts would not be followed by others who were as able and significant. Gladstone therefore expressed his fears that the next generation of English Catholics would probably prove to be unintellectual Ultramontanes;

> For myself I lament all this deeply. It is impossible not to feel, objectively and historically, a strong interest in the *old* Anglo-Roman body. Suffering from proscription, and in close contact everywhere with an antagonistic system, it refused all extremes, and remained loyal in its adhesion, devout in religious duty, moderate and rational in its theological colour. All this is gone, and replaced by what Tennyson might call its 'loathsome opposite'.

Some English Catholics were also aware that the victory of Ultramontanism might have a detrimental effect on the life of the Church.

Bishop Goss of Liverpool, for instance, expected the Vatican Council to:

> change the patriarchal sceptre into a dictator's truncheon, and the Bishops who went to Rome as princes of the household to confer with their august Father will return like satraps dispatched to their provinces where they may find awaiting them for obedience the very decrees which they had refused to sanction in Council.[4]

The Bishop hoped that when further opposition became obviously useless, the opponents of the definition would leave Rome and by so doing provide another argument against recognising the assembly of bishops as an ecumenical council.

It is therefore hardly surprising that some of the issues raised by the development of Ultramontanism should dominate this survey of English Catholicism. The term Ultramontanism is used to describe that tendency within the Catholic Church which would centralize authority in the Roman See. It became a definite movement partly as a reaction against Gallicanism which attempted to restrict papal authority over national churches or local bishops. Following the French Revolution, however, Gallicanism became discredited by its associations with erastianism, schism or even heresy, and Ultramontanism spread rapidly. Originally the Ultramontane movement included Liberal Catholics who opposed the interference of the state in ecclesiastical affairs and who hoped that papal authority would enable the Church to meet the challenge of the age more effectively than rather conservative local hierarchies. But in time, the more authoritarian and reactionary forces came to dominate the movement and traditional as well as Liberal Catholics found themselves on the defensive.

Although it is hardly original to discuss English Catholicism during the nineteenth century under the obvious headings of Wiseman and Newman, Manning and Vaughan, these four cardinals so dominated the period that it is impossible to imagine the development of English Catholicism without them. Such an approach, however, is not without its dangers and I have tried to describe the external, national and international, background to the 'Catholic Question', before discussing various aspects of the internal life of the Church where it would certainly have been possible to arrange the material differently. A further difficulty is that of emphasising the role of individuals and the consequent temptation of making comparisons, at least implicitly. The general opinion that Newman was the greatest English Catholic among his contemporaries is understandable, but not inevitable. His obvious rivals in the present context were archbishops of Westminster and it is always difficult to do justice to administrators, if only because the faults of a system often seem more obvious to an historian than its virtues. Yet it is probably because the Church in England was led by such great men during the nineteenth century, that the same Church today still suffers in some ways from their limitations.

Of course, any attempt to cover the history of English Catholicism during the last century within the length of the present book inevitably involves a degree of arbitrary selection and the danger of an imbalance in the final result which is also open to criticism. No effort has been made, for example, to deal adequately with the development of the Catholic press except in the light of more general issues. Yet the Catholic magazines and newspapers which appeared during the nineteenth century are a most valuable and almost inexhaustible source of information. About fifty different Catholic magazines, some obviously more successful than others, began during the first half of the century when Catholic publishing shared the general expansion associated with the growth of lending libraries and which only ended with the success of the newspapers.[5] Even during the second half of the century, numerous magazines, pamphlets, official publications and even novels could be used to illustrate the development of Catholicism.

It has also proved impractical to cover all the extensive primary sources, but I have attempted to make full use of the secondary and often recently published material.[6] At the same time, I must express my appreciation, however inadequately, to the archivists and librarians who so kindly allowed me to use the books and documents in the archives of the archdioceses of Westminster and Birmingham, the dioceses of Clifton and Nottingham, the Birmingham Oratory and the Catholic Record Society, the University Library, St Edmund's and Fisher House, Cambridge, the English College, Rome, and St Edmund's, Ware, Upholland College and Ushaw College. I owe a particular debt of gratitude to Canon G.D. Sweeney and the late Fr Stephen Dessain. Later acknowledgments will reveal the extent of the generous help which I was fortunate enough to receive from these and other individuals, while thanks are also due to Miss Jean Bowes Gwatkin.

Ushaw College,   J. Derek Holmes
Durham

Notes

1. H.E. Manning, "The Work and the Wants of the Catholic Church in England", an article published in the *Dublin Review* new series I (1863) 162, and reprinted in his *Miscellanies* (London, 1877) I: 65-6.

2. J.H. Newman, "The Second Spring", a sermon preached at the first Provincial Synod of Westminster and reprinted in his *Sermons preached on various occasions* (London, 1900) 179-80.

3. W.E. Gladstone, *Correspondence on Church and Religion* (London, 1910) II: 61.

4. F.J. Cwiekowski, *The English Bishops and the First Vatican Council* (Louvain, 1971) 170.

5. See the lists in the *Tablet* 57 (1881) 139, 181, 220, 259-60, 301, 341-2, 380, 458.

6. Whenever original sources or contemporary publications have been used full details will usually be found in the notes, whereas the full details of other printed material will be found in the bibliography.

William Ullathorne, as Bishop of Birmingham

Chapter I: The emancipation of English Catholics

The history of the Church in the nineteenth century must be seen against the background of three of the greatest revolutions of all time. The consequences and the implications of the American and the French Revolutions tended to dominate political developments, while social and economic conditions increasingly reflected the progress of the Industrial Revolution. England was the first country to be immediately or directly affected by all three revolutions, though their ultimate effects on the political, social and economic life of mankind were fundamental and universal in spite of regional or chronological variations. But although the political and economic revolutions of the eighteenth century eventually and inevitably transformed relations between Church and State throughout the world, their immediate effect in England was to delay the movement towards civil and religious liberty.

The Agricultural and Industrial Revolutions led to social and economic problems, and an increasing association of political and social reform with the Dissenting Churches. This development was linked with the growing conflict of interest between urban industrialists and rural landowners in which the Nonconformist Churches tended to be identified with the former and the Established Anglican Church with the latter. As a consequence of the revolution in France the British Government began to suspect that all members of social or political reform groups were potential revolutionaries and once England was at war with France, these conservative fears ensured that the reform of religious or political grievances would be delayed or refused and their advocates subjected to further repression. Supporters of political or religious reform could be condemned both as traitors and enemies of religion, and the prejudices which had been created during the war continued even after it.

It seemed inexpedient to grant concessions to disaffected groups when the enemies of religion were conquering Europe. In 1790, for example, Charles James Fox argued in favour of repealing the Test and Corporation Acts which effectively excluded Nonconformists from taking part in central and local government. Edmund Burke would have supported this move ten years earlier, but having witnessed the destruction of the French Church and nation, he became convinced that English Nonconformists were to some extent associated with the forces of revolution and subversion, and he refused to tolerate any further concessions. The Catholic Relief Acts of 1791 and 1793 were not necessarily exceptions to this general pattern, but might also be seen as evidence that it was possible to give support even to English Roman Catholics when European religion and civilization seemed in danger of collapse. As Philip Howard later pointed out in an address to the Anglican bishops:

> In such an awful crisis, it is surely an incumbent duty on every man who has any remaining zeal for the religion of Christ, to set aside all controversial differences, and, with that brotherly love so constantly urged by its divine author, to unite in the defence of the common cause.[1]

A few of the French clergy and laity who found refuge in England from 1791 until the beginning of the nineteenth century also helped to strengthen the Catholic Church in parts of England and to modify some of the prejudices of Protestant Englishmen. However many of them were no help at all and some of them proved positively harmful so that it is an exaggeration to claim that 'The building up of the Catholic Church in England began when the French priests got down to fulfilling their apostolic responsibilities'.[2] The first bishop to flee from France landed in England on 3 March, 1791, and the first wave of clerical exiles included about three thousand priests and some sixteen bishops. Hundreds of French priests arrived in London and were able to walk unmolested in the streets of the city only a dozen years after the Gordon riots. Other groups of French priests were to be found in Lewes, Winchester, Carshalton, Guildford, Farnham, Bath and Bristol, while a few ventured into the Midland and Northern Districts.

By 1797, there were about five and a half thousand priests and almost six thousand laymen exiled in the United Kingdom. Many of them received financial support from the British Government as well as from voluntary collections and the Oxford University Press produced an edition of the Vulgate, but not the Roman Breviary, for their use. French priests helped to establish missions at Brighton and Southampton, Chelsea and Tottenham, while there were no less than eight French chapels in London itself. At the beginning of 1800, some five and a half thousand French priests were receiving help from the Relief Committee, but about a tenth of these had returned to France by the end of November. During the following year, another two thousand priests returned and by the end of 1802, only nine hundred priests remained and several French churches in London were closed. Nevertheless, some priests and laymen decided to stay and the French influence remained strong in their London congregations for some time to come, manifesting itself in their patterns of devotion as well as in the profession of their faith, though in due course this would be largely superseded. The Abbé Jean Jacques Morel, for example, settled in Hampshire during 1796, where he spent the remaining fifty-six years of his life and although his original congregation was almost entirely French, it gradually became increasingly English over the years.

Another consequence of the French Revolution was that English Catholic institutions as well as French religious congregations sought refuge in England. Many of these moves were made very reluctantly and sometimes at the cost of considerable sacrifices which even seemed to threaten the very existence of the institutions concerned. Nevertheless the reestablishment of some forty religious houses, schools and seminaries previously scattered throughout Europe would eventually prove to be an important factor in the transformation of the Catholic Church in England during the nineteenth century. Had it not been for the Revolution, it is doubtful whether these various establishments would have returned to England at that time, while the provisions of the Act in 1791 forbidding the foundation of colleges or convents in England might well have been enforced. As it was, when Sir Henry Mildmay introduced a hostile Monastic Institutions Bill in 1800, the Bishop of Rochester prevented the measure from passing through the House of Lords.

Meanwhile, the English Catholic community also reflected the increasing impact and consequent tensions of the Agrarian and Industrial Revolutions which provided opportunities for some Catholics, the bold and the fortunate, to succeed, though others, the unlucky and the less adventurous, might fail. The Catholic gentry had a good record for adopting agricultural improvements in the past, if only because this enabled them to cope more easily with the fines imposed upon them. But not all of them were financially able to take advantage of the various enclosures which could often prove extremely costly. The Catholic gentry in the seventeenth century had a solid tradition of industrial enterprise in iron-forging, coal-mining, glass-making and soap-making. The Brookes of Madeley began the first iron forges at Coalbrookdale, the Duke of Norfolk owned Sheffield, Worksop and Glossop as well as other properties in Lancashire, while the Earl of Shrewsbury received increasing sums of 'unearned income' from the 'Black Country'.

Although by 1830, the number of Catholic peers had declined, those who survived were generally well-off and self-assured; economic developments would increase their large fortunes, while their numbers would be reinforced by converts from Anglicanism.

Although the Old Catholic community would be transformed beyond recognition after 1850, it has been argued that the period from 1800 marked 'a golden age of the English mission'[3] which achieved an unequalled measure of success. By 1800, the Catholic clergy had established an organisation of men and resources, however limited, which enabled them to cope more successfully than the Anglican clergy with the great transition which was taking place in the country. From about 1770 until 1850, the Catholic community dramatically changed; numbers multiplied about ten times and the rural population slowly declined, as the urban population of Catholics rapidly and sometimes dramatically increased. The number of Catholics was increasing, not simply as a result of the population explosion and economic developments, but also because of the efforts which the clergy had been putting into the task of popular catechising since about 1700. This numerical and geographical transformation inevitably resulted in occupational and social transformation as gentry, farmers and agricultural labourers were replaced by professional men and business men, mechanics and industrial workers.

Catholics seem to have played only a small part in the inventive and technological development of industry between 1760 and 1830. Catholics occupied a bigger but still modest place among the industrial entrepreneurs, though a Catholic was the first chairman of the consortium which established the Stockton and Darlington Railway, and members of another Catholic family were associates of George and Robert Stephenson. Many Catholics, however, owned workshops in the textile, pottery, steel, iron and glassmaking industries, and a few in the soap, furniture, distillery, metalwork and flax-spinning industries. Many other Catholics seized the opportunities offered in trade, business and banking. Catholic tradesmen who wished to succeed were forced to move from supplying the needs of their aristocratic co-religionists into the tough world of general competition. Inn-keeping had always proved to be one of the staple occupations of Catholics who, with the improvement in communications, now provided the post-horses and coaching-services which were needed. Finally, between 1760 and 1830, the number of Catholic lawyers and doctors, already relatively large, multiplied.

The changes which were taking place can best be seen in the expanding industrial towns. In 1770, local Catholics celebrated Mass in the house of the owner of the first cotton spinning factory in Blackburn. A public chapel was established first in 1773 and then in 1781 and the somewhat ambiguous position of Catholics at the time might be indicated by the fact that it was thought necessary to appoint beadles armed with staves to prevent interruptions from unfriendly visitors. Yet these same beadles wore uniforms of blue cloth and red facings with a cape covering their shoulders which hardly suggests that they adopted a particularly retiring attitude. The local Catholics were to be found in most of the trades and occupations associated with industrialization. Some of them were able to join the *nouveaux riches* by seizing the opportunities offered during the Industrial Revolution. One local Catholic established an engineering and foundry business in 1794, while another was a partner in a firm which, at least in part, leased its mill from the Archbishop of Canterbury. A hand loom weaver from Chorley was the grandfather of a prosperous solicitor and a successful doctor who were practising in the middle of the nineteenth century.

At this time, Catholics seemed to be able to make progress in the legal or medical professions without losing their sense of community or suffering from increasing social divisions and in spite of the rapid growth of the congregation, Catholics in the Blackburn area continued to form a closely knit community. By the middle of the nineteenth century, however, although Catholics could still move from trade to the professions within a generation and continued to take their parochial duties very seriously, there is evidence of increasing social divisions among them which possibly reflected the situation in the country as a whole as well as changes in local conditions. At the same time, Catholics at the beginning of the century were hardly isolated from the life of the local community. Local newspapers were increasingly sympathetic in reporting Catholic news and Protestants attended Catholic Charity Sermons. The self-confidence of Catholics in Blackburn can be illustrated by the fact that they built a large new Church in a prominent position in the town during the years immediately before Catholic Emancipation and from the publicity given to the celebrations associated with its opening in the local press. In such an area, the passing of the Emancipation Act would arouse little hostility.

The transformation of English Catholicism at the turn of the century was inevitably accompanied by a shift in the balance of power within the community from the aristocracy and the gentry to the clergy or more specifically to the episcopacy. The various bodies which came into existence to represent the interests of the English Catholics between 1778 and 1829 illustrate the changing balance of power in the community as a whole. The Catholic Committees of the eighteenth century were almost exclusively formed from the ranks of the laity, the aristocracy and the gentry, whose interests tended to lie in the midlands and the south. This provoked a reaction which would eventually unite those members of the clergy, classes and regions who had felt excluded and by 1791, the bishops were strong enough to take political action themselves in order to ensure that the Relief Bill did not simply represent the views of the Committee. The Catholic aristocracy and gentry could no longer successfully claim to determine the relations between the Catholic community and the outside world. *The Catholic Board* formed in 1808 to agitate for political rights included the vicars apostolic and representatives from the clergy and the laity in the north of England. By 1820, Bishop John Milner, the intransigent and hostile opponent of the English Cisalpines, was able to win support from the Irish and the increasing number of Irish immigrants for his policy of securing the political rights of Catholics without making any concessions to the English Government. When Milner died in 1826, it had become obvious that the aristocracy and gentry were no longer in a position to oppose effectively the extension of episcopal, and in due course Roman, jurisdiction.

It is often argued that the controversial literature at the time of Catholic Emancipation illustrates the fact that the expression of radical political opinion had been muted as a result of the events of the French Revolution. On the whole, the controversy tended to be theological or apologetic rather than political and the usual arguments in favour of Catholic Emancipation were those of expediency rather than principle. Roman Catholics at the time would not wish to associate their claims with more radical political demands, while their social and political isolation during the previous century would in due course be reflected in their reluctance to seize the opportunities which became open to them after Emancipation. However, even the most cursory reading of contemporary Catholic periodicals would illustrate that none of these historical claims are supported by the evidence. Obviously, many Catholics did not wish to be associated with political radicals and were neither prepared nor equipped to indulge in political activities following the grant of Emancipation. But as early as 1812, Bishop Thomas Smith was apprehensive of the 'mischief' arising from the meetings of the *Friends of Religious Liberty* in which, he claimed, many Catholics seemed to join 'and to make themselves conspicuous'. He questioned what they meant by 'general liberty of Conscience', a principle which he felt 'may be certainly carried to unwarrantable lengths'.[4]

The point is that Catholics were divided on the political implications as well as the best means of securing their civil and religious demands. Some of them made fervent and even obsequious protestations of loyalty:

God is our witness with what sincerity and fervour we pray that the British Constitution and the reign of the illustrious House of Brunswick over us may last for ever, and that our august and beloved Prince Regent's sway may daily increase in happiness and glory.

During the following year, the same magazine reported the 'atrocious' attempt which had been made on the 'sacred person' of the Regent; this was described as an example of the efforts being made to inflame public opinion among 'the labouring classes' which 'would inevitably plunge the country into the horrors of a French Revolution!!' Some Catholics had earlier associated the penal legislation in force against them with the repressive legislation adopted as a result of the French Revolution, but later Catholic demands for reform were carefully distinguished from the events which had occurred in France.[5]

At the same time, the great historian, John Lingard, explicitly referred to events in America:

If then, the authority of those who framed the American constitution, be of any weight, let it be taken entire, and it will be found to contain the most pointed condemnation of all that for which the anti-catholics contend.

As he later explained,

In the United States, the Catholic Clergy perform their sacred functions, and exercise their spiritual authority without molestation. The government meddles not with the appointment of their bishops, or their correspondence with foreign prelates. In the eye of the law, every creed is equal. No one is singled out as a particular object of jealousy and restriction. As long as religion interferes not with the civil power, the civil power interferes not with religion.[7]

Other Catholics identified their demands with the claims of civil and religious liberty, and raised the question of political reform. On more than one occasion, Catholics were encouraged to make a calculated appeal to public opinion and to demand 'a rational reform in the commons house of parliament',[8] while those Catholics who supported a closer identification of religious and political reform joined the *Friends of Civil and Religious Liberty*. The local *Catholic Association* in

Preston received little support from the 'respectable' classes and became more 'popular'; its proceedings became so irregular 'in entertaining political and other objectionable questions' that 'it was deemed most prudent to dissolve the Association'. However, it was still proposed, unsuccessfully in the event,

> That this Committee, viewing with the deepest concern the present perilous state of the kingdom, do most earnestly exhort the Catholics of every class, to come forward, as Englishmen, and join their fellow-countrymen, of all denominations, in calling for a Constitutional Reform of the Commons' House of Parliament, embracing a restoration of civil rights to every Briton without distinction of creed.[9]

During the struggle for Emancipation, the Catholic Question inevitably became part of the Irish Question since the British Government was directly responsible for Irish Catholics who formed more than a third of the total population of England and Wales. This was the background to the threat made by Sydney Smith:

> Whatever your opinion may be of the follies of the Roman Catholic religion, remember they are the follies of four millions of human beings, increasing rapidly in numbers, wealth, and intelligence, who, if firmly united to this country, would set at defiance the power of France, and if once wrested from their allegiance with England, would in three years render its existence as an independent nation absolutely impossible.[10]

Although English Catholics had secured measures of relief before 1829, it is highly unlikely that they could have achieved full emancipation at this time. Individual Englishmen might support the movement towards civil and religious liberty, but the grant of Catholic Emancipation was a political settlement resulting from the situation in Ireland which explains both the repression of the later seventeenth century and the concessions in the early nineteenth century. On both occasions, Irish Catholics threatened the unity and security of Britain, and they were able to exert greater political pressure on the British Government than their English co-religionists.

During the war with France, the Society of United Irishmen, most of whose members were northern Presbyterians, encouraged a French invasion of Ireland. Catholics, on the other hand, hoped that their loyalty might win concessions and by the Franchise Act of 1793, they were given the vote on the same conditions as Protestants. This increased political influence was even more important later because there were more forty shilling county freeholders in Ireland than in England. However, further relief was not immediately forthcoming and as a result Catholics tended to support the United Irishmen during the rebellion of 1798. When this was suppressed, William Pitt hoped to end any future threat by uniting Ireland with England, a policy which had previously proved effective in the case of Scotland. Irish Catholics in general did not oppose this policy because it seemed that an English Parliament would be more likely to grant Catholic Emancipation than an Irish Parliament which merely represented the Protestant Ascendancy. Furthermore, Pitt had also given the impression which was interpreted as a pledge, that the Act of Union would be followed by Catholic Emancipation. The King, however, refused to violate his coronation oath and Pitt resigned. When he was again appointed to the position of Prime Minister in 1804, it was on the condition that he would not raise the question of Catholic Emancipation.

Inevitably Irish demands included national grievances and the Irish tended to be more 'popular' or 'radical' than many of the English Catholics. The English Catholic aristocracy and gentry were simply interested in political emancipation, whereas the Irish Catholics who already had the vote were also concerned with the future of the Irish nation and the Established Protestant Church of Ireland. A meeting of English and Irish Catholics at the beginning of 1810 brought some of these divisions into the open and for a time they ceased to work together. It was in this context that Lord Stourton is reported to have exclaimed: 'What have we to do with the Irish? We have nothing to do with them but to pray for them'.[11] The basic divisions centred on the means to be adopted in an effort to secure Emancipation and the 'securities' or guarantees which Catholics might be prepared to give in order to maintain the Protestant Establishment. Two parties emerged. Those Catholics who were prepared to accept conditions were opposed by a more popular movement demanding unconditional Emancipation and this party was ultimately successful not only in Ireland, but even in England.

The most controversial proposal was that of allowing the British Government a veto over the election of Catholic bishops. The Irish were especially opposed to this guarantee and Daniel O'Connell, Secretary of the General Committee, became the leader of the anti-vetoist party. In 1813, a Bill which included a long Cisalpine oath and provision for a veto was even approved by the Roman authorities, but it was rejected by Irish Catholics; 'I am sincerely a Catholic', O'Connell remarked, 'but I am not a Papist'. Two years later, the Pope suggested a further compromise involving a modified veto. This was accepted by the English vicars apostolic, but O'Connell bitterly attacked them and described Dr Poynter as 'Poynter by name, but Spaniel by nature'.[12]

Catholic Emancipation was largely a result of the political pressure which Catholics in Ireland, unlike those in England, could exert on the British Government. But this interpretation of events must not be allowed to under-estimate the significant contribution made by English Catholics particularly in the work of educating public opinion to the point that it was prepared to accept Catholic Emancipation at least as a solution to a political crisis in Ireland. Edward Blount, secretary of the *Catholic Association* in England, himself replied to the claim:

> that the English Catholics are few in number, and insignificant in the scale of national importance. Nothing can be more untrue − nearly a million of men spread through the various classes of society; some adorning the very highest; many possessing large properties, and all, in their respective situations, deserving honour and esteem, never can be unimportant, unless they forget themselves.

On the invidious comparisons made with the Irish Catholics, he retorted:

> Our stake is not less than theirs, nor are our means inferior to theirs. They have the advantages of numbers, no doubt; but we are at the seat of Government, inter-mixed with every class of society . . . and possess a facility for grappling with the public mind which they do not.[13]

The description of the Old Catholic community as a *gens lucifuga*,[14] so enthusiastically endorsed by the later Ultramontanes, seriously underestimated the extent to which Catholics could overcome the disabilities of penal legislation as well as their ability to fight for their civil and religious rights. Many of the penalties and restrictions theoretically in force against Catholics could in practice be reduced to inconveniences or irritations. In theory, Catholics were excluded from a military career, the legal profession and from politics. But many Catholics found service in foreign armies and could legally serve in Hanoverian or Hessian regiments on British pay. In the later part of the eighteenth century, Captain Edward Huddleston and Major Richard Huddleston were in the Cambridge Militia, William John Mawhood was a lieutenant in North America, while Henry Howard of Corby, after a lifetime of effort and too old for field service, ended as a captain in the West Yorkshire Militia.[15] Until the Relief Act of 1791, Catholics could not be called to the Bar, but according to Lord Eldon, who was trained in conveyancing by a Catholic, Catholics formed the cream of that branch of the profession.[16] James Booth, a conveyancer, acted for Lord Temple during the 1750s and Charles Butler, Secretary of the Catholic Committee, even acted as an unofficial agent of the Crown; in 1779, he prepared Lord Sandwich's defence of the Admiralty's administration of Greenwich Hospital.

The fact of property was often more important than penal legislation or political restrictions and as a result of inter-marriage as well as a period of unprecedented agricultural prosperity, many of the Catholic gentry were extremely wealthy. The social and economic status of the Petres or the Norfolks guaranteed their political influence and significance. They were able to nominate Members of Parliament to the 'rotten' boroughs under their influence or control and by 1809, the Petres had given some £15,000 to Whig election campaigns. Catholic names appeared on voting registers and they were sometimes able to vote, though this would depend on the attitude, particularly the political attitude, of the returning officer involved, and whether local officials actually required them to take the necessary oaths. Of course, it was in the interests of Catholics themselves as well as those who helped or employed them, not to reveal the extent to which they were able to evade the legal restrictions technically in force against them. There were several obvious reasons to explain why Catholics emphasised their 'grievances'; sometimes as an excuse for inefficiency or laziness, but mostly as part of their propaganda campaign to secure 'relief' from the 'intolerable' measures to which they were subjected.

In order to secure relief from their grievances, the Old Catholics published tracts, wrote to the press, organised petitions and made use of their social contacts and personal friendships. These personal friendships were especially important and they also enabled the Catholic gentry to influence and take part in the social, economic and political life of the country which they felt to be their right as gentlemen. The Anglican Puseys of Pusey, for example, were on the friendliest terms with the Roman Catholic Throckmortons of Buckland whose domestic chaplain in the 1760s was regarded as the friend and natural ally of the Anglican rector of Bletchley. John Lingard, one of the last representatives of the Cisalpine tradition, was a close friend of the local Anglican parson in Hornby, while a Protestant contemporary described the late Edward Weld as being

of an agreeable person, sweet, modest, and humane temper; easy, affable, and obliging behaviour. He lived in great credit and hospitality, and maintained a good correspondence and harmony with the neighbouring gentry; nor did difference in opinion create any reserve or distance. His charity and generosity were not confined to those of his own persuasion, but universal; and his character, in every social relation of life, truly amiable. Though he ever behaved as a peaceable subject, he was ordered into custody in 1745, on account of his name being mentioned in a treasonable anonymous letter, dropped near Poole — a malicious piece of villany, which none but a bigot and zealot would practise; and which will endanger the life, fortune, and reputation of the most blameless and inoffensive. An immediate and honourable discharge was a most convincing proof of his innocence. His worth, and the favours I received from him, demand this testimony of my respect and gratitude to the memory of a friend.[17]

At the beginning of the nineteenth century, however, the English Catholics were increasingly divided both socially and politically. The Old Catholic aristocracy and gentry tended to be moderate and conservative in their approach and demands, whereas the rising professional and middle classes, mechanics and workers were inclined to support more radical and popular reforms. Correspondents in Catholic periodicals began to criticise the 'indifference' of the Catholic aristocracy and there were attacks on the Corn Laws and the Game Laws, taxes and tithes, franchises and sinecures at a meeting held in Wigan. The *Catholic Board* was still largely influenced by the gentry who paid an annual subscription of five guineas; it was a model of restraint and moderation in advancing the Catholic claims. But the development of the *Catholic Association* illustrated that the interests of the Catholic middle class who were tempted to unite the cause of emancipation with that of political reform were not necessarily the same as those of their more aristocratic co-religionists.

In 1823, O'Connell and R.L. Sheil revived the *Catholic Association*. The *Association* was not immediately successful either in Ireland or in England and some measures of relief were introduced between 1823 and 1824 quite independently. But it was to have a great influence on English politics during the next six years and eventually secured the passing of Catholic Emancipation. In June, 1823, the *Catholic Board* was succeeded by the *Catholic Association*. Edward Blount, the Secretary of the *Association*, was a member of the gentry and wished to restrict membership by charging a 'rent' of a guinea. However, less wealthy Catholics were in their turn able to follow the example of the

Irish and a group of mechanics in Stockport who collected a guinea so that one of their number could become a member of the *Association*. These more radical members were more willing than the Catholic nobility or gentry to follow the example of the Irish *Association* and to adopt more direct and energetic policies in an effort to achieve their aims.

In Ireland, the *Association* was supported by a 'Catholic Rent' of a penny a month which enabled it to defend its members from oppression and to prosecute those who injured the person or property of Catholic priests. The *Association* not only published its own tracts and helped to establish the *Truthteller*, but replied to attacks in the anti-Catholic newspapers and subsidised pro-Catholic publications. Catholics were now able to support more effectively those Protestant Members of Parliament committed to Catholic Emancipation and to organise petitions to Parliament. O'Connell himself took care to keep the English informed by inserting the *Association's* important business as advertisements in English newspapers. He encouraged English Catholics to form their own *Associations* and branches quickly spread especially in Lancashire.

The *Association* in England also bought space in magazines and newspapers to advertise the Catholic claims; advertisements and addresses were stitched into magazines like the *Edinburgh* and the *Quarterly*. The *Association* publicized the philanthropy of wealthy Catholics such as the Duke of Norfolk when he laid the foundation stone of an Anglican Church or Lord Petre who subsidized the decoration of another and Sir Edward Vavasour whose quarries provided material for the reconstruction of York Minster. In 1826, well over 100,000 copies of the famous *Declaration* and *Address* were printed and distributed to newspapers, periodicals and reading rooms throughout the country. The *Association* took advantage of the improved means of communication and used such focal points as churches and chapels, taprooms and coffee houses to circulate Catholic propaganda. In 1826, the Catholics of Salford and Manchester distributed 14,000 tracts, the *Metropolitan Defence Society* distributed another 15,000 handbills, while in Newcastle and Bristol, Norwich and Warrington, Sheffield and Canterbury, the *Friends of Civil and Religious Liberty* printed and circulated a flood of material in support of the Catholic claims.

The main difficulty facing Catholics and their supporters was that few political leaders were sufficiently convinced of the importance of Catholic Emancipation to be willing to antagonize the social and political

31

Cardinal Wiseman

forces ranged against it. George III and George IV were convinced that Catholic Emancipation could not be reconciled with the coronation oath. At the other political and social extreme, 'King Mob' could always be relied upon to answer the call of 'no popery'. Even many sensible men were hostile to Catholic Emancipation as a result of their conviction that the Revolution of 1688 had brought about the freedom and greatness of Britain, and because of their respect for the stability of English historical institutions. To such men, persecution might be intolerable, but justice meant fair treatment in the courts, not political equality.

Furthermore, at this time, party divisions were confused and political issues could not be identified with party differences. Members of Parliament voted according to their own convictions and interests on every issue, but especially on the Catholic Question. In any case, although supporters of the Catholics often secured majorities in the Commons, their opponents enjoyed the favour of the King and the Lords, and neither group could form a stable government without the other. It was therefore agreed in 1812 that ministers should be free to express their own opinions, while the Government itself adopted a policy of neutrality on demands for Emancipation. This agreement allowed minor concessions to be made to Catholics, but at the same time ensured that it was politically impossible to grant full Emancipation. Supporters and opponents of the Catholic claims had to work with each other, so the issue of Emancipation was left unresolved.

In 1821, the Lords' refusal to pass further relief proposals was significant for several reasons. In the first place, it was becoming obvious that Catholics could only succeed if they were strong and united. This conviction was reinforced by the fact that although Catholic supporters had secured a majority in the Commons for the first time since 1813, it became impossible to repeat this success two years later. By 1823, many prominent supporters of the Catholic claims had joined the Government and were therefore bound to accept the political compromise in spite of their personal convictions. This stalemate could only be broken by a powerful and external pressure. A third factor influencing the general situation between 1822 and 1827 was that the reaction which had followed the war with France was declining; the 'Liberal Tories' were repealing repressive measures and granting limited reforms.

Supporters of Catholic Emancipation were always conscious of the fact that at least part of the reason for the opposition to the Catholic claims resulted from popular misconceptions or misrepresentations of

Catholic beliefs and practices. Opponents expressed their doubts about the political loyalties of 'papists' and accused Catholics of not keeping faith with heretics or believing in exclusive salvation; accusations which reflected traditional Protestant suspicions of Roman Catholicism. Catholics were corrupt, intolerant and idolatrous, in spite of Lord Binning's protest that 'it was not civil to call people idolaters; particularly when it happened not to be true'.[18] The opponents of Catholic Emancipation also used arguments based on the alliance of Church and State — England's 'Protestant Constitution' or 'Our Happy Constitution in Church and State'.[19] Catholic Emancipation was considered to be incompatible with the Bill of Rights, the Act of Settlement, the Union with Ireland and the coronation oath taken by the King to support the Anglican Church by law established. Yet if the argument descended to defending the Protestant Ascendancy, Catholics could be scathing;

> those who affect so great an alarm for the Protestant ascendancy in both houses of parliament, betray a very mean opinion of the goodness of the Protestant cause, opposed as a system of religion against the Catholic system, by supposing that Catholics, if admitted to the common rights of society, will ever be able to outweigh them, who now count their thousands where we count our hundreds.[20]

Specific answers and proposals were made by Catholic apologists in order to reply to Protestant difficulties. While Catholics admitted that some popes might have occasionally exceeded their spiritual authority in intervening in secular affairs, they maintained that this was not part of their Catholic belief and pointed out that,

> the most zealous Catholics in former periods treated this stretch of papal power as an usurpation. Our Catholic ancestors, and particularly the Gallican clergy under the monarchy, were ever the most formidable opposers of this pretended jurisdiction of the Pope in the civil concerns of states.[21]

Expressions of support from non-Catholics, especially from non-Catholic clergymen, were gratefully recorded in the Catholic press.[22] One of the earliest of these apologists was the Whig cleric Sydney Smith. In an obvious attempt to answer some of the constitutional and practical difficulties which had been raised, he commented that 'Gog and Magog have produced as much influence on human affairs as the Pope has done this half century past', and he expressed the hope that Catholic priests might be tamed by receiving Government salaries on the grounds that 'all men gradually yield to the comforts of a good income'.[23]

In due course, the vicars apostolic were asked to prepare a formal statement of Catholic belief on the points in dispute and particularly on the question of allegiance to a Protestant ruler. In 1826, the Catholic bishops issued a *Declaration* that Catholics held no principles or opinions incompatible

> with all the civil duties which, as subjects, they owe to their sovereign and the constituted civil government of their country; and with all the social duties which as citizens, they owe to their fellow-subjects, whatever may be their religious creed.

There were eleven sections in the *Declaration* including discussions 'On the Charge of Idolatry and Superstition', 'On the Doctrine of Exclusive Salvation', 'On Keeping Faith with Heretics', and 'On allegiance to our Sovereign and obedience to the Pope'. In this last section, the bishops distinguished between civil and spiritual authority. Neither the pope nor any other ecclesiastical authority could directly or indirectly interfere with civil duties nor try to enforce spiritual obligations by secular means. Catholics could not be dispensed from their obligations in conscience to obey 'the civil government of this realm'.

> Hence we declare, that by rendering obedience in *spiritual* matters to the Pope, Catholics do not withhold any portion of their allegiance to their King, and that their allegiance is entire and undivided; the *civil* power of the state, and the *spiritual* authority of the Catholic church, being absolutely distinct, and being never intended by their Divine Author to interfere or clash with each other.[24]

The Irish bishops made a similar *Declaration* and the Catholic laity added an *Address* which was adopted at the annual general meeting of the *Catholic Association*. The authors of the *Address* consciously and explicitly appealed to the 'liberal' and 'enlightened', deplored the use of force or persecution by members of any religion and recommended that the principles of religious freedom should be adopted in Catholic as well as in Protestant countries. The penal legislation and prejudices of the British people were described as an unparalleled example to the enemies of liberty throughout the world.

> Bearing equally with you our fellow subjects, the burthens of the country, and upholding equally its institutions, and its glory we claim to be admitted to a full participation in all the rights of British subjects. – Every principle or practice hostile, in the remotest

degree, to those institutions, we most explicitly disclaim. Year after year we repeat the humiliating task of disavowal; still we suffer the penalties of guilt. We ask you is this to endure for ever? Are we always to remain the victims of misplaced suspicion? The doors of the Constitution are shut against us, as long as we continue true to the dictates of our consciences; but if we abandon the Faith of our fathers, resign every honourable feeling, and become perjured men and apostates, then are all our disqualifications removed; the sanctuary of the British Constitution is thrown open to us; we become senators, privy-counsellors, nay, guardians of the morals of the people, and dispensers of public justice! God forbid we should purchase such distinctions, however valuable, at the price of dishonour. In the hour of danger, when our country needs it, we mingle our blood with yours. We desire no ascendancy, religious or political. If our country falls, we ask to fall with her; if she prospers, we claim to share her prosperity.[25]

Over the years, several measures were suggested apart from the provision of clerical salaries as means of securing the loyalty of the Catholic clergy and laity. In spite of his opposition to the veto, O'Connell himself was quite prepared to compromise in an effort to achieve his main aim of political emancipation. In 1825, for example, he agreed to two such 'securities', the disfranchisement of the Irish pauper forty-shilling freeholders as well as the payment of Catholic priests by the British Government. The King and the Lords, however, again opposed the relief proposals and it seemed impossible to form a Ministry committed to Catholic Emancipation. Nevertheless, it was after the failure of these measures that the Prime Minister declared, 'the *crisis* cannot be averted for many months ... Whenever the *crisis does* come, the Protestants must go to the *wall'.*[26] There was a general election in the following year and although a candidate who supported Catholic Emancipation was at a disadvantage, he was usually elected if his other views were acceptable and he himself personally popular. Anti-Catholicism was not sufficiently strong or co-ordinated to influence the election as a whole. 'No popery' might be widespread in the country and there was in fact a small anti-Catholic majority in the new parliament, yet even in the forthcoming crisis, anti-Catholicism was not sufficiently organised or united to be effective.

The increasingly liberal policies adopted by the Tory Government encouraged the Nonconformists to press for the repeal of the Test and Corporation Acts. A Bill releasing Protestant Dissenters from the obligation of subscribing to the Thirty-nine Articles and receiving the Sacrament on being appointed to public office received the royal assent in May, 1828. One of the arguments raised against granting this concession was that it would inevitably and immediately be followed by Catholic Emancipation and it was certainly a moral boost to the Catholic cause. The first precedent against the old notion of the Constitution had been established and Lord John Russell commented,

> It is really a gratifying thing to force the enemy to give up his first line, that none but Churchmen are worthy to serve the State, and I think we shall soon make him give up the second, that none but Protestants are. Peel is a very pretty hand at hauling down his colours.[27]

Supporters of Catholic Emancipation took advantage of the successful Bill in favour of the Nonconformists to introduce the same parliamentary motion on Catholic relief which had been rejected in 1827. This time it was carried by six votes, though it was subsequently rejected by the Lords. Thus the House of Commons seemed balanced in favour of Emancipation at the moment when events were moving out of its control

The views of Lord Wellington, Leader of the Government, were identified with those of King George IV, the Tories and the Protestant Ascendancy. The chief member of his Cabinet was 'Orange Peel' who was generally considered to be the leading anti-Catholic in the Commons and an opponent of any concession to Irish nationalism. Even Peel, however, was becoming convinced of the necessity and inevitability of reform. He had already made some concessions to English Catholics, adopted more liberal political views and was in any case too moderate to identify himself with the extreme Protestants with whom he was about to break on the Catholic Question. Consequently, when Peel and Wellington were faced with Irish demands, a divided Cabinet and a Commons' majority in favour of reform, they quickly decided to settle the issue once and for all.

William Huskisson, one of the more liberal members of the Cabinet, offered to resign over an issue of parliamentary reform. Wellington eagerly accepted this resignation which was followed by others, in order to change his Cabinet. This move was generally regarded as a triumph for the extremists, but some contemporaries, including Huskisson himself, were apparently convinced that Wellington was hoping to win the neutrality if not the support of the extreme Tories in settling the Catholic Question without splitting the party. However, Wellington's speeches and actions were governed by his desire not to alienate the extreme Protestants, by his ignorance of what the opponents of the Catholic claims might do, and by his doubts about the attitude of a reluctant King. In the event, therefore, his intentions were so obscure that both extreme Protestants and Irish Catholics felt certain that he would never grant Emancipation.

As a result, the *Catholic Association* decided to oppose the election of any candidate who supported the Government. William Vesey Fitzgerald who had consistently supported Catholic Emancipation had to seek re-election in County Clare on his appointment as a new member of the Cabinet. Irish Catholics at first simply tried to find another Protestant supporter of Emancipation to stand against him, but when their invitations were refused, O'Connell decided to stand himself. By this act, Catholics consciously rejected the constitutional means they had previously adopted in favour of a more revolutionary approach; a Catholic was prevented by law from taking his seat in Parliament. From the first day of the poll, it became evident that Fitzgerald was fighting a losing battle and O'Connell was elected with a majority of just over a thousand or a third of the votes. Catholics drummed the message home:

> No longer, dear V-sey, feel hurt and uneasy
> At hearing it said by thy Treasury brother,
> That thou art a sheet of blank paper, my V-sey,
> And he, the dear, innocent placeman, another.
>
> For, lo, what a service we, Irish, have done thee; —
> Thou now art a sheet of blank paper no more;
> By St. Patrick, we've scrawl'd such a lesson upon thee
> As never was scrawl'd upon foolscap before.[28]

Clearly, it was now impossible to promote an Irish member of parliament to the Cabinet or give a peerage without creating a similar situation. A general election might result in the return of many Catholics unable to take their seats at Westminster which might lead to the existence of an unofficial Irish Parliament or even proposals to end the Union. Irish demands for Catholic Emancipation were already being associated with popular democratic claims and might easily be identified with the forces of a nationalist revolution. Thus, in order to avoid rebellion, to restore law and order, and to remove the threat to the Tory Government, Wellington and Peel decided to introduce a Relief Bill. In announcing this change of policy, Peel felt obliged to seek re-election from his Oxford constituents who taunted him,

Oh! Member for Oxford! you shuffle and wheel!
You have altered your name from R. Peel to Repeal.[29]

He lost the election in Oxford, but was returned for the pocket borough of Westbury.

Wellington and Peel spent the next six months attempting to secure the support of their divided party and a hostile King in favour of a new policy suppressing the *Catholic Association*, disfranchising the forty-shilling freeholders and destroying the popular influence of the Irish leaders by granting Emancipation. During this delay and before the Government could announce its policy in Parliament, an anti-Catholic protest movement led by the extreme Protestants in the Lords organised Orange, Pitt and Brunswick Clubs, held public meetings and circulated petitions. Their main success was in Ireland where both Catholics and Protestants were becoming increasingly aggressive. But in spite of the fact that most of the ordinary people were basically anti-Catholic, the leaders of the protest movement tended to be conservative and refused to indulge in unconstitutional activity. Since they were unwilling to challenge the King's Government or demand the reform of Parliament, their movement ended in failure when George IV finally gave his assent to the Bill.

There were in fact three Bills. A Relief Bill gave Catholics the same status as Protestant Dissenters, while two others, probably unnecessary and certainly unfortunate, suppressed the *Catholic Association* and disfranchised the Irish forty-shilling freeholders on the grounds that they were subject to clerical control. Some Catholics, such as the journalist William Eusebius Andrews, opposed the Disfranchisement Bill; he referred to 'the Bill of Pains and Penalties misnamed the Emancipation Bill' and chose to regard its provisions as the revival of another persecution. When the Royal Assent was given, the *Truthteller* appeared with a thick black margin and the heading, 'Extinction of Civil and Religious Liberty in Ireland, through the Political Turpitude of the Catholic Aristocracy, Squirearchy and Lawyers'.[30] Most Catholic leaders, on the other hand, only showed a nominal resistance to the renewed restrictions on Catholic voters and on the whole accepted the Bill as the price to be paid for securing their main aims, the relief of penal legislation and the admission of Catholics to public office. In spite of its limitations, most Catholics were content to give a general welcome to the Emancipation Act, though it might seem from Bishop Bramston's New Year Pastoral of 1830 that he regarded it as another burden to be borne rather than the lifting of a yoke.

By passing the other two bills, the Government probably hoped to win over those members of the Tory party who considered that the Relief Bill was a deceitful betrayal of principle. For much the same reason, the Government also decided to close Jesuit houses and abolish Religious Orders of men by insisting on registration and forbidding the admission of any new members under pain of banishment or transportation. This measure, which helped to win many votes, was never put into operation, though other legal restrictions remained in force and Emancipation was far from complete. Catholics were excluded from offices such as Regent and Lord Chancellor. The use of ecclesiastical titles by Catholic bishops was restricted. It was still illegal to perform religious ceremonies or to wear religious habits in public. Catholic charities continued to be regarded as superstitious, while Catholic soldiers and sailors were still expected to attend Anglican services.

On the other hand, the idea of securing Catholic 'guarantees' by vetoing episcopal appointments or paying clerical salaries was dropped on the grounds that this would cause further trouble. Catholic members of Parliament, however, had to take a new parliamentary oath pledging themselves not to subvert the ecclesiastical establishment. This oath was to become an important factor in the future crisis between Church and State, and in the development of the Oxford Movement, because the Irish members distinguished between the Irish Church and its property; 'Surely', O'Connell argued, 'religion is not a thing of pounds, shillings and pence'.[31] The difficulty was that English Catholics were simply concerned with ending their civil or political disabilities, whereas Irish Catholics had a whole range of social, economic and national grievances of which exclusion on religious grounds was only one. Emancipation which was a final objective for many English Catholics was only a first step for most of their Irish colleagues.

Furthermore, the remaining restrictions on English Catholics were not as serious as those affecting Irish Catholics who were still unable to take their rightful place in the life of the nation as members of the police force or judges on the bench. There was also the glaring injustice of a Catholic population paying tithes to an alien and established Protestant Church. With the passing of the Emancipation Act, English and Irish Catholics no longer needed to work together and their political aims actually diverged. In spite of the gratitude which English Catholics showed to their Irish allies, O'Connell himself was black-balled from membership of the Cisalpine Club, ironically soon to become the Emancipation Club, though it is now known that only two people voted against him.

It is not difficult to understand contemporary and later criticisms of the Emancipation Act of 1829 in view of the restrictions on Catholics which remained in force. The Act undoubtedly deprived Catholics of some of the benefits which they had enjoyed since the process of modifying the penal laws had begun. Mgr Ward has argued that English Catholics gained most of their religious liberties in the eighteenth rather than the nineteenth century, and incidentally, he would date the rapid development of Catholicism from 1791 rather than 1829. Although the laity were emancipated in 1829, freedom of worship had been granted in 1791, while the clergy and the Religious Orders were in a better position under the acts of 1791 and 1793 than the act of 1829. Furthermore, the actual repeal of the penal laws, he pointed out, only began in 1844.[32]

Perhaps the most serious grievance and one which continued almost throughout the nineteenth century, resulted from the various marriage acts. Lord Hardwicke's Act of 1753 only recognized the validity of marriages celebrated according to the rites of the Anglican Church. The Nonconformist Marriage Act of 1836 allowed Catholics to be married before their own priests but these marriages did not carry any civil consequences and their children were regarded legally as illegitimate. Consequently, 'illegitimate' children who were chargeable on the parish where they were born, could be separated from their parents who might be returned to Ireland as paupers. It was also a felony for a priest to celebrate a marriage without a registrar and many Irish Catholics were married in Protestant churches simply because it was financially cheaper. According to one commentator, even by the end of the century, 'lamentably few' marriages, particularly but not exclusively 'mixed' marriages, were contracted in Catholic churches largely as a result of the poverty of the Irish. Even those who could afford the cost might still avoid the trouble and added expense of going to the registrar by being married in a Protestant church.[33]

The exaggerated reactions to the passing of Catholic Emancipation are not at first easy to understand. A duel was arranged between the Duke of Wellington and the Earl of Winchilsea who had referred to the Duke's insidious design of establishing popery, though the Earl retired from the field without firing a shot. When Lord Kenyon heard that ten bishops had voted in favour of the Bill, he prayed that God would 'grant His protection to the Church in its deserted state'; his aunt could hardly believe that she was 'still in poor old England' because the 'world seems altered in every way' and the Duke of Wellington deserved to be hanged.[34] The *Birmingham Argus*, specially edged in black, announced to its readers:

> Died, full of good works, deeply lamented by every HONEST BRITON, MR CONSTITUTION. His decease took place on the 13th of April in the year of our Lord 1829, at the House of the *Incurables.*[35]

Cartoons appeared showing Wellington and Peel burying the Constitution or 'KISSING the POPE'S TOE!!!'

Yet fears that the passing of Catholic Emancipation marked the end of the old Constitution were not entirely without foundation and might well have played an important part in later manifestations of anti-Catholicism which frequently involved constitutional issues, particularly following the development of ultramontanism and the rise of the Irish Question. The struggle for religious freedom must be seen in the wider context of political reform and the *Catholic Association* was an example of a successful movement or agitation which was consciously followed by later advocates of political or economic reform. Once inequality on grounds of religion was abolished, inequality on grounds of landed property or local custom would also be questioned. The social and economic interests involved in the struggle over constitutional reform lay behind the conflict between Anglicanism and Dissent. 1828 and 1829 were significant dates in the history of the privileged and constitutional position of the landed class as well as in the development of the supremacy of the House of Commons. The Duke of Cumberland therefore was not entirely wrong when he remarked on the repeal of the Corn Laws about twenty years later, 'England's downfall began in 1829'.[36]

After the passing of the Emancipation Act, several Catholic peers took their seats in the Lords and the eldest son of the Duke of Norfolk was returned to the Commons for one of his father's pocket boroughs. In July 1830, five Catholics were returned for English constituencies and there were ten Catholic members from Ireland. In the parliament of 1831, there were eight English Catholic members, yet by the end of the nineteenth century, there were still only five Catholic members representing English constituencies. Although this fact might illustrate that the direct political impact of English Catholics during the nineteenth century was limited, it does not necessarily reflect the extent of their political influence or their efforts even in the 1830's. Between 1833 and 1837, for example, the editors of *The British Catholic Colonial Quarterly Intelligencer* attempted to associate the interests of the British Catholics with those of the nation. They attempted to win the support of the British Government and public opinion for Roman Catholic missionaries from England and Ireland who might be instrumental in spreading the gospel, destroying idolatry and preventing anarchy in the British empire; they somewhat self-consciously referred to 'our humble efforts in the cause of *Christianity, Humanity*, and British interests . . . our weak but sincere endeavours, to promote the united cause of *all British Christians'.*[37]

Yet in spite of the political or constitutional implications of the various reform measures which were passed at the time, freedom of conscience and civil and religious liberty were still limited in many respects. The rights of Jews, infidels or atheists had been ignored and Dissenters remained subject to serious grievances. Catholic Emancipation in particular failed to achieve all that was expected and even some of the non-Catholics who had supported it were later disillusioned. One obvious reason for their disappointment was that Emancipation had been regarded as a remedy for the Irish Question, whereas it was in fact immediately necessary in order to prevent civil war and only removed one of the outstanding problems. The Government adopted the policy of Emancipation because of the danger of revolution and the threat to the Union. Ultimately, the solution to the Catholic Question was a matter of political expediency or empirical necessity and the motives of the Government as well as its solution were political and secular. Catholic Emancipation neither resulted from, nor promoted the development of religious toleration; 'Popery continued its traditional role of red-rag to John Bull'.[38]

Anti-Catholicism was widespread during the nineteenth century and its manifestations reflected its long history as well as developments both within the Church and in society at large. All the major anti-Catholic demonstrations, particularly in the middle of the century, took place throughout the English-speaking world. The same accusations and arguments were used in England and America, in Canada and Australasia. Canadian workers condemned the Maynooth Grant in 1845 and the insolent 'papal aggression' six years later. In 1855, the Massachusetts State Legislature passed a series of laws discriminating against Catholics and appointed a 'Nunnery Committee' to investigate alleged evil practices in convents and seminaries. This was remarkably similar to the English parliamentary enquiries of 1853 or 1870.[39] American and British Protestants also united in supporting the Italian nationalists and condemning the papal government.

The prejudices of the ignorant combined with the presumptions of the educated. All reasonable men became convinced that such an irrational religion as Roman Catholicism could hardly survive. Catholics were unenlightened, intolerant bigots whose religion was opposed to sound economic progress and liberal political developments. The widespread belief that Catholics were superstitious, idolatrous and morally corrupt seemed confirmed by the publication of the *Syllabus of Errors* or the definition of papal infallibility, and was substantiated by the history of Fr Achilli, the accusations of Joseph McCabe or the fictions of Maria Monk. Catholics were again accused of divided loyalties as the development of Ultramontanism reinforced Protestant doubts about the compatibility of their civil and religious allegiance.

The Protestant working classes could easily be roused to violence, especially as their economic conditions declined when Irish immigrants accepted lower wages or co-operated in breaking a strike. Other demonstrations were occasioned by the political claims of Catholics, particularly Irish Catholics, or when local Anglican clergymen adopted Catholic beliefs or practices. The most serious anti-Catholic demonstrations usually occurred when the working classes were roused by the better educated. The most influential of these agents were the clergy, especially the popular dissenting clergy and those anti-Catholic preachers, sometimes including former Catholic priests, who travelled extensively on both sides of the Atlantic. Another important means of anti-Catholic propaganda was the cheap religious press and perhaps the most notorious book in this context was the *Awful Disclosures* of Maria Monk. This was first published in 1836 and was widely read in Britain as well as in her native North America. When the unfortunate Maria gave birth to a second illegitimate child, her supporters claimed that this had been 'arranged' by the Jesuits in an effort to discredit her! Yet it seems impossible to dispel a credulous curiosity even today. The completely fictional *Disclosures* were used against Al Smith and John F. Kennedy in their presidential campaigns and are still being reprinted in England.

Much of the anti-Catholic literature combined biblical fundamentalism, apocalyptic prophecy and offensive apologetic, manifesting attitudes of incredulity and fear, shock and alarm, with occasional suggestions of pornography. Favourite subjects included 'the strange and unnatural habits of celibacy', auricular confession — 'that master-engine of the Papacy', and the Society of Jesus — 'this vile conspiracy against mankind'.[40] The Jesuits were not simply creatures of flesh and blood, but fought with the power of Satan himself; they severed themselves for ever 'from every tie of kindred' and crushed 'every affection of the heart'. As confessors, the Jesuits controlled the consciences of entire households, dictated the last wills and testaments of dying patients, and persuaded poor deluded young women to enter convents:

> to say prayers by the score, which she cannot construe, to rise at midnight to attend a service which she cannot understand, to address her prayers, not to her Creator and Redeemer, but to saints of whom some were madmen, and some knaves, and many are nonentities; to put her trust in crosses and relics; to practise the grossest idolatry; to believe that the food which is innocent on Thursday's, becomes sinful on Friday's; and if her devotions aspire to the higher honours of her profession, to torment herself with whip-cord and a horse hair shift!

Among the standard accusations was that of charging for the forgiveness of sins and 'the following shocking items' were 'extracted from the Romish "Taxa Cameroe".'

	£	s.	d.
The price of absolution to a Layman, who stole holy things out of a holy place . . .	0.	10.	6.
Do. For a Priest guilty of stealing holy things . . .	0.	10.	6.
Do. For a Priest for the vice of simony . . .	0.	10.	6.
Do. For a Layman murdering a Layman . . .	0.	7.	6.
Do. For him that killeth his father . . .	0.	10.	6.
Do. Or mother, or wife, or sister, or kinswoman, if the murdered person be of the laity . . .	0.	10.	6.
The murderer of a Priest must seek absolution at Rome			
Do. For a Priest to keep a Concubine, and also his dispensation to save him from being *irregular* . . .	0.	10.	6.
Do. For nameless crimes . . .	0.	7.	6.
Do. Dispensation for marrying first cousin . . .	2.	14.	0.
The Common fee for absolution of sin of ordinary nature . . .	0.	5.	0.

Most Catholic apologists attempted the fruitless and unending task of answering specific objections and those books or pamphlets which survive are merely gathering dust on the shelves of Catholic libraries. John Henry Newman, on the other hand, was much more realistic and attempted to expose the underlying irrational prejudices behind the forces of anti-Catholicism. In his brilliant satirical lectures on *The Present Position of Catholics in England*, he pointed out that the fundamental difficulty was that the Catholic Church was considered 'too absurd to be inquired into'; 'too corrupt to be defended, and too dangerous to be treated with equity and fair dealing'; the Church was 'the victim of a prejudice which perpetuates itself, and gives birth to what it feeds upon'; 'Catholics are to be whitewashed! What next?'[41]

Even during the nineteenth century, however, anti-Catholic prejudice was based on outdated social and political patterns. Some of its manifestations were significant precisely because they were associated with important changes in relations between Church and State, religion and society. This was particularly true of the political and social concessions made to English and Irish Catholics, though even in this case, the Orange Order was the only anti-Catholic institution which survived. Of course, in spite of a decline especially among the better educated, anti-Catholicism did not totally disappear and might even survive a general decline in religious belief.

At the beginning of the period, however, intolerance was only one of the problems which faced the newly emancipated English Catholics who found themselves in a series of tragic dilemmas because 'solutions' to immediate difficulties often seemed to exaggerate more fundamental problems. The most immediate and pressing needs were to provide men and money for an ever increasing population, but even these comparatively simple and obvious demands were complicated by the fact that Catholics in England did not form a homogeneous community. The Old Catholic community was being transformed not only as a result of economic and political developments, but by the arrival of Irish immigrants, Oxford converts and foreign missionaries.

The English Catholics found it extremely difficult to accept the foreign clergy and many of the new converts, and almost impossible to cope with the flood of Irish immigrants. The various groups which formed the Catholic Church in England had very different interests and needs. Priests trained in the older traditions of rural Catholicism or as chaplains to Old Catholic families were too few and unfamiliar with the problems involved to satisfy the demands of the converts or the needs of urban immigrants. Furthermore, in spite of their notoriety, there were never enough Irish priests or foreign missionaries in either numbers or ability to supply what was needed.

There was also the problem of money. Although some English Catholics were extremely wealthy and remarkably generous, it was quite impossible to provide all the money which was required. In a vain attempt to satisfy the different claims of immigrants who needed cheap chapels, romantic idealists who wanted to revive Gothic architecture and well-to-do converts anxious to impress the English upper classes, the unfortunate bishops usually found themselves in debt. The correspondence between the Earl of Shrewsbury and Bishop Walsh of the Midland District helps to illustrate the financial problems of Catholics in the middle of the century, the incompetence of many ecclesiastical authorities as well as the generosity of some of the Catholic laity.

During the 1840s, the Bishop reported that the finances of his District were in a deplorable state – 'From misapplication of Funds, though well meant at the time for the good of religion, from misplaced confidence in others, my great misfortune from undertaking too many new Missions and from various unexpected most serious pecuniary lapses' such as the death of one benefactor and the religious profession of another. Unless the District received £600 immediately and a further annual income of £1,500 to £2,000, Oscott would be lost, the Cathedral and Bishop's House with a combined debt of £4,000 would be seriously threatened, and various missions both inside and outside the District as well as several individual Catholics would be ruined. Walsh dreaded the public scandal of a Catholic bishop who was known to have been proposed as Archbishop of Westminster also being known as 'a defaulter in money matters!' He therefore made a direct and emotional appeal to Shrewsbury and through him to other wealthy Catholics:

the holy catholic religion which is so extensively flourishing in Birmingham, and in the neighbourhood will receive an awful check, perhaps its death blow ... Catholics will be disheartened and disinclined to contribute towards religion; Converts will be scandalized and discouraged; Protestants will triumph ... To prevent so dreadful a calamity, I would most cheerfully, *most gratefully* live on bread and water and enduring the remainder of my life in solitude and penance offering up the prayers of a contrite and humble heart to the throne of mercy in behalf of religion; – But with my distressing complaints and feelings in consequence of the sacred character I bear, to be cast into prison, to hear profane and wicked conversation of low persons, etc. is frightful to me. Still even this dreadful state I would endeavour to submit to with resignation provided I should be the only sufferer and religion be thus rescued from scandal.[42]

A few years later in 1853, Bishop Ullathorne was actually imprisoned for debt, though as a shareholder rather than as a bishop. In 1856, Ullathorne again faced further serious financial difficulties as a result of the death of some benefactors and the loss of a large legacy through a flaw in the will.

It was, of course, inevitable, as a result of the general economic situation, that 1848 should prove to be a disastrous year in financial terms. The collections for poor and new parishes taken in one church at the time show that these collections were declining as Irish immigration was increasing. In 1844, the collection amounted to £68 and increased to £77 in the following year. But in 1846 the collection declined to £50 and only amounted to some £8 in 1847. The local Bishop was himself aware that this dramatic decline was a result of contemporary economic conditions rather than any lack of zeal or generosity.[43] In the same year, Wiseman himself reported that:

> I am quite out of condition as to funds. To tell the truth I am out of pocket on all sides. I have not sent my account with the College, really because I have not heart to do it, as you will see that I am creditor to a large amount somewhere *above* £1,500 . . . I have no intention of pressing anything on the College, either for interest or principal, unless it shall be one day in circumstances to settle with me without loss or difficulty.[44]

Meanwhile the tensions within the small community of English Catholics were getting worse. The Oxford converts, for example, increased the numbers, prestige and influence of English Catholics, but also emphasized the social and intellectual limitations of some of the Old Catholics who were accused of being a hundred years behind their non-Catholic equivalents, as proud as Lucifer and as ignorant as they were proud.[45] To this was added the threat of theological and devotional divisions. Following their doubts and uncertainties as Anglicans, most of the converts were attracted by the increasingly popular Ultramontane theories of Roman and papal supremacy which were sometimes accompanied with the introduction of Italian devotions or Roman vestments as manifestations of the new spirit. The Old Catholic priests and bishops, on the other hand, for financial as well as practical reasons, dressed plainly, lived simply and carried out their pastoral and liturgical duties with the least possible ceremony. The Old Catholics were now to be accused by new converts and continental missionaries of being lacking in devotion, of disloyalty and even of 'Gallicanism', though their lives and histories should have provided sufficient evidence of their devotion to the Church of their ancestors. Exuberant Italian devotions, demonstrative 'Catholick' revivals and increasing talk of an imminent conversion of England did not appeal to men who could remember former hostilities and the difficulties of penal legislation.

Until 1778, Catholics could not legally inherit or purchase land, and bishops, priests and school teachers could still theoretically be sentenced to life imprisonment. Even after the Relief Act of 1791, Catholics were warned that they incurred the penalties of *praemunire* for receiving such religious objects as holy pictures and crosses, missals, rosaries and breviaries. Personal friends of Bishop Challoner could still remember his last days during the Gordon riots and when Joseph Berington first dressed in black, he was accused of risking a fresh persecution. Consequently, public processions or clerical collars seemed at worst provocative and at best unnecessary or superfluous. Lingard, for instance, did not want to be *suffocated* with a Roman collar and when the London Oratorians were pelted in the streets, he thought that they were simply paying the penalty 'of setting good sense at defiance'.[46]

Some of the bishops recorded the criticisms made to them about the foreign missionaries:

> I have heard language used by Dr Gentili blamed — with how much justice I cannot say — especially as I well know that every *reformer* of morals is sure to meet opposition — he is strong against Balls, especially the Polka etc. and I believe your Lordship does not *love* them — he is said to give offence by *plain language* in his instruction on the 6th commandment but I believe if it gives offence to some it also does much good — these Missioners are callous to all *human respect* in any of its bearings — this is *good* — but I think it may go too far — I have not, as I said, been present at any instruction at a Mission or sermon but the impression on my mind from what I have heard is that it will be prudent in the Missioners in their zeal to do good, not by anything outré, or unguarded, to give those *who are disposed to do* it, *an opportunity of blaming their Ministry* — It would be a great pity to lessen the repute in which these Missions are at present held — I think it important for *a public good*, that the Missioners should unite with their zeal so much prudence, mildness and dignity that others may not with an *appearance of justice* be able *to gainsay* them.[47]

For their part, the Italian missionaries joined some of the Irish clergy in sending unfavourable complaints about English Catholics and their priests to the Roman authorities. There they found a ready sympathizer in Nicholas Wiseman who was so willing to identify himself with the movement to Romanize the Church in England. Wiseman fully supported the adoption of Roman or Italian devotions to replace the older devotions which had developed as part of the English Catholic tradition. He preferred the attitudes of the new converts or the Italian religious to those of the Old Catholics and, in spite of the costs involved, he also favoured a policy of magnificent expansion.

Notes

1. P. Howard, *Address to the Right Reverend the Archbishops and Bishops of England and Ireland* (London, 1801) 3.
2. F. Heyer, *The Catholic Church from 1648 to 1870* (London, 1969) 196.
3. J. Bossy, *The English Catholic Community 1570-1850* (London, 1975) 322.
4. Smith to Poynter, 26 January 1812, Archives of the Archbishop of Westminster (AAW) A.51.
5. *Catholicon* III (1816) 38; IV (1817) 40.
6. *Orthodox Journal* I (1813) 81; VIII (1820) 293-311.
7. J. Lingard, *A Review of Certain Anti-Catholic Publications* (London, 1813) 32; *Observations on the Laws and Ordinances, which Exist in Foreign States* (Dublin, 1817) 16.
8. *Orthodox Journal* VII (1819) 421; see also *Orthodox Journal* VIII (1820) 49-53, 89-107, 129-41; *Catholic Spectator or Catholicon* III (1825) 120-21; 283-5.
9. *Catholic Miscellany* VII (1827) 60, 64-5; VIII (1827) 271-5.
10. "Peter Plymley", *Letters on the Subject of the Catholics, to my brother Abraham, who lives in the country* (London, 1807-8) second letter 23.
11. B. Ward, *The Eve of Catholic Emancipation* (London, 1911) I: 120.
12. G.I.T. Machin, *The Catholic Question in English Politics* (Oxford, 1964) 15; Ward, *Eve of Emancipation* II: 148.
13. Quoted by R.W. Linker, 'The English Roman Catholics and Emancipation: The Politics of Persuasion' *Journal of Ecclesiastical History* 27 (1976) 176.
14. Newman, *Sermons on various occasions* 172.
15. Linker's account of Howard's career should be contrasted with that given by J.C.H. Aveling, *The Handle and the Axe* (London, 1976) 268.
16. Aveling, *Handle and Axe* 269.
17. G. Oliver, *Collections, illustrating the History of the Catholic Religion in the countries of Cornwall, Devon, Dorset, Somerset, Wilts, and Gloucester* (London, 1857) 48-9.
18. U. Henriques, *Religious Toleration in England 1787-1833* (London,

1961) 155.

19. Henriques, *Religious Toleration* 155.

20. *Catholic Magazine and Reflector* I (1801) 227.

21. *Letter to the Lords and Commons of Great Britain on the subject of the Catholic Claims, by The British Observer* (London, 1805) 16.

22. *Catholic Miscellany* II (1823) 85-9, 164-5, 182-6, 237; *Catholic Spectator or Catholicon* II (1824) 29-30; *Orthodox Journal* V (1817) 162; VII (1819) 74-9.

23. Quoted by Henriques, *Religious Toleration* 161.

24. *Declaration of the Catholic Bishops, the Vicars Apostolic and their Coadjutors in Great Britain* (London, 1826) 4, 14.

25. *An Address from the British Roman Catholics to their Protestant Fellow Countrymen* (London, 1826) 3-4.

26. A. Briggs, *The Age of Improvement 1783-1867* (London, 1960) 200.

27. Briggs, *Age of Improvement* 231.

28. *Catholic Miscellany* new series (1828) 300.

29. Briggs, *Age of Improvement* 232.

30. Ward, *Eve of Emancipation* III: 260, 264, 272-3.

31. W.O. Chadwick, *The Victorian Church* (London, 1966) I: 23.

32. Ward, *Eve of Emancipation* I: viii-ix, 2; III: 259; *The Sequel to Catholic Emancipation* (London, 1915) II: 72; see also W.J. Amherst, *The History of Catholic Emancipation* (London, 1886) I: 180-3.

33. J. Mòrris, *Catholic England in Modern Times* (London, 1892) 90.

34. Machin, *The Catholic Question* 177, 180.

35. Briggs, *Age of Improvement* 230.

36. Machin, *The Catholic Question* 193.

37. *The British Catholic Colonial Quarterly Intelligencer* 2 (1834) 81-2.

38. Henriques, *Religious Toleration* 262.

39. C. Butler, *The Life and Times of Bishop Ullathorne* (London, 1926) II: 162-4, 172-3; E.R. Norman, *Anti-Catholicism in Victorian England* (London, 1968) 20-1, 84-5; *The Conscience of the State in North America* (Cambridge, 1968) 90, 99.

40. D. Massy, *Dark Deeds of the Papacy contrasted with Bright Lights of the Gospel* (London, 1851) 5-6, 8, 22, 28-9, 169, 196.

41. J.H. Newman, *The Present Position of Catholics in England* (London, 1903) 11-12, 79.

42. Walsh to Shrewsbury, no date, Ushaw College Archives W.S. 64. For several years, Wiseman had been largely responsible for the financial affairs of the District and Walsh had only recently discovered 'the awful deficiency'. But in a later letter dated the 4th of August 1848, Ushaw W.S. 65, Walsh made it clear that his original reference, presumably about the misapplication of funds, did not refer to Wiseman. See also D. Gwynn, *Lord Shrewsbury, Pugin and*

the Catholic Revival (London, 1946) 27.

43. M. Conlon, *St Alban's Blackburn* 1773-1973 (Chorley, 1973) 22, 26.

44. Wiseman to Bagnall, 30 March 1848, Archives of St Edmund's College Ware.

45. J.M. Capes, *To Rome and back* (London, 1873) 233, 254-5, 294-5; see also E.S. Purcell, *Life of Cardinal Manning Archbishop of Westminster* (London, 1896) I: 656-7, 663-5.

46. M. Haile and E. Bonney, *Life and Letters of John Lingard 1771-1851* (London, n.d.) 353.

47. Mostyn to Griffiths, 25 May 1846, AAW.

Pope Pius IX

Chapter II: Wiseman and the Roman restoration

Nicholas Patrick Stephen Wiseman had been one of the first students to join the Venerable English College in Rome when it had re-opened in 1818. There his vocation to serve the Church in England was combined with a deep devotion to the See of Peter. It is perhaps significant that linguists and artists, historians and antiquarians interested him more than theologians. Be that as it may, two influences on his always imaginative and impressionable mind were especially important – the historical associations of early church history and the frequent sight of the Pope: 'It was something above earthly to see an Emperor and Empress, a queen, dukes and princes of the highest blood kneeling before the sovereign vicar of Christ'.[1]

Wiseman was both confident and intelligent, and his career was remarkably rapid and successful. In 1827, he published three dissertations under the title *Horae Syriacae* which helped to establish his reputation as a scholar and after a personal and direct appeal to the Pope, he succeeded in being appointed Professor of Oriental Languages in the Roman University. Incidentally, for a time, Wiseman's faith seems to have been tried by his study of the early findings of biblical and scientific criticism. In 1835, he collected his studies over the years in a series of lectures *On the Connexion between Science and Revealed Religion* which were so advanced that as late as 1860, the distinguished English scientist, Sir Richard Owen, believed they could easily be supplemented in order to bring them up to date. In 1827, Wiseman was appointed Vice Rector of the English College, the official English preacher in Rome, and in the following year, when only twenty-five years old, Rector of the Venerabile.

As the leading representative of English Catholics, Wiseman met many visitors to Rome, but two visits in particular seem to have been especially significant. In 1831, he showed a sympathetic hospitality to the French leaders of the Ultramontane revival, Lamennais, Lacordaire and Montalembert, when they made their futile appeal to the Holy See in favour of their positive attitude towards liberal democracy. Two years later, Wiseman met two leaders of the Oxford Movement, John Henry Newman and Richard Hurrell Froude. Both of these meetings were to have a profound influence on Wiseman's attitudes and subsequent career, but he does not seem to have considered them separately; they were seen as two different aspects of the same phenomenon. Wiseman began to hope that the revival of Catholicism on the continent might be paralleled in England. For some time after the French Revolution, it seemed that only Catholicism could satisfy the human need for religion; Protestantism and the developments of the Reformation appeared to be coming to an end. The conversions of Englishmen like Kenelm Henry Digby, Ambrose Phillipps de Lisle, Augustus Welby Pugin and George Ignatius Spencer confirmed Wiseman's growing optimism. This was reinforced by Spencer in particular who kept the Rector informed of the progress of the Oxford Movement and the Catholic revival in England and it was Spencer who successfully urged Wiseman to direct his attention towards serving the Church in England.

In 1835, Wiseman returned to England through Munich and Paris where he met leading members of the continental Catholic revival. He had paid a brief visit to England three years before, but apart from this, had not revisited the country since he left at the age of sixteen. Consequently, the most formative years of Wiseman's life had been spent at the very centre of Catholicism, not at the periphery in England. His sympathies and attitudes were inevitably Roman, while his ignorance of England and Anglicanism was even greater because of a mistaken impression that he understood them perfectly.

On arriving in England, Wiseman began a tour of Catholic families and institutions. He was perhaps inevitably surprised to find that his fellow Catholics seemed disinclined to seize the opportunities which he probably exaggerated were now open to them after Emancipation. He himself later claimed that the 'shackles were removed, but not the numbness and cramp which they had produced';[2] time was needed to overcome the sense of social and political isolation, though Wiseman must have also known that English Catholics were often encouraged to adopt a modest if not retiring attitude by their own ecclesiastical authorities who were in a better position to judge the situation than their 'Roman' visitor. Wiseman was also surprised to see how little interest English Catholics took in the Oxford Movement at home or in the revival of Catholicism abroad. But the four vicars apostolic, short of priests and desperate for money, attempting to govern a large area with an ever increasing population, were less concerned with the apparently academic discussions of intellectuals in Munich or Oxford than with the necessity of securing Wiseman's help for the reorganization of the English mission and the restoration of a proper diocesan hierarchy.

Yet Wiseman's visit has generally been regarded as a starting-point of the expansion and development of English Catholicism over the next few decades and he himself had an immediate and sensational success which David Lewis believed marked the beginning of the serious revival of Catholicism in England. In a series of lectures originally intended for the congregation of the chapel at the Sardinian Embassy, Wiseman found himself explaining his religion to a large audience of interested non-Catholics. The influence of romantic writers and political reformers had helped to modify the prejudices of some educated Englishmen, while this was the time when Thomas Arnold thought that no human power could save the existing Anglican Church which, according to Thomas Mozley, was 'folding its robes' to die with what dignity it could.[3]

No doubt Wiseman was aware of these factors, but he would also be aware that they coincided with his own ideas of an English Catholic revival – Lacordaire was speaking in France and Möhler in Germany, now Wiseman was speaking in England!

> I have two lectures every week. The effect has been a thousand times beyond my expectations. The chapel is crowded to suffocation, every seat is occupied half an hour before the compline, and if it were three times as large it would be full . . . Every one agrees that a most successful experiment has been made, and that proof has been given of the interest which may be thrown round the Catholic doctrines by a little exertion.[4]

The 'experiment' was repeated with even more success during the following Lent at Moorfields and again Wiseman's lectures, it is said, contributed to changing the whole character of English Catholicism by giving confidence to Catholics and removing Protestant ignorance.

It is true that English Catholics saw Wiseman and their Church being treated with interest and respect. In 1836, Wiseman was asked to write on Catholicism for the *Penny Cyclopaedia*; he helped to establish the *Dublin Review* as well as a Catholic Institute which would defend poor Catholics and reply to Protestant attacks. But not all English Catholics welcomed these developments. One opponent of the Institute protested against 'factious laical intrusion' and found it

> impossible to admit that the defence and maintenance of our religious and moral fame should be confided to those persons, or any of them, whose conduct has excited, and, in no small degree, furnished excuses for that outcry against which they profess to complain. Let

them defend themselves, if they will and can; but let not 'the Catholic inhabitants of Great Britain' be thus untruly connected, at the eleventh hour, with their past misdeeds, or held forth, prospectively, as accountable for their future courses.[5]

Furthermore, Wiseman's personal influence was being exerted in a particular ideological way. Older Catholic periodicals and magazines often tended to reflect the moderation of the Old Catholics and their natural reserve in expressing their loyalty to the papacy or in their descriptions of continental devotions. The *Dublin Review*, on the other hand, would reflect Wiseman's enthusiasm for the Holy See and for his understanding of the international Church, Catholic and Universal.

On returning to the English College, Wiseman's thoughts were increasingly directed towards England and he even became anxious to leave Rome! During the summer of 1839 he paid another visit and from then until the end of his life, the Church in England became his primary concern. His energy and enthusiasm on this occasion were quite remarkable. Within six weeks, he preached about ninety times for an hour at a time and travelled over one and a half thousand miles. But the way in which he described what he saw was most significant; a 'new splendid church' was 'quite worthy of ancient days' and on the whole 'would not have done dishonour to Rome'; a procession in Huddersfield so impressed him that he reported 'It was like an Italian more than an English day'.[6]

Wiseman's sympathy for continental Catholicism, foreign devotions and religious orders, was one of the factors which soured his relations with the English bishops and clergy during his last years in Rome. He was also associated with, though not always personally responsible for, the criticisms made by various missionaries and the irritation of the Roman authorities with the vicars apostolic. In 1838, two edicts were issued in favour of the regular clergy. These edicts were regarded as a direct insult to the English bishops since their jurisdiction over the religious orders was reduced and the latter were apparently allowed to open new missions without episcopal permission. On this occasion, Wiseman was criticised as an inefficient agent and accused of working with those who opposed his ecclesiastical superiors. Meanwhile, the English bishops reacted unfavourably to some obviously unrealistic proposals for the administration of the Church in England and the colonies, and this was interpreted as manifesting a lack of zeal and respect for the Holy See. As a result of these and further misunderstandings, the bishops decided that their future representative should not be associated with the English College and when the clergy adopted a similar resolution, they felt so strongly on the issue that they offered to open a subscription in order to provide a salary for the new agent.[7]

Throughout this period, the attitudes of religious and their relations with the bishops provided a constant source of conflict and misunderstanding. Wiseman himself tended to sympathize with the religious orders and since Pope Gregory XVI was a Camaldolese monk, the reports and criticisms of the religious in England received a sympathetic hearing in Rome. Bishop Ullathorne, himself a former religious, later wrote that:

> Certain foreign ecclesiastics gaining their earliest experience of the English mission, were also writing off their first impressions of work done by the English Bishops and Clergy, of the inaccuracy of which they were only convinced at a later time, and when the mischief was done.[8]

The religious themselves encouraged the idea that they should be entrusted with a greater share of the government of the English mission and it was even suggested that future bishops should always be chosen from the ranks of the religious. One of them wrote:

> I want an increase of *Regular* Bishops in England. For the promotion of real piety, for the reconversion, for the *real* conversion of England, sufficient protection must be given to Regulars, and this can scarcely take place till there are more Regular Bishops, who will control the Clergy in their blind opposition to Religious Bodies.[9]

The secular clergy, for their part, strongly defended their right to be ruled by secular bishops. In 1840, the secular clergy sent a petition to Rome opposing the election of religious as bishops, while the clergy in Manchester prepared petitions and protests when it was rumoured that one of the regular clergy was to be appointed as their bishop. This traditional rivalry between secular and regular clergy existed in almost every sphere of activity. On one occasion, Wiseman himself remarked: 'While I was in the North, I found the feeling strong, among the more zealous and devout of the Clergy in favour of a *secular* body of missionaries for retreats and missions'[10]

In 1839, Wiseman again offended the vicars apostolic when, without consulting them, he planned the establishment of a missionary body of priests and obtained indulgences for a confraternity of prayer for the conversion of England. Wiseman tried to secure papal approval for the formation of a group of missionaries who might speed the conversion of the country and bring about a religious revival among English Catholics. Wiseman's address to Gregory XVI was later reprinted by his opponents under the title *Dr Wiseman's Character of the English Mission* with a short but devastating introduction:

> The following Document was presented to the late Pope, by Dr Wiseman, in the year 1839. The extraordinary nature of its statements surprised the Holy Father; and, to ascertain its correctness, copies were made, and transmitted to each of the then Vicars Apostolic, with a request that they would signify their opinion of it. The answer returned by the prelates was to the effect that they knew nothing of the scheme proposed by Dr. Wiseman; that they had *not* therefore given to it their 'unanimous', or indeed, *any*, 'consent'; and that most, if not all, of the statements contained in the Petition were *opposed to the truth*![11]

The Roman authorities failed to appreciate conditions in England and proved too willing to listen to criticisms of the bishops from new converts and foreign missionaries as well as some of the Old Catholics like the Earl of Shrewsbury. The vicars apostolic were in fact devoted in carrying out their pastoral responsibilities in a very difficult situation. A non-Catholic clergyman reported seeing Bishop Griffiths

> get out of an omnibus in Piccadilly, seize his carpet bag, and trudge straight home with it to Golden Square ... A very pleasing, venerable, episcopal-looking man, very like any other Bishop, save that none of ours would touch a carpet bag with his little finger.

Frequently exhausted by their pastoral duties, they were reluctant or unwilling to take on the added burden of preparing long reports in an unfamiliar language and they were, in any case, sometimes quite unable to supply the information or answer the questions asked by the Roman authorities. In 1840, for example, Bishop Walsh told Lord Shrewsbury, 'my poor head is weakened by the important letters in Latin, French and English I have been writing on the Coadjutorship'.[12]

As a result of the pressure of work, the bishops sometimes failed to acknowledge letters, while their lack of familiarity with Roman procedure and the proper formalities seemed further evidence of that lack of zeal and respect of which they were so unjustly accused. Bishop Riddell of the Northern District who died of cholera contracted when ministering to his people made no secret of his feelings when writing to Wiseman only a few weeks before his death.

It is shameful that such influence has been made use of to prejudice persons in authority in Rome against the Bishops. I really think it would be well to urge the Pope to send over some one to look into the state of things. As to one complaint: Want of sufficient money, of Religion, of Churches, and Priests; there is no doubt there is great truth in it, and in the large towns there are not half enough priests; but I can't make out how this can be laid to the charge of the Bishops. For example: in this District, there are few monied men, and as regards the gentry, we can't get anything from them. Then again, how can the Bishops do much with their own slender means? If Dr M[ostyn] and myself had not something of our own, we could not live, for all that we get, is the Interest of £2,000 left by a lady for the support of the Bishop. I think myself that more may be done in the way of conversions, if the Clergy would consider themselves not only as Pastors but as Missionaries, but we all know the difficulty of making converts amongst the respectable classes.[13]

In later years, Wiseman himself would have his own problems with the Roman authorities and once again the chief factor would be their irgnorance of conditions in England. As Bishop Grant once complained, 'The Bishops must write more detailed accounts of their districts, as they say at Prop. that they have more precise news of China than of England'.[14] There were also personal factors. Cardinal Barnabo, the Prefect of Propaganda, had 'a reputation for keeping nobody's secrets'. Furthermore, there were differences of attitude. Spencer Northcote referred to 'the manifest jealousy and touchiness they [Propaganda] seem to exhibit in everything that might look like a desire to be independent of them'.[15] At the end of 1839, however, Wiseman still enjoyed

the satisfaction of hearing His Holiness approve of all I have done in England, and of the points I have there chiefly inculcated. There is a wonderful sympathy for our unfortunate country excited everywhere, in France, Belgium and Italy. Prayers for its conversion are increasing everywhere. Whatever we do seems to excite universal interest. All this augurs well, but we must labour hard in England, if we hope for any good to be done.[16]

For some time, the prospect of the conversion of England or even of reunion with the Anglican Church aroused exaggerated hopes and occasioned further internal difficulties within the Catholic community. Referring to Bishop Walsh's reservations about the restoration of the

Cistercian Order in England, de Lisle told Lord Shrewsbury, 'we must await awhile until the reunion of the Anglican Church has put a little new blood into our degenerate body, before we can expect such work as Abbey Churches to rise up.'[17] In 1831, de Lisle told Spencer that he expected England to be Catholic again in about fifty years. If the Old 'Catholics' were more zealous and less apathetic, the conversion of the country would not take so long. He also reported that remarkable events would probably take place before the end of 1832, though he did not expect the complete conversion of England in so short a time! Ten years later, de Lisle informed Shrewsbury that leading Anglicans were determined to bring about reunion, but needed a little time! The Archbishop of Canterbury and the Bishop of Oxford had apparently approved of a scheme, but other bishops were still holding out. Wiseman himself, who, according to de Lisle, 'perfectly concurs with me in everything', had sent a correspondence with some of the Oxford leaders to Rome and although this was confidential, 'you may rest assured that the reunion of the Churches is certain'.[18] Consequently, Bishop Baines' famous pastoral of 1840 opposing an organized crusade of prayer for the conversion of England should not simply be seen as a manifestation of the suspicions or resentments which later met some of the Oxford converts, nor as evidence of an over-cautious or 'national' Catholicism. It should be seen as a realistic protest against the wishful thinking and unrealistic hopes as well as the enthusiastic adoption of foreign devotions which were increasingly associated with Wiseman and his friends.

Although Bishop Griffiths asked for prayers for the conversion of England in two pastoral letters in 1839 and 1840, the vicars apostolic did not support the idea of an organized campaign partly because of the extreme language being used by some of the converts; these condemned their former co-religionists as 'heretics' who were only prevented from joining the Church by the lack of zeal among Catholics themselves. The new converts also attached undue importance to the wearing of medals and scapulars, and eagerly accepted reports of 'miracles' and 'prophecies' usually foretelling the imminent conversion of England. The Old Catholics, for their part, denied that their prudence resulted from any lack of zeal, rejected the exaggerated hopes and fervent devotions of the new converts, and expressed the fear that such 'aggression' might provoke the forces of anti-Catholic prejudice.

Bishop Baines himself did not discuss the possibility of corporate reunion, but simply pointed out that in 1839, some 221 people, or less than one per cent of the Catholic population, had been converted in the

Western District. On the basis of those figures, it would take two centuries to convert a million people. Consequently, even presuming that all Catholics remained faithful to their religion, the conversion of England would still take thousands of years. The language of the Bishop's pastoral, however, was stronger than many of those who supported him would have liked and it is therefore not surprising that the Roman authorities should have taken exception to it and ordered him to retract various interpretations.

Bishop Griffiths was also strongly criticized by the Pope for a piece which was published in the *Catholic Directory* during the following year. The Vicar Apostolic of the London District expressed his scepticism of 'a body of schismatics returning with sincerity to the true faith'. The Pope harshly and unjustly condemned him in a public letter addressed to the London Clergy:

> no belief is more deadly, none can prevail among you more likely to quench the admirable zeal for church building than that maintained recently by your Bishop ... To what can it tend, such an opinion as this, utterly unsuited to the present time, except to check and discourage that noble band of Catholics, which with such effort of soul, such generous abundance of gifts, presses forward the building of churches? What, I repeat, can be the result of your Bishop's remarks but to hold back spirits eager for conversions, spirits more lofty than his own? And what country on earth, I should like to ask your sapient Bishop, was ever by the same cunning devices of its rulers robbed of the faith of its fathers, as your unhappy land has been? ... If, therefore, this Bishop of yours, where everything is so clear, is the only man who cannot see the sky brightening in England, all the more must you and we take care, Beloved Sons, that you and the laity of England may not have your eyes darkened by the clouds that overshadow his.[19]

Nevertheless, in spite of the obvious differences between Wiseman and the English bishops, by the end of 1838, Bishop Walsh enlisted the support of Lord Shrewsbury in asking the Roman authorities to appoint Wiseman as his coadjutor. Walsh made the point that all the vicars apostolic agreed that Wiseman should return to England and that, as the oldest bishop, Walsh himself had the first claim on Wiseman as his coadjutor. It is interesting that although the other bishops wished to have Wiseman in their Districts, Walsh reported that they did not necessarily want him as their coadjutor.[20] It is therefore not surprising that Wiseman's eventual appointment as coadjutor bishop and President of Oscott in 1840 was not greeted with universal approval especially since the significance of his appointment was evident both at home and abroad. The *Univers* announced: 'The universal knowledge of the illustrious Anglo-Roman has fixed on him the eyes of Europe . . . [He is now] going to take his place among the new Augustines whom a new Gregory sends forth to achieve a second time the conquest of England'.[21]

Several English priests had already criticized Wiseman and his attitudes. In 1835, the President of Sedgley Park found him 'distant and formal, the result of Roman pomposity'.[22] In 1839, an unfriendly critic reported, 'Wiseman has clearly set his sail for the breeze of the Bishopric — his ambition has got the better of his discretion'.[23] These suspicions of Wiseman's ambition endured throughout his life. When in 1850, Wiseman referred to 'our great frailty', an unsympathetic commentator asked, 'Is that man conscious of his frailty, who has ever sought to raise himself by grasping at honours, dignity, and power. O Le Drole!'[24] On the other hand, Wiseman received enthusiastic support from those English Catholics who shared his Ultramontane convictions. The President of the English College in Lisbon asked Bishop Walsh,

> Please to present my most respectful compliments to your excellent Coadjutor Dr Wiseman. In him we have the Spectacle so often exhibited in the Catholic Church and no where else of first rate abilities together with most extensive learning, directed solely to the honour and glory of him who gave them, because accompanied with humility and piety the Daughter of that virtue. I cannot but think that God intends mercy to England when I see him raise up in it such Persons as Dr Wiseman, Mr Digby, Mr Spencer, &c. &c.[25]

One of the principal reasons why Bishop Walsh consistently sought Wiseman's help in the Midland District was in order that he might work with members of the Oxford Movement and Wiseman himself was very anxious to return to England for the same reason. As Rector of the English College, Wiseman had tried to prepare his students for the 'Oxford Controversy' and when he moved to England, he hoped that Oscott would provide a haven for converts and a meeting place for those Tractarians who were interested in making personal contact with Roman Catholics. Oscott was to become a centre which would attract 'Catholic' members of the Church of England to the Apostolic See; it was to be a 'beacon light' and a reflection of 'dear Rome'.[26] In spite of this evident romanticism, Wiseman was not entirely unsuccessful. After being converted, Peter Le Page Renouf took a position there which was analogous to an Oxford Fellowship providing board, lodging and expenses. His father later visited him and seems to have been reassured and even impressed by his son's situation. Unlike Newman and the young Acton who were critical of some aspects of their life at Oscott, Renouf was very satisfied and even attempted to compare it with Oxford, though this should probably be seen as the enthusiastic reaction of a recent convert. Wiseman himself later estimated that the District had spent over £75,000 on the care of converts.

In July, 1839, Wiseman published his famous essay on St Augustine and the Donatists which Newman described as 'the first real hit from Romanism . . . it has given me a stomach-ache'. Wiseman pointed out that according to the Fathers, the apologetic question was essentially one of fact. If a particular church was out of communion with others, these became the judges over it. Although Newman later replied to the article, he 'had seen the shadow of a hand upon the wall . . . [and] . . . He who had seen a ghost, cannot be as if he had never seen it'.[27] Two years later, Wiseman published his *Letter on Catholic Unity*. In spite of the fact that his direct argument was somewhat less than irenic and in spite of the 'triumphalism' which so often threatened to vitiate even his best work, Wiseman also revealed some genuine ecumenical sentiments.

Members of the Oxford Movement contemplated reunion as a duty if the Catholic Church reformed certain abuses, but, Wiseman maintained, the impression that the Church sanctioned abuses was the result of misunderstanding and consequently reunion with the Holy See which would 'give vigour and energy to a languid and sickly existence' was a stern practical necessity. Furthermore, Wiseman argued, there were 'sufficient instances of persons, whose prejudices have been most violent against Rome, but were overcome in Rome, and by Rome itself'. At the same time, Wiseman recognized past corruptions and present deficiencies in the Church. He demanded a gentle charity and condemnation 'by each one on himself' rather than a condemnation of each other, and he explicitly suggested that explanations rather than retractions were needed.[28]

English Catholics were not unfamiliar with the reception of converts and both Bishop Douglass in 1790 and Bishop Griffiths in 1837 had reported to Rome on the frequency of conversions. However the converts from the Oxford Movement were different in several ways from those who had been received before, particularly in view of the numbers involved as well as their social position, influence and education. In 1843, Wiseman reported that more converts had been received during the past twelve months than in the previous ten years. He himself had recently baptized a lecturer on astronomy in Nottingham who expected fifteen of his pupils to follow his example. Wiseman had also received thirty-six people in Birmingham and would receive fifty more in a few weeks time. He was about to go to Wolverhampton where he would receive another twenty and a great deal was also being done, he reported, in many other places.[29] At the end of the year, Bishop Walsh reported that there were about a hundred converts under instruction in Nottingham, half of whom were about to make their profession of faith.[30]

Some of the Old Catholics who remembered the difficulties of former years found it difficult to accept that members of the Oxford Movement could be sincere, especially when High Churchmen began to claim that the celebration of Mass was part of the worship of the Church of England. A writer in the *Orthodox Journal* wondered how Anglican Ministers could have co-operated in the persecution of Catholics for the last three hundred years, if the teaching of the Anglican Church was what they now stated it to be.[31] But in spite of the scepticism of the Old Catholics, more influential converts were received into the Church than they had ever imagined and the sympathetic approach adopted by Wiseman was largely responsible for many of these. Newman later contrasted Wiseman's large and generous view of the Tractarians with the open hostility of a couple of Catholic priests who publicly accused Newman, Pusey and their friends of malice and treachery, cunning and guile, in their hatred of Catholicism. Newman was also able to record that one of the Catholic bishops who had previously been most suspicious had sent an expression of sorrow for his mistrust as he lay dying.[32]

The different attitudes adoped by English Catholics towards members of the Oxford Movement were reflected in a letter written to Wiseman during 1846 by Edmund Winstanley:

> From what passed between us when Your Lordship was here you will perceive that my opinion respecting the Oxford Movement coincided with that of Your Lordship. I sickened over the view Dr Baines took of the affair as also over the various articles published by those who entertained the same cold and damping sentiments. Lucas is one of these miserable croakers. Would to God he would keep his ice within his own breast and not attempt to freeze his readers. What good can result to our sacred cause from such empty, *sophistical* reflections as those of the *Tablet* of December 20? But he is a snarler and is never so eloquent and talkative as when he is blaming and satirizing. The good old fashioned and devout Catholics

of the North of England amongst whom I was bred almost identified the conversion of England with their faith: they firmly believed that this happiness, this *miraculous* effusion of God's mercy on England, had been merited by the blood of her martyrs and the sufferings of her Confessors, and had been revealed to our forefathers.[33]

Conversions were in fact frequently associated with miracles and with relics especially by the Ultramontanes. Bishop Walsh once informed Lord Shrewsbury,

> I have just had the consolation of administering the holy sacrament of confirmation to thirty apparently devout Catholics, most of whom are converts. Amongst the latter are the father, brother and uncle of the young lady who was cured in so extraordinary a manner by holy water, which circumstance occasioned their conversion. The young lady herself was confirmed with them.[34]

In 1848, Wiseman himself reported that Gladstone's sister had been cured by the application of a relic of Blessed Philomena and referring to the Catholic attitude towards relics he declared; 'I shall not think Ushaw Chapel *complete* till it is *replete* with holy authentic relicks. A large traffic in the antechapel when on certain days they could be exposed with veneration, lights etc., would perhaps be the best way of keeping them'.[35] On a later occasion, he wrote of 'our poor country, to which the Saints were returning through their relics'.[36]

The opportunity of realising Wiseman's dream occurred a few years later. At the end of 1859, Mgr George Talbot informed the President of Ushaw that he had seen 'the finest collection of valuable Relics that exists in the world in the possession of a private individual, and which he is obliged to dispose of by selling the Reliquaries'. As Talbot pointed out, it was quite impossible to *buy* relics, but it might be necessary to pay for the silver reliquaries and the expenses of the collectors. Talbot claimed that this collection of some 20 relics of our Lord, 3 of the Blessed Virgin and 860 of various saints, was the richest in the possession of any individual or community in the world and was even better than the collections in the Roman Basilicas. He also expressed the opinion that nowhere would 'so magnificent a collection' be more appreciated than at Ushaw, and the cost, a matter of £1,000, could not be better spent 'than in thus giving an impulse to the veneration of Relics in England';

> one cannot tell what blessings will accrue to England from the Relics of so many great Saints being transported there. St Ambrose

says that the possession of the bodies of Saints is a pledge that our prayers will be heard by them; therefore, I cannot help thinking that the Saints, whose Relics you will possess, will redouble their prayers for the conversion of the English.[37]

The reception of converts, however, gave rise to other problems such as the practical difficulty of finding employment, especially for married clergymen. This was a constant source of worry to Wiseman, while the danger, exemplified in the cases of J.M. Capes, E.S. Ffoulkes or R.W. Sibthorp, that some of the 'verts might return to the Church of England if only for a time, as well as the lack of co-operation and even opposition from the Old Catholics threw him into fits of depression when he felt completely isolated. Wiseman's sentiments at these times are very revealing. Sibthorp's return to Anglicanism was a severe blow to Wiseman and for a time made him ill. He attributed Sibthorp's defection to mental illness resulting from an accident which had altered all his ideas 'in the most extraordinary manner, as upon Church architecture etc'.[38]

And yet I had been careful to consult the Holy See through Propaganda before acting in this case. It was no small reason to me to go to Rome for the purpose of reassuring myself on this and other points connected with moral practical theology, in which I saw that my practice was at variance with that of others. I had almost become shaken in regard to them by seeing myself so completely alone, and blamed accordingly. I consulted there those on whom I could rely, and was encouraged by their answers.[39]

Wiseman was also encouraged by the 'providential' intervention of a sick man who, ignorant of the situation, apparently told him to go on, using the same methods and in spite of opposition, which Wiseman interpreted as referring to his attitude towards converts.

The position of the converts was one of the factors behind Wiseman's 'Romanizing' policies. The continental revival of ultramontane Catholicism, the growth of civil toleration in England, the development of Tractarianism within the Anglican Church and the political influence of O'Connell and the Irish, were different and sometimes diverging forces with which Wiseman was in personal contact and which he hoped to unite in support of English Catholicism. Thus, in spite of the suspicions or distrust of the Old Catholics, Wiseman continued to sympathize with members of the Oxford Movement, while refusing to break with O'Connell, though Newman, for example, was very critical of the Irish leader. Newman had 'an unspeakable aversion to the policy and acts' of O'Connell and could hardly contemplate joining a Church which had so associated with Whigs and Irish agitators in attacking the Church of England.[40] However, Wiseman himself believed that these divergent groups might be united by a general increase in their sense of loyal devotion to the See of Peter. English Catholics must lose their traditional or 'Gallican' reserve, while Oxford converts must study in Rome and so receive the highest ecclesiastical approval for their future work. However, events did not run smoothly and divisions seemed to multiply.

The practice of the liturgy at the beginning of the century was undoubtedly in need of reform. Church music tended to be somewhat operatic and the Bavarian Chapel became known as the 'Shilling Opera' – the price of the best seats.[41] Famous singers from the opera companies could be heard during the season and reports in Catholic magazines sometimes read like theatrical reviews. These operatic celebrations were often attended by Protestants and performed by indifferent Catholics, some of whom were occasionally living scandalous lives and who might perform their roles without staying to attend Mass. Members of the choir entered and left the church as they did in the theatre, organists read their newspapers and in the absence of a soprano, bass singers might attempt to sing falsetto.

Pugin and de Lisle had three main aims, the conversion of England, the revival of plain chant and the restoration of Gothic architecture. At first, they looked to Wiseman for support and he certainly allowed Pugin considerable freedom at Oscott in spite of the financial embarrassment which resulted. De Lisle for his part identified those who violated rubrics and wore worsted chasubles in defiance of the Church with those who opposed the zealous men working for the conversion of England and those who vowed that Wiseman should never be a bishop in England! Everything was becoming identified in one integral whole and even minor details became significant. When one unfortunate priest wore an old French cope, Pugin is reported to have asked him, 'What is the use, my dear sir, of praying for the conversion of England in that cope?'[42] In any case, Pugin felt that there was little point in providing decent vestments for English priests; when they wore his chasubles, they did not look like priests and the chasubles did not look like chasubles.

Pugin was extreme in his enthusiasm as Mgr Ward has pointed out;

He called out for Gothic shops and Gothic railway arches, as being the only lasting and suitable kind, and he drew a Gothic railway station to contrast with the then new arch-entrance to Euston. In his own house, all the furniture was Gothic, and he even designed Gothic moulds for the cook to use in making his puddings and jellies. He was not insensible to the humour of his actions, and on one occasion he wrote to a friend that his wife was about to present him with a Gothic baby.[43]

Again, Pugin was not unaware that medieval rood screens served the practical purpose of protecting monks from draughts and that it was not traditional in the Latin Church to exclude the people from the altar. Yet his enthusiasm for rood screens became almost proverbial. When Wiseman opposed the building of a rood screen, Pugin wrote 'what a miserable state of things the grand division between the sacrifice and the worshippers, between priest and people to be attempted to be abolished by those who should be foremost in their restoration'.[44]

In due course then the Gothic revival came into conflict with the Romanizing movement. Some of the Ultramontanes feared that the restoration of British or medieval liturgies and practices might lead to an attempt to emphasize the national character of English Catholicism. Wiseman himself reflected their opinions when he expressed his fears lest

the revival of medieval studies should lead to the undermining of religious union, by the setting of nationalities in opposition to the universality of Christianity, points of the circumference in rivalry with the centre, admiration of the branches to the contempt of the trunk.[45]

Furthermore, the adoption of Roman devotions and the use of Roman ceremonies demanded Roman architecture. English priests began to adopt the dress of the Italian clergy, wearing cassocks and birettas at all times. Latin was pronounced in the Italian way, nicknamed by its opponents as 'chees and chaws'.[46] Extreme Romanizers even imitated the carelessness which was then prevalent in Rome, saying Mass quickly and carelessly, talking freely at the altar or in the choir, even spitting in church or allowing dogs to run about there, as they were in Rome, on the grounds that this illustrated their sense of feeling at home in church or, in the case of one individual, because collar bells had a devotional effect.

Pugin later deplored what he called Wiseman's *pagan* taste and he received a formal discouragement from the Holy See following an ultramontane complaint about the Gothic revival. Pugin also became disillusioned with some of the Oxford converts after seeing the 'disgusting' and 'horrible' London Oratory and when he discovered that the Oratorians were not sufficiently enthusiastic about rood screens and plain chant. De Lisle was reported to have *cursed* the Oratory near a statue of the Virgin Mary, or as Faber put it, 'Opposite *Mamma's image*', while Faber himself denounced De Lisle as a Gallican and a Puseyite.[47] An ominous confusion was developing between doctrinal or theological issues and matters of devotion or ritual, while opponents were simply being condemned as pagans or heretics.

In 1847, Bishop Griffiths died and Wiseman was appointed Pro-Vicar Apostolic of the London District. This appointment became permanent in 1849 on the death of Bishop Walsh. The appointment of Wiseman was again not universally popular, though one of his correspondents declared that not even 'St Peter in person would give universal satisfaction'.[48] Wiseman's supporters were known as the Chelsea party and his opponents who included several of the most prominent clergy were known as the Moorfields party. The controversy was complicated by the fact that it became confused with differences over the restoration of a canonical hierarchy and as a result some of the clergy might have changed sides. Bishop Walsh was the senior candidate for the Archbishopric of Westminster, Bishop Briggs was regarded as 'the next senior Bishop' and Wiseman as 'the Junior Bishop'.[49] The petitions themselves were often confusing and perhaps occasionally deliberately misleading, but it is impossible not to recognize the ironic tone of one 'defence' of Wiseman:

It puts forward, as the chief and almost only reason, why Dr WISEMAN should be made Archbishop of Westminster, a qualification which would fit him, at most, for a missionary Apostolic. 'Ten years ago', say the petitioners, 'Dr WISEMAN preached in London every Sunday for several months, and three times a week during one Lent, and, therefore, he is more fitted than any of the other Vicars Apostolic to be made Archbishop of Westminster'. Had the petitioners declared him a man of consummate prudence, of unimpeachable integrity, had they characterized him a *St Charles Borromeo*, in his hatred of all novelties and innovation, and like him, an unexceptor of persons, and a stern, uncompromizing defender of sacred and long established customs, had they even spoken of his practical knowledge of the English Mission, of his personal experience in the cure of souls, and of his great knowledge and tender solicitude of the working Clergy, the Address would then have carried weight with it.

But it says little more than that he has preached a few times to overflowing congregations, and is, therefore, fit to be made Archbishop of Westminster.[50]

This petition reflected the existence of a deliberate and often organized resistance to Wiseman's 'Romanizing' innovations. Wiseman's opponents were not necessarily opposed to reform as such, but maintained that it should be based on English rather than Italian or Roman customs. To attempt to transform 'Englishmen into Romans' was, according to Lingard, for example, both impracticable and undesirable.[51] The introduction of continental devotions or fundamental and vigorous schemes of reform were regarded as alien to the English character or provocative to English opinion and would also have been opposed by Wiseman's predecessor. Most of the influential clergy criticized Wiseman as a 'Roman' intrusion supported by the new converts. Yet within three years, he succeeded in winning over most of his opponents, even if at times he had to show an unexpected firmness:

There is here a clique of underground but determined opposition. The head, an ex-Jesuit, has got into my hands, and I am applying the screw gently and peaceably, till today I have got him fixed in this dilemma, that he must either retract all his assertions and make a complete submission, or leave the District. Either will be a total discomfiture of the party here.[52]

Within two years, Wiseman established eleven new missions, ten religious communities, two orphanages and a grammar school for seventy boys. Devotional and charitable associations spread rapidly, the numbers of conversions and communions increased dramatically, and within a year some 15,000 Catholics were reported to have returned to the practice of their religion as a result of missions and retreats. A mission was organized among the thieves and prostitutes in one of the worst areas of London and when 'the devil interrupted the work by causing the stairs to break', a Protestant policeman apparently expressed the opinion that the Government 'ought to support it'.[53]

Wiseman's move to London was an indication, not only of the growing pastoral needs of English Catholics, but also of the need to reorganize their ecclesiastical administration. Since 1753, they had been governed by a constitution, only once partly modified, which had been established when there were comparatively few Catholics scattered in small groups throughout the country. By the middle of the nineteenth century, their numbers had increased considerably and included a number of new converts and a mass of Irish immigrants. The eight vicars apostolic whose authority was vague and undefined had to deal with major problems of reorganization as well as lesser difficulties such as the control of the continental missionaries and the new religious orders. But canon law did not apply within vicariates and the vicars apostolic were not even able to hold an episcopal synod to deal with minor difficulties. Consequently in 1845 and in 1847, the English bishops had asked the Holy See to restore a diocesan hierarchy, the ordinary form of ecclesiastical government.

In 1848, de Lisle referred to 'the deplorable Divisions that reign amongst the members of our Body' which, he felt, were at least partly the result of confusion about the rights of clergy and laity which must therefore be defined.

> I firmly believe that half the scandals and divisions, that arise amongst us, would thus be put an end to; or rather that they never would arise, but for want of a clear understanding in reference to these matters. Once that our Hierarchy shall be established, and that the Canon Law shall become operative amongst us, all will know their respective Rights and Duties: but in the absence of positive Law there is necessarily a confusion of ideas, and consequent collisions of the most unseemly character in practise.[54]

When the restoration of the hierarchy was planned in 1847, many Catholics petitioned that Wiseman should be appointed to Westminster and when it was later announced that he was to be raised to the cardinalate, which normally implied residence in Rome, further representations were made to prevent his separation from England. There were many critics of Wiseman whose opinions were known in Rome. Gentili, for example, thought that he would divide English Catholics and recommended Ullathorne as the most suitable candidate for Westminster.[55] Nevertheless, English Catholics in general seem to have been horrified at the prospect of losing a man who in spite of his enthusiasm for Rome, converts and foreigners, enjoyed an international reputation as a scholar and a national reputation as their leading apologist. Wiseman was considered to be the only man with sufficient ability and authority to lead the new hierarchy. Furthermore, appeals and petitions in favour of Wiseman's return were supported in Rome by the Pope's adviser on English affairs, Mgr George Talbot.

Talbot effectively influenced the Pope for almost twenty years in his attitude towards English Catholics. He became an inflexible supporter of Wiseman and Manning, and an opponent of the other bishops who deeply resented what one of them called, The 'backstairs influence' which was used unfairly against them. Ullathorne bluntly described Talbot as *'the pest* of the English Bishops'.[56] It is impossible to estimate the distortion and damage suffered by English Catholics as a result of the influence of this far from able convert who had only a superficial knowledge of their situation and who considered himself, unlike them, to be thoroughly Roman: as he wrote in a moment of political crisis, 'I long to die a martyr for the Pope and the rights of the Holy See'.[57] Ullathorne believed that Manning's 'intriguing interference' and attempts to influence Rome according to his own way of thinking had weakened Roman administration, and because of his 'onesided' information had resulted in decisions which were 'prejudicial' rather than 'beneficial'[58] Talbot cannot have caused less damage. Whatever his motives, and on one occasion he wrote, 'I declare before God, in everything I do, I act from principle, for the greater Glory of God and the Salvation of Souls', he was a fanatical schemer, incapable of appreciating another point of view, who identified opposition to his own policies and those of his friends with disloyalty to the Holy See. His attitude and approach during the controversy between Wiseman and Errington, for example, seem revealed in the significant remark which he made, 'As it is a matter of the greatest importance for the Church in England, we must leave it in the hands of God, when we have done all that lies in our power'.[59]

Meanwhile, if a normal episcopal hierarchy was becoming increasingly necessary for the government of the English Catholics and although it might well have been restored before 1850, the actual timing proved nothing less than tragic. The restoration of the hierarchy was already a controversial issue between the Tractarians who claimed to have the only authentic bishops in England and the Roman Catholics who were ruled by vicars apostolic. Far more important, however, was the fact that the restoration was introduced at a particular time, in such a way, by certain people, so that it seemed to be a direct attack on the Church and State of England. Newman's conversion in 1845 had encouraged the hopes of optimistic Catholics and the Gorham case in 1850 seemed to make it impossible for other Tractarians to resist any longer the arguments of Rome. The Privy Council scandalized High Churchmen by deciding that unorthodox views on baptism were not contrary to Anglican doctrine and as a result the Church of England seemed in a state of crisis if not collapse.

In order to avoid the inevitable protests which would follow a restoration of the hierarchy, the Roman authorities had decided that the restoration should only take place under a Whig government, at a time when Parliament was not sitting and without breaking the law by avoiding the use of existing Anglican titles. Several years earlier, Mark Tierney had added a further warning:

> however we may calculate on the temper of the Government and the real object of the change, when properly understood, the measure should be introduced *quietly*, not ostentatiously. There should be no public or outward demonstration. In fact it should be not so much a change, as a silent and almost imperceptible transition.[60]

Although the conditions laid down by Rome were fulfilled, the announcement was almost immediately seen as a direct challenge to the Church of England and on 14th October, 1850, the *Times* began to attack. Wiseman was 'an English subject, who has thought fit to enter the service of a foreign Power and accept its spurious dignities', while his appointment to Westminster was 'a clumsy joke'; 'one of the grossest acts of folly and impertinence which the Court of Rome has ventured to commit since the Crown and people of England threw off its yoke'.

The publication of the exuberant Wiseman's exultant pastoral, *Out of the Flaminian Gate*, made matters even worse. The 'greatest of blessings' had been bestowed on England 'by the restoration of its true Catholic hierarchical government, in communion with the see of Peter'. Until Rome decided otherwise, Wiseman himself would govern and:

> continue to govern, the countries of Middlesex, Hertford, and Essex as ordinary thereof, and those of Surrey, Sussex, Kent, Berkshire, and Hampshire, with the islands annexed, as administrator with ordinary jurisdiction . . . The great work, then, is complete; what you have long desired and prayed for is granted. Your beloved country has received a place among the fair Churches, which, normally constituted, form the splendid aggregate of Catholic Communion; Catholic England has been restored to its orbit in the ecclesiastical firmament, from which its light had long vanished, and begins now anew its course of regularly adjusted action round the centre of unity, the source of jurisdiction, of light, and of vigour. How wonderfully all this has been brought about, how clearly the hand of God has been shown in every step . . .[61]

This pastoral was perhaps Wiseman's greatest practical mistake. Several Catholics, including some of the vicars apostolic, had already urged that the restoration of the hierarchy should take place quietly as Tierney had recommended. Ullathorne believed that 'if it could have been quietly promulgated amongst ourselves at that period, we should have settled down in peace'.[62] But Wiseman's language was almost calculated to arouse the passions of anti-Catholic prejudice.

Wiseman's pastoral was published on the 7th of October and read in the London churches on the 17th; two days later, the *Times* asked:

Is it, then, here in Westminster, among ourselves and by the English throne, that an Italian priest is to parcel out the spiritual dominion of this country – to employ the renegades of our National Church to restore a foreign usurpation over the consciences of men, and to sow divisions in our political society by an undisguised and systematic hostility to the institutions most nearly identified with our national freedom and our national faith? Such an intention must either be ludicrous or intolerable – either a delusion of some fanatical brain or treason to the Constitution.

The Archbishop of York spoke of an 'unparalleled aggression', the Bishop of Oxford of the 'indecent aggression', the Bishop of Chichester of this 'audacious aggression' and the Bishop of London, who asked his clergy to preach controversial sermons, of a 'subtle aggression'. All but two of the Anglican bishops considered it necessary to protest to the Queen against,

this attempt to subject our people to a spiritual tyranny from which they were freed at the Reformation; and we make our humble petition to your Majesty to discountenance by all constitutional means the claims and usurpations of the Church of Rome, by which religious divisions are fostered and the labours of our clergy impeded in their endeavours to diffuse the light of true religion.[63]

The laity joined the clergy in organizing protest meetings; legal attempts were made to prove that the papal brief was invalid; the Mayor of Boston suggested that Wiseman should be exiled under the Aliens Act as a Spaniard; Lord Winchilsea urged the Government to declare war on the Papal States; an Anglican clergyman from his pulpit demanded the death penalty for priests hearing confessions. On Guy Fawkes Day, anti-Catholic mobs roamed the streets, breaking the windows of Catholic churches and pelting Catholic priests. An effigy of the Pope bearing the legend 'Oh, No, Pio No No' replaced that of Guy Fawkes at York, and the Pope, Wiseman as well as other bishops were also burned in effigy at Ware, Salisbury and Peckham.

The Tractarians were also subjected to this popular hostility. It was widely believed that the Pope had been encouraged in his 'aggression' by the weakness of Protestantism and the existence of 'traitors' within the Church of England. Queen Victoria had long since learned to treat Roman Catholics with tolerance and justice, and she deplored the recent abuse to which they had been subjected. But both the Queen and her Prime Minister, Lord John Russell, who incidentally had been aware of the proposal to restore the hierarchy for the last three years, feared and suspected the Puseyites. Russell's own attitude was revealed in an unfortunate letter which unintentionally seemed to direct the anti-Catholic prejudice towards the Tractarians who, unlike the Roman Catholics, usually supported his political opponents.

Another result of this public letter was that Russell, again unconsciously, committed himself to carrying penal legislation against Catholics in spite of the fact that this was a constitutional anachronism and although he himself had devoted his life to advancing the principles of toleration; furthermore, his own Government depended on the votes of Irish Catholics. When the Cabinet eventually and reluctantly planned the legislation to make territorial titles for Catholic bishops illegal, the actual bill was modified and harmless, and was repealed some twenty years later. What was significant was that the attitude of Wiseman and the impetuosity of Russell, the progress of Irish immigration, the development of Ultramontanism and the Oxford Movement, and the demands of a hostile public had forced the Government to pass the last act in English history intended to discriminate between Christian denominations.

In the meantime, Wiseman insisted on returning to the country and on 20 November issued his famous *Appeal to the English People*. This pamphlet appeared extensively in five daily newspapers including the *Times* and was a clear, direct and precise answer to the various attacks on the restoration of the hierarchy. He explained, for instance, the internal nature of the new reorganization which did not affect the royal prerogative. He demanded toleration as a right and by implication the establishment of a canonical hierarchy as essential to Catholicism. But Wiseman's *Appeal* was also aggressive and helps to illustrate the extent to which Wiseman was capable of showing contempt for the Church of England which he attacked on several counts. He made a deliberately offensive contrast between the concern of Catholics for the Westminster slums and the interest of the Anglicans in the wealth, titles and dignities of the Abbey. He accused the Anglican bishops and clergy of taking advantage of the crisis; they were associating 'their pretensions with the rights of the Sovereign', attempting to regain their lost influence and to replace 'by one burst of fanaticism' the position which they had lost over the years.[64] The danger to civil and religious liberty came from those who were using the present crisis to try to revoke the grant of toleration, though Wiseman expressed his confidence that the English people were too enlightened to be fooled in this way.

In spite of the favourable reaction which Wiseman's *Appeal* received in some quarters, the *Times* among others remained critical. The *Appeal* appeared in the *Times* on 20 November and on the following day, the newspaper asked,

> And why is it only when the unmistakable response of the people of England has shown him that his inflated pretentions will tend but little to the glorification or advancement of himself and his Church, does he first inform us that counties do not mean counties, but the Roman Catholics residing in them; that England is not restored to the Roman Catholic Church, but that her scanty Romanist population has received a new form of government? It is because the Roman Catholic Church has two languages, an esoteric and an exoteric — the first couched in the very terms of that more than mortal arrogance and insolence in which Hildebrand and Innocent thundered their decrees against trembling kings and prostrate emperors; the second, artful, humble, and cajoling, seizing on every popular topic, enlisting in its behalf every claptrap argument, and systematically employing reasoning the validity of which the sophist himself would be the last to recognize. But, let her speak what language she will, the spirit of that Church is unchanged. Pliable and ductile without, she is stern and unbending within. Within her pale is salvation, without is heathen darkness.

Wiseman's controversial skills played only a minor part in moderating the agitation. Sensible men became ashamed of hooligan prejudice, as Wiseman himself recognized, while other groups apart from Catholics were interested in bringing the controversy to an end. The Whigs did not want to offend the Irish, High Churchmen resented the outburst of Protestant opinion and expressions of prejudice offended those who supported the principles of religious toleration.

Nevertheless, 'papal aggression' had important and lasting consequences for the history of English Catholicism. Wiseman himself believed that 'the unnatural effervescence caused by the Hierarchy . . . instead of impeding is wonderfully forwarding the cause of religion'.[65] He chose to regard Manning's conversion as one of the first fruits of the restoration of the hierarchy and the prelude to an even larger movement towards the Church of Rome. Not unnaturally, Wiseman's opinions were also shared by his friends and allies. When Winstanley heard that the English hierarchy was about to be restored, he expressed his fears that it would 'not be carried into effect without great difficulty, not to the entire satisfaction of every one'.[66] He later remarked:

> I perceive from the public papers that the Legions of Hell are still howling and raging through the Land, and endeavouring to stem the tide which has long been bearing England towards Rome. But nothing can resist the Almighty, who, in his mercy, has, I firmly believe, decreed the conversion of this Country. How consoled must your Eminence have been in the midst of your severe trials by the splendid conversions which have lately taken place at Leeds and elsewhere, and which are taking place daily. Thus the gigantic efforts Protestantism is making to uphold itself only serve to hasten its downfall. Parliament may, and I suppose will so far yield to the outcry of bigotry as to pass some Bill against us; but this Bill will prove nugatory; and in spite of it the sacred Hierarchy will stand and produce the intended happy effects.[67]

But if English Catholics gained some converts and a degree of public recognition, the price to be paid was a revival of intolerance and the loss of a few of their number. The Duke of Norfolk and Lord Beaumont maintained that it was impossible to accept the new hierarchy without violating their civil obligations. The former told the latter that 'Ultramontane opinions are totally incompatible with allegiance to our Sovereign and with our Constitution' and he became an Anglican.[68] On the popular level, Catholic workers and servants were subjected to increased manifestations of anti-Catholicism, England in general became more conscious of its Protestantism and Evangelicalism was strengthened within the Anglican Church. It is possible that in spite of Irish immigration, Catholic Emancipation might have eventually enabled Catholics in England to avoid the aggressive and isolated attitudes which are characteristic of a minority in a hostile environment, but as a result of 'papal aggression', Catholics firmly closed their ranks and felt as besieged as ever.

Perhaps the most perceptive contemporary account of the situation was that given by Mark Tierney to Charles Newsham then in Rome.

> We are here in an awful state of excitement, brought about by the very unwise return of Dr Wiseman as Cardinal Archbishop to this country. The cause of religion, I am convinced, is thrown back at least a century by this proceeding. Had the hierarchy been re-

THIS IS THE BOY WHO CHALKED UP "NO POPERY!"—AND THEN RAN AWAY!!

Punch cartoon

established quietly and without ostentation, nothing would have been thought of it: but the appearance of so obnoxious a person as a Cardinal, the pomp and style of an archbishop, and, above all, the lordly tone of power and domination discernible in the Pastoral, by which, 'from out of the Flaminian Gate', the new Cardinal announced his elevation and proclaimed his authority, has so inflamed the minds of the people of all classes and of all denominations, that I really tremble for the result, and certainly look forward for the passing of some restrictive laws against us, as soon as Parliament shall meet. Of course, the outcry and the opposition are most dishonest. Every tale is awakened, every forgotten slander is raked up, every infamous calumny is renewed . . . But the falsehood and the dishonesty of all this does not make it either the less distressing or the less mischievous. Religion suffers as well as its professors; and that which the Pope intended as a boon and a blessing to us, has, by the imprudence of the principal person employed, been converted into a positive misfortune. Even the Cardinal's *Manifesto*, as it is called, is not, in my opinion calculated to do much good. As a piece of composition, as a splendid display of rhetoric, it is worthy of all praise: but its statements are not always correct, and the bitterness of its sarcasms, so unsuited to the character of a Christian prelate, has already excited the very worst of feelings against us, or perhaps more correctly against the cause.[69]

As a result of Wiseman's behaviour at this time and in spite of the efforts of Sir George Bowyer who was employed by the Cardinal to explain the restoration of the hierarchy to the Government, Wiseman lost the confidence of the secular authorities and other bishops had to undertake most of the official business conducted with the Government. The main significance of this development was that it became one of the factors in Wiseman's subsequent disputes with his episcopal colleagues; his own interventions in politics were rare and limited. It was too early for him to share and he probably would not have sympathized with Manning's attempt to associate Catholicism with the rise of the working class, while political interventions on behalf of Catholic claims might have alienated more support than they would have gained. Nevertheless, Wiseman did make some attempts to secure relief from the remaining social and political grievances of English Catholics and he eventually won concessions from different Governments on grants for Catholic poor schools, the appointment of Catholic school inspectors, the establishment of Catholic reformatories and the appointment of priests as official and salaried chaplains to prisons and the armed forces.

Papal aggression also had another significant political effect. It helped for a time to bring about a closer union between English and Irish Catholics who had previously suspected that Wiseman was too friendly with the British Government and who were always determined to resist English attempts to rule Ireland through Rome. The traditional support which Catholics had given to the Whig and Liberal parties tended to decline with the public agitation which resulted in the Ecclesiastical Titles Act and as the Liberals began to support the Italian Nationalists against the Pope. In 1858, Wiseman did what he could to help the Derby and Disraeli Ministry; he urged Irish Members of Parliament to support it and used his influence on behalf of the Conservatives at Waterford and in other constituencies.

Another consequence of papal aggression was Newman's trial for libel. In his lectures *On the Present Position of Catholics in England*, he had successfully ridiculed the more extreme forms of anti-Catholic prejudice and had condemned a former priest, supported by the Evangelical Protestant Alliance, as an immoral liar. Wiseman himself had already exposed Achilli in the *Dublin Review* for June, 1850, but the Cardinal was unable to provide Newman with sufficient evidence for the trial as a result of his usual carelessness and inefficiency. In spite of the fact that few reasonable men believed Achilli, Newman was only able to defend himself by condemning the Catholic Church in Italy where a priest had indulged in sexual offences even in a sacristy. But if Newman's accusations could be shown to be false, he himself would then stand condemned as a liar who used Italian whores to commit perjury.

In the event, Newman was condemned by an anti-Catholic jury and a prejudiced judge who lectured him on the deterioration in his character since his conversion. The dilemma into which the anti-Catholic fanatics had apparently forced Newman was resolved by the evident unfairness of a trial condemned as a mockery by the *Times* and the wide support which Newman received from his fellow Catholics throughout the world. As a result Catholics regarded the outcome as a moral victory. The *Times* commented:

> It is a great thing, no doubt, that in Protestant England the principle embodied in the national faith should triumph over its Roman Catholic adversaries; but it is a still greater thing that justice should be administered with purity and impartiality . . . We cannot afford to buy controversial success at the price of our reputation for a calm

and immaculate administration of justice . . . in the case of Dr. Newman . . . We consider that a great blow has been given to the administration of justice in this country, and Roman Catholics will have henceforth only too good reason for asserting, that there is no justice for them in cases tending to arouse the Protestant feelings of judges and juries . . . We now take our leave of this painful subject, trusting we may not soon again be called upon to comment on proceedings so indecorous in their nature, so unsatisfactory in their result — so little calculated to increase the respect of the people for the administration of justice, or the estimation by foreign nations of the English name and character.[70]

It would however be wrong to leave the impression that all legal decisions at the time were subject to anti-Catholic prejudice. In the Court of Arches during 1849, an ordained convert, Pierce Connelly, had successfully pleaded for the restoration of his conjugal rights with his wife Cornelia who had become a nun. In 1851, while the Ecclesiastical Titles Bill was being debated in the Commons, the Privy Council decided in favour of his wife. Since the husband could not afford another trial in the Court of Arches which he was technically allowed in this unique case, he contented himself with indulging in anti-Catholic propaganda. His later petition to the Commons was laid aside as improper and indecent. It is perhaps worth recording that the Bishop of New Orleans warned Cornelia that what her husband 'has attempted in vain in England he would obtain in this country'.[71]

There were of course immense practical problems as well as apologetic difficulties involved in the restoration of the hierarchy. Bishop Thomas Joseph Brown of Newport and Menevia even tried to resign. He had never been enthusiastic to change his vicariate into a diocese which, he felt, was not yet ready to form part of a restored hierarchy. The distances involved and the shortage of priests made it impossible to form a chapter of secular priests and Brown was allowed to form a canonical chapter composed of Benedictine monks. Bishop Errington of Plymouth faced similar difficulties and he was permitted to establish a smaller chapter.

The titles and sees chosen for the new hierarchy illustrate the different and even conflicting interests of English Catholics. Whereas Hexham and Beverley were historical titles appealing to the romantic past, Clifton and Salford were near industrial or commercial centres and successfully avoided using local Anglican titles. The choice of Birmingham, Liverpool, Nottingham, Northampton and Plymouth reflected the practical needs of the emerging society, while Westminster or Newport and Menevia combined the use of ancient titles with an attempt to satisfy contemporary needs. The choice of Westminster was probably unnecessarily provocative. Englishmen would not quickly forget that Wiseman had assumed as his title 'the very seat of our English Legislature'[72] while Lingard regarded it as 'ridiculous' to choose the title of a bishopric created by Henry VIII for a Catholic archdiocese.

An immediate practical difficulty was that of finding suitable bishops and it was a year before all the vacancies were filled. A few years earlier, one of Gentili's arguments against restoring the hierarchy had been the difficulty of finding enough qualified men and, in Newman's opinion, English Catholics were not ready for a hierarchy and found it impossible to fill the sees when it was restored. Wiseman himself was conscious of the fact that the number of candidates was limited and he expressed the hope that the new bishops would be more than simply soft, good and respectable. In the event, although the new bishops proved to be hardworking and devoted pastors, it would seem that none of them were truly great men and few were more than competent.[73]

Even Wiseman himself who is said to have found English Catholics a persecuted sect and left them a Church, was far more successful in encouraging or initiating projects than in completing them. He has been justly described as a very bad man of business who occasionally manifested a great capacity for business. Newman described him as 'full of resource and suggestion', but 'too busy to be strenuous about any thing'.[74] Unfortunately, the Catholic community needed a business-like administrator to plan for the future and to make the best use of their limited resources as well as an exuberant enthusiast to encourage their self-confidence. Wiseman had neither the inclination nor the aptitude for administrative details, while the time and energy which he devoted to apologetics and propaganda, public lectures and foreign correspondence meant that diocesan affairs were neglected and an increasing number of complaints against him began to reach the Roman authorities.

Wiseman's lack of administrative ability coupled with his impulsive generosity contributed in no small measure to the difficulties and conflicts which plagued the Catholic community during the next few years. Without consulting the Irish bishops, he hoped to obtain a titular bishopric for Newman when the latter was appointed Rector of the Irish University. But when the plan miscarried, Newman never received a word from Wiseman in explanation.

In 1857, Wiseman asked Newman to prepare a new translation of the

Bible, but when time and money had been spent in preparation, and when the work had actually begun, Wiseman began to avoid a definite commitment and then silently withdrew, again without explanation. Distressing as these particular instances might be, they are only typical of Wiseman's behaviour and relatively insignificant in the history of English Catholicism compared with some of the other conflicts and misunderstandings which resulted from Wiseman's policies and personality.

The restoration of the hierarchy involved the formation of a definite ecclesiastical constitution for the Church in England. The possibility of lay control which might have existed during the previous century had since disappeared and most priests were no longer simply chaplains of the local gentry. On the other hand, the establishment of a clerical regime did not of itself define the rights and duties of bishops and chapters, religious orders and secular clergy, and Wiseman was not the sort of leader who was capable of working out such a piece of technical and detailed administration. The situation was further complicated by the fact that over and above administrative difficulties, more serious questions such as the struggle between the Old Catholics and new converts, and even more fundamental controversies which resulted from the rise of Ultramontanism were already beginning to cut across other party lines.

During the eighteenth and early nineteenth centuries, English-speaking Catholics tended to see the restoration of a normal hierarchy as a national or even occasionally as an anti-Roman measure by the grant of constitutional self-government through synods of bishops with 'ordinary' canonical jurisdiction. Consequently, in 1843, Wiseman himself had opposed a movement in favour of the restoration of the hierarchy organized by Daniel Rock. Incidentally, Wiseman's opposition to the restoration of the hierarchy at this time illustrates his capacity for diatribe in attacking those who disagreed with him as well as his lack of realism in reacting to unwelcome situations.

Now for the Brotherhood — I wonder how you could have been induced to join it. I have reason to believe that *not one* priest in our district has acceded to it, and that not on account of the attack upon me (unworthy of such an honour) in their circular, but because they know first that such was not the right path, and second because it came unsanctioned by the Bishops . . . I say therefore . . . that it is a most uncanonical, unecclesiastical, uncatholic device and attempt; it hath neither antiquity, nor present propriety, nor future promise to recommend it; it is a filthy imitation of the anti-corn law league, of its agitations, deputations, assemblies, speechifyings, resolved first and second, petitions (acephalous) and bullyings (of the Holy See). It is the fungus-growth of a modern upheaving spirit, that will not be content to dig foundations but must blow them up with gun powder. Do not think I am *warm* about it; but to tell the truth I dread the idea of any Oxford man getting hold of the scheme: they who so reverence obedience and subordination, and hate the radical and chartist practices and modes of acting.[75]

English priests traditionally supported a re-establishment of the hierarchy and a return to the normal canonical government of the Church since this would give them a voice in the election of their bishops if only through the chapters and the status of parish priests instead of missionaries who could be removed at the will of the vicar apostolic. In 1790, one group of English Catholics petitioned the Holy See that all their future bishops 'shall be Ordinaries, and that none of them or even their Coadjutors shall be chosen without the advice and consent of their respective clergy'.[76] Almost fifty years later, the short-lived *Catholicon* still gave qualified support to this demand but described as 'the great and legitimate object of general desire, THE SUBSTITUTION OF CANONICAL BISHOPS FOR UNCANONICAL VICARS APOSTO-LIC'.[77] Even in 1851, the clergy in one of the northern deaneries passed a resolution asking the bishops to grant several privileges, the first of which was 'The election of Bishops by the general voice of the Parochial Clergy'.[78]

However, the English hierarchy was actually re-established at a time when Catholicism was peculiarly Roman or even Italian and increasingly Ultramontane, and the ecclesiastical constitution of the English Catholic community remained unsatisfactory. The Church in England remained a missionary Church under Propaganda so that, in this respect at least, episcopal authority and independence were restricted. On the other hand, the powers of the bishops increased in other ways and some Catholics were opposed to the restoration of the hierarchy precisely because it gave too much power to the bishops. The parochial clergy still lacked security of tenure and failed to gain a voice in the election of their bishops. The rights of the chapters were almost marginal. The canons could suggest three names as candidates for vacant sees, but these were often ignored by the other bishops and even by the Pope himself. As a result, older advocates of hierarchical government like Tierney and Rock who believed that election by the senior clergy was an integral part of any scheme, usually considered that a true hierarchy of bishops, priests and ministers, had not in fact been restored. They continued to petition the Roman authorities unsuccessfully over the next few years and, according to Mgr Ward, the sense of disappointment among the secular clergy had not quite disappeared even at the beginning of the twentieth century.[79]

But if the bishops enjoyed greater authority over their priests, the first resident English Cardinal since Pole attempted to exercise almost supreme and apparently autocratic control over the other bishops. The first synod which Wiseman typically hoped to make 'a new and stronger bond between the English Church and the Holy See',[80] was the emotional occasion on which Newman preached his famous sermon 'The Second Spring'. Ullathorne praised Wiseman's conduct of affairs and spoke of the unity and harmony shown by the bishops.[81] But this appearance of unity was deceptive and the synod, like the new polity of which it was an important element, disappointed the hopes which had been raised. Wiseman soon had to face opposition and complaints, legal struggles and appeals to Rome involving such issues as episcopal rights over seminaries, negotiations with the Government, the introduction of a genuine parochial structure, his appointments especially of converts, and the privileges of the new religious orders.

Wiseman was accused of being responsible for various innovations of being arbitrary in exercising authority and of indiscreetly arousing Protestant hostility by his public behaviour. Undoubtedly, Wiseman's standards of taste and etiquette were Roman and he loved to process in medieval splendour; he delighted in liturgical ceremonial or elaborate ritual and closely studied rubrical details. On Easter Sunday in 1851, he attended St George's Southwark 'in full robes, *just as I should have gone to the Capella* at St Peter's'.[82] When he visited the English Benedictines at Douay, he surprised them with the size of his retinue; successive carriages brought a bishop, the Cardinal's secretary and doctor, attendant priests, servants and luggage. The liveries of his servants and his carriage were elaborate, his notepaper more splendid than was usual at the time, and he surprised some High Church guests by serving four fish courses during Lent.

Wiseman's love of display and public behaviour were widely known and, after his death, it was said in Italy that he was still suffering in purgatory for his faults in this respect. Eventually Cardinal Antonelli urged Wiseman to avoid giving offence by unnecessary display and to discharge his religious duties in a quiet manner without irritating public opinion. Wiseman became less ostentatious and more accessible, and in due course was even accepted as a notable and distinguished figure on the London scene. It is only fair to add that this transformation of public opinion was largely due to Wiseman himself, while his success as a controversialist and lecturer did much to reconcile non-Catholics to the resident Cardinal and the restored hierarchy.

There were, however, more important difficulties than those which resulted from Wiseman's exuberance. Almost immediately after the restoration of the hierarchy, the Archbishop of Westminster became involved in a long quarrel over the property of the divided London District with his friend and successor at the English College whom he had himself recommended as the first Bishop of Southwark. What is significant about this rather technical point is that Wiseman and his friends should have proceeded to identify Bishop Thomas Grant with the 'old party' which opposed them.[83] Wiseman's policies and enthusiasms aroused the suspicions and opposition of some other bishops and English Catholics, but now administrative difficulties were becoming confused with more fundamental problems and even with ideological differences.

During 1854 and 1855, Wiseman became involved in a particularly bitter and unpleasant controversy which began when he removed all the priests from Islington in order to reform the parish and introduce Roman devotions. This was mentioned in a series of articles in a French Catholic periodical, possibly written by one of the priests concerned, who complained that the real reason for his removal had been his opposition to Ultramontanism. These articles also attacked the restoration of the hierarchy as a consequence of Wiseman's personal ambition and described it as disastrous to the real interests of English Catholics; Wiseman's policies it was claimed were arousing renewed Protestant hostility and dividing English Catholics most of whom disagreed with his Ultramontane views.

In the course of this controversy, Wiseman was sued for libel as a result of a mistranslation which suggested that one of his opponents had been 'expelled' from the Jesuits. One of the trials occasioned further manifestations of that anti-Catholic prejudice which had been evident in the Achilli trial. Wiseman himself commented:

> I consider it almost a privilege to have been treated as I have been during this week. The conduct of the judge, and the behaviour of the jury sympathizing with every coarse jest of counsel, and every impertinence of witness proved from the beginning that the cause was prejudged. What however was most painful was the deliberate perjury committed by two priests; one such as to throw on me the

charge of having forged a document for the trial. It is to get rid of this imputation only that I should think of taking any further steps; but never will I put my cause into a jury's hands.[84]

However, public opinion reacted against the prejudiced verdict which was set aside by the Court of Exchequer and the case was finally settled out of court. Furthermore, Wilfrid Ward believed that the attitudes and actions of Wiseman's critics in this case, indirectly contributed to the success of Ultramontanism by discrediting some of its opponents.

As has been indicated already, Wiseman believed that the only influence which could unite the varied and conflicting groups which formed the English Catholic community was that of Rome, and therefore of himself as the obvious representative of Rome. What he apparently failed to appreciate at first was that his Roman attitudes and his support for Ultramontanism created other grounds of friction which would become increasingly acute and cut across existing divisions. When Lingard died in 1851, the *Tablet* criticized some of his writings and 'the Gallican element pervading his History that made it agreeable to heretics'. In time, 'Dr Lingard's History will sink somewhat in public estimation' since he belonged to a school whose influence was now declining:

> It will not be owing to inaccuracies, or misrepresentations, or to obsolete style, but to another feeling, to the growing dislike to his school, to the abandonment of local peculiarities, and a more healthy sense of the strength and beauty of Rome; to a more child-like dependence on the Holy See, and a keener appreciation of St. Peter's presence; to a more lively apprehension of his mysterious power, and a more profound and self-abasing reverence for the Sovereign Pontiff on his throne.[85]

Tierney described this as an 'infamous article' and spoke of his determination 'to destroy the venom which the satellites of Golden Square are beginning to pour out on his memory'. Tierney had no doubt that Wiseman himself was at least indirectly responsible for these criticisms since he had been heard to express similar sentiments a thousand times,

> and it is what they are prepared to vomit out against every one, whose powers excite their jealousy, or whose calm sense of religion make that religion what it should be, — 'a reasonable service', instead of a blind undiscriminating fanaticism.[86]

On a later occasion, Tierney deliberately and perhaps wickedly quoted Wiseman's earlier defence of Lingard; in 1829, Wiseman had described an attack on Lingard by one of the early Italian Ultramontanes as *'the drivelling of a mad ultra'*. Tierney also challenged Wiseman's opinion that Lamennais not Lingard had been created a Cardinal *in petto* at the consistory of 1826.

The increasing Ultramontane character of English Catholicism was reflected in episcopal correspondence and appointments. At the end of 1859, Bishop Brown of Shrewsbury wrote to Talbot defending English Catholics from the charge of being isolated or nationalistic.[87] He granted their spirit of reserve, but this, he maintained, was a result of former persecutions and contemporary difficulties which those at a distance could too easily ignore. The bishop reported that the priests in one mission were insulted daily and the windows of another church frequently broken. It was unjust to describe this spirit of reserve as a lack of devotion to the Holy See. The English were not a talkative people, but no other nation in the world was more devoted to the Chair of Peter. Since the Restoration of the Hierarchy, English Catholics had obeyed every wish and command of the Holy Father which was manifest in the sacrifices of effort and money which they had made to carry out the various synodal decrees. Meanwhile, accusations that they were not Roman simply discouraged English Catholics and encouraged Protestants.

In 1860, Wiseman wrote to Propaganda expressing the fear that unless 'a real *Roman*' was appointed to the diocese of Beverley, 'all will go wrong'. When Robert Cornthwaite was appointed in the following year, Talbot expressed his satisfaction on the grounds that Cornthwaite was 'thoroughly Roman, which nowadays is a very necessary qualification'.[88] Cornthwaite himself expressed his complete agreement with Talbot that the main point to be preached, defended and enforced was the privileged position of the See of St Peter. The new bishop confided that he spoke in public and private, in season and out of season on this subject, and expressed the hope that all his people were true and loyal subjects of the Holy Father.

The opposition among the Old Catholics and their vicars apostolic to the introduction of foreign religious orders had not simply been because of a lack of enthusiasm for Italian devotions or a Roman 'spirit', but because the religious owed allegiance to their own superiors, were largely independent of the bishops and consequently increased their difficulties in administering their districts. Similarly, Wiseman's support or encouragement for new converts or religious orders was not simply because they would help to advance his Roman ideals, but because the growing needs of the English Church provided increasing opportunities for the religious to make their own contributions to the Catholic community. Nevertheless, different policies were easily confused and it is in fact difficult to decide to what extent they should be distinguished.

In spite of Wiseman's enthusiasm for magnificence or his love of splendour, he showed a practical social concern and was genuinely anxious to provide more priests, missions and schools for the immense poverty-stricken immigrant population in the slums of his diocese. He reported enthusiastically on the progress of work among the poor. In one area where two of the three or four thousand inhabitants were 'habitually drunk, fighting and scandalous', almost everyone returned to their religious duties after the opening of a mission. The people became 'most orderly' and the Ragged School soon closed. Wiseman himself visited the area, promised to provide priests to hear confessions and to say Mass, and 'preached on perseverance, especially in sobriety, going to their duties, peaceableness, and not sending their children to Protestant schools'.[89]

As a result of personal experience, Wiseman knew that the most immediate help available could only be provided by one of the various religious communities, but the introduction of foreign communities or the foundation of English branches created further internal difficulties with the diocesan clergy or the Old Catholics. In any case, existing orders were often short of vocations, restricted by their constitutions or too independent of the local bishop to meet all Wiseman's needs. In an ingenious attempt to solve these difficulties, Wiseman occasioned a major controversy. When the Cardinal persuaded Henry Edward Manning to form the congregation of the Oblates to provide a body of men prepared to engage in almost any pastoral activity, Wiseman was not simply introducing a new convert, a new religious community or a new means of intervening within the established system, but an extraordinary and dominating personality who would soon clash with a self-styled defender of the old order.

In 1855, Wiseman secured as his coadjutor, his old friend George Errington who had assisted him both in Rome and at Oscott. In spite of Errington's own misgivings, he had been appointed titular Archbishop of Trebizond with right of succession to Westminster. The Cardinal intended that the Archbishop should be regarded as his equal and in turn, the Archbishop insisted that there should be no appeal from his decisions. But it is difficult to imagine the emotional and impulsive Wiseman not intervening, especially since by all accounts,

Errington was an exact canonist and rigid disciplinarian, a stern and inflexible official of independent and authoritarian judgment.

When Errington made the first visitation of the archdiocese since the restoration of the hierarchy, he set about introducing new methods and reforming any abuses or irregularities which came to his attention. Almost inevitably, there were complaints to which the more sympathetic Wiseman tended to yield. Errington did not share Wiseman's enthusiasm for new converts and when the Coadjutor visited the diocesan seminary, he restricted the teaching of W.G. Ward who thereupon resigned. Ward, a layman and Ultramontane convert, had been one of Wiseman's most deliberate and significant appointments in advancing the 'Roman spirit' or the 'new system' and since the Cardinal had already frequently reversed his Coadjutor's decisions, Errington now decided to treat this issue as a test case.[90]

At the same time, in order to avoid any scandal which might result from an impossible situation, Errington offered to resign. Talbot wrote to both men on behalf of the Roman authorities in order to prevent a break between them and he warned Wiseman of the danger of giving the impression that he could not even agree with his own nominees such as the Bishop of Southwark or the Archbishop of Trebizond.[91] This conciliatory approach, however, did not last long. Meanwhile, it was agreed that Errington should administer the diocese of Clifton until a new bishop was appointed. At the time, this diocese was almost bankrupt and was probably the most difficult episcopal charge in the country; George Oliver later paid tribute to Errington 'who, during a very critical period, presided over the dioceses of Plymouth and Clifton with indefatigable zeal and enlightened judgment'.[92]

During Errington's absence from Westminster, Manning who was already attracting the most able and zealous younger priests, and who was, if anything, even more anxious than Wiseman to strengthen the links between the Church in England and Rome, was appointed by the Pope as Provost of the Westminster Chapter. Wiseman himself had hoped for this, but Errington was staggered and dismayed. Manning had spent most of his Catholic life in Rome and was only known to English Catholics as a friend of the Cardinal or a favourite of the Roman authorities. This suggested, unfairly in fact, that he was a man of unscrupulous ambition and afterwards Wiseman was falsely seen, especially with his advancing illness, as being completely under Manning's influence in that 'Romanizing' movement which the new Provost represented or symbolized.

Appreciating Errington's reluctance to rejoin Wiseman, Talbot offered him the Archbishopric of Trinidad which Errington wanted to accept, but Wiseman successfully appealed to him to return to Westminster. Meanwhile, Ward had withdrawn his resignation and although this pleased Wiseman, he did not dare to tell his Coadjutor. Wiseman broke this news when he accompanied Errington to the railway station as the Archbishop was on his way to make a second visitation of the seminary, and then only when Errington was in the train leaving Wiseman on the platform. Thereupon, any sense of mutual confidence between the two prelates became impossible, though differences over Ward were taking second place to an increasingly acute conflict over Manning who combined his position as Provost with that of Superior of the Oblates, and who was suspected of attempting to establish the control of the Oblates over St Edmund's, Ware. Some years later, Wiseman denied that he had ever intended to put the seminary under the exclusive direction of the Oblates, but Manning at one stage certainly hoped and expected that he would do so, and Wiseman's agent in Rome was later instructed to point out that the presence of the Oblates was a means of influencing the younger clergy in Roman and Ultramontane attitudes.

Not only Errington, but most of the Canons, the Vicar General and Wiseman's own Secretary were concerned at the extent of Manning's authority and influence, while the Cardinal's financial and ecclesiastical support for the Oblates was resented as encroaching on the rights of the secular clergy. Errington himself was critical of the idea of establishing another religious community independent of the local bishop and he was convinced that Manning was introducing an independent congregation which would attract its best members at the expense of the finances and the manpower of the diocese. Furthermore since one of the aims of the Oblates was to introduce the Roman seminary system into England, Errington also feared that his future clergy would be educated in the new spirit of Ultramontanism. The Canons eventually alleged that Manning's congregation infringed certain canonical laws and reminded Wiseman of some rules which he had previously drawn up in favour of the Chapter. Both sides, however, appreciated that this was not merely a controversy over technical regulations and when Wiseman found his own ideals defended by Manning and the converts against the traditional hostility of the Old Catholics to Roman innovations, he ignored both canon law and previous practice, and simply annulled the Chapter's proceedings.

When Errington came forward as the champion of the Canons in their appeal to Rome over control of St Edmund's, Wiseman retaliated by dismissing his Vicar General and replaced him with an obviously incompetent successor. The Holy See referred the controversy back to England, but it could hardly be settled at home. Wiseman, therefore, asked Talbot whether another see might not be found for his Coadjutor and hinted that some means of forcing his resignation must be found. Wiseman was convinced that if he was succeeded by Errington, the old order would be restored and his life's work largely ruined, while the Chapter was not only personally hostile but anti-Roman and would destroy all hope of a truly loyal clergy which was Roman in spirit and devotion.

This view was widely shared. F.W. Faber claimed that if Errington became Archbishop of Westminster, 'the Holy See will have to reckon that it will take fifty if not a hundred years to restore England to the pitch of Ultramontanism which she has now reached.'[93] Manning considered that the controversy involved nothing less than the 'ascendancy of a Roman over every other kind of spirit' and 'whether England shall be organized and assimilated to the living devotions and spirit of Rome, or perpetuate itself upon its own insular centre'.[94] It is, therefore, hardly surprising that Wiseman who was described as 'the instrument under God to *Romanize* England' should have enjoyed the positive support of the Pope who, it was promised, would grant all his requests and receive him 'with open arms'.[95] The encouragement and support given by Talbot to Wiseman might even have prevented a reconciliation; as Talbot told one of his correspondents:

> You quite frighten me by saying that there is a chance of his coming to a reconciliation with his Coadjutor. It would be simply making a fool of the Holy Father, the Propaganda, and your humble servant, and would be a sheer triumph for the retrograde party in England. I have sent his Eminence an Autograph Blessing from the Holy Father which I hope will console him. I am satisfied that when he comes to Rome he will have completely his own way. He has only to remain firm.[96]

Consequently, in spite of other relevant factors and although both sides were undoubtedly influenced by genuine convictions about the welfare of the Archdiocese of Westminster, the implications of the conflict were far more fundamental and it became a turning point in the struggle between traditional English Catholicism and the new Roman Ultramontanism. Errington for his part certainly shared many of Manning's aims and would have supported some of his policies, but Errington also regarded himself as the defender of English traditions against Manning's Roman innovations. Furthermore, Errington must have been alienated by the methods and the insinuations of his Ultramontane opponents. Priests who were critical of the Coadjutor were given to understand that the authorities would welcome any complaints and these were forthcoming.

In Rome, Talbot simply threatened Errington with dismissal if he was not prepared to resign and helped to prevent the possibility of an equitable compromise by unjustly accusing the Archbishop of 'anti-Romanism, Anglo-Gallicanism'.[97]

> As for your Coadjutor, I have thought it more straightforward and open on my part to tell him what my opinion of him is. I told him plainly that I thought him radically Anti-Roman in Spirit and Anglo-Gallican, although I did not for a moment suppose that he would maintain any Gallican proposition or even the Gallican theory. Therefore I said that he could not ever agree with your Eminence whom I looked upon as my beau idéal of a Roman Bishop.[98]

This accusation of Gallicanism apparently convinced Errington that if he co-operated by resigning, he would not only confirm the truth of such a false assertion in his own case, but also compromise those who had supported him. He therefore declined when repeatedly offered other episcopal sees. When the Pope personally appealed for Errington's resignation, he again refused unless the Pope gave an express command which finally came after a Commission of three Cardinals, including one of Wiseman's friends, had issued a hostile report in 1860.

Three charges were brought against Errington; he had been opposed to the Oblates — mostly to their presence in the seminary, he had supported the Canons against the Cardinal and had again opposed him at the third Provincial Synod. This last accusation was crucial, at least according to Talbot. By opposing Wiseman at the Synod, Errington had given to the Roman authorities who had already decided to demand his resignation, a good reason for doing so, 'whereas before there was nothing [tangible?] to be laid hold of, so as to remove him from his present position, if he should shew fight'.[99] In fact, the only reasons offered for depriving Errington of his right of succession were his disagreements with the Cardinal and a general concern for the welfare of the province of Westminster. But as Frederick Rymer pointed out, the first difficulty could have been solved by suspending Errington's rights during Wiseman's lifetime, while the second reason was not considered to be an obstacle when Errington was offered a succession of appointments from Trinidad to Edinburgh.

Furthermore, the primary cause of Wiseman's quarrel with his Canons was the presence of the Oblates in St Edmund's and they were soon removed, perhaps even as a result of advice from Rome. The main issue at the third Synod had been the control of the seminaries which was eventually decided against Wiseman. In these circumstances, Rymer concluded his vindication of Errington by asking whether:

> loyalty to the Holy See requires that every Catholic should at once yield compliance with every wish of the reigning Pontiff, no matter what may be his personal character, no matter what representations or misrepresentations may have been made to him, no matter under what influences he may be acting, no matter how opposed to canon law nor how injurious to the general discipline and welfare of the Church his wishes may be.[100]

Although Errington was finally defeated, Wiseman discovered that as a result many of his own priests were hostile, while the other bishops were determined to resist any further interference within their individual or collective areas of jurisdiction. There were, of course, several reasons for the growing misunderstandings between the Cardinal Archbishop and the rest of the hierarchy. Wiseman's own position and personality, the fact that other bishops were his former students irritated by his continued autocratic manner in dealing with them, the circumstances of his appointment and the fact that another bishop had to act as the episcopal representative in dealing with the Government, all contributed to the conflicts within the hierarchy. Two particular issues were in question, the legal basis of Catholic property and the control of the seminaries. But the main point at issue was whether the bishops were to have a decisive or merely a consultative voice in the adoption of policies affecting the development of English Catholicism. Misunderstandings deepened as Wiseman asserted himself. The bishops began to hold discussions among themselves without reference to Wiseman, Manning and Vaughan who alone shared his confidence. Wiseman accused them of hauling down the Tiara and Keys, and displaying their Confederate flag, the Gallic cock that crowed against St Peter! In 1862, most of the hierarchy found pretexts for declining his invitations to the annual Low Week meeting and these were interpreted as 'conspired and deliberate insults towards the head of the Hierarchy' who asked Manning to report the matter to the Prefect of Propaganda.[101]

In all appeals to Rome, Pius IX himself sympathized with Wiseman, while the skills of Manning or the influence of Talbot seemed deciding factors in the Cardinal's favour. The other bishops, therefore, sometimes felt the need to adopt dramatic counter-measures, and, although his motives are far from clear, Ullathorne at one stage offered to resign which had the effect of securing a full and fair hearing for the bishops' case. Herbert Vaughan however made a typically unfavourable comment, 'Mgr *Ego Solus* . . . has come out in his true colours, Anglican and Gallican in the strongest way'. Vaughan's opinions were supported by Manning who described Ullathorne's criticism that Rome was continually restricting original episcopal privileges as *'purus fructus Gallicanismi'*.[102] In an address to the English bishops assembled in Rome for the canonization of the Japanese martyrs, the Pope ordered them to take the largest mountain in the Alps to cover their disagreements. Wiseman, optimistic as ever, chose to regard this speech as the end of an 'unhappy attempt to make void the Hierarchy and return to Vicarial regimen'. But the hostilities of the bishops were not immediately forgotten. When he left his colleagues after the audience, 'Not a hand was kindly held out. I had almost to lift some up dead from the side'.[103]

But in spite of the Pope's personal sympathy for Wiseman, the Bishops were in the event more successful. The decision on Catholic property was closer to their views than those of Wiseman or Manning, while Propaganda practically confirmed the decrees of the Synod on the control of the seminaries. This was contrary to Wiseman's hopes that the local diocesan bishop would enjoy complete jurisdiction over the local college and in spite of the fact that both Manning and Talbot believed that a decision in favour of Wiseman's position on this issue was of fundamental importance for the future of the Church of England. Finally, although attendance at the Low Week meeting was made compulsory, as Wiseman wished, the agenda was to be circulated in advance and the decisions made by a majority vote or by referring the matter to Rome. Thus the Cardinal's authority had been 'supported' in a way which restricted his previous practice; the other bishops had decisive votes, not merely consultative voices.

These disputes might be seen as the inevitable faults of a new system of ecclesiastical government which could not be expected to be successful at once. On the other hand, several unhappy features might have been avoided. In the first place, the Roman authorities allowed delays and procrastinations which failed to avoid immediate unpleasantness without solving real problems. According to Butler, the curial officials, perhaps as a result of the claims of English Ultramontanes, seem to have been more concerned with avoiding the dangers of an imaginary schism than with the long term interests of the English Church.[104] This dispute over the property of the London District went on for some seven years before being decided in favour of the Bishop of Southwark. Another important element which has already been mentioned was the personality of Wiseman himself. The very existence of the restored Church was due more to him than to anyone else, but his understanding of that Church and his own place within it was bound to lead to an impatient irritation on the part of others. Finally, Wiseman became increasingly dependent on Ultramontanes like Talbot and Manning who, accepting the confusion of issues which resulted from the rise of Ultramontanism, were unwilling or unable to indulge in compromise and who suspected their opponents of unworthy motives and conspiracies, while accusing them of heresy.

At the same time, Manning's success between 1858 and 1863 when he acted for Wiseman in Rome has been exaggerated and so has his part in the removal of Errington which was not, as was sometimes suggested, the result of any personal ambition. Although Manning fully supported the Cardinal and shared his conviction that the succession of Errington would be disastrous, Manning was only indirectly involved as Provost of the Chapter and Superior of the Oblates. Both Wiseman and Manning were convinced supporters of Ultramontane attitudes or policies and worked for the triumph of that Roman spirit which one had introduced and the other would maintain. Their fault was to identify Ultramontanism with Catholic truth. Nevertheless, there can be little doubt that Manning's influence strongly contributed to Wiseman's increasing intransigence at this time and that much of the opposition from the Bishops and the Clergy was in fact opposition to Manning. Wiseman's ideas about seminaries or his opinions of the clergy were not inspired by the Provost, but the Cardinal was apparently encouraged to adopt extremes which were not typical of his earlier years. Newman described the Wiseman of 1840 as 'a man of genial temper and large mind . . . averse to harsh measures'.[105] Butler has argued that Manning had a similar temperament to the autocrat which Wiseman had unconsciously become and that the Provost gave uncompromising rather than the moderate advice which might have avoided the sorrows and sadness of the Cardinal's later years.[106]

On Wiseman's death, the *Daily Telegraph* pointed out that although he was 'a rigid Ultramontane', the friend of Lacordaire or Montalembert was not an obscurantist.[107] Wiseman attempted to meet the intellectual difficulties of the day and if he accepted *Quanta Cura*, he could never have inspired it. The newspaper claimed that Wiseman had been in favour of establishing a Catholic College at Oxford and had only reluctantly acquiesced in the suppression of the *Rambler*. According to

Wilfrid Ward, although Wiseman retained his earlier and more liberal sentiments, the influence of Manning became increasingly evident in practice as a result of the Cardinal's ill-health and sense of isolation, the development of Ultramontanism and the rise of the Italian Question. When Newman first planned to establish an Oratory at Oxford, Wiseman had encouraged him. When de Lisle proposed schemes for reunion and joined the *Association for the Promotion of the Union of Christendom*, Wiseman was sympathetic. Yet in both cases, he ultimately decided in favour of Manning's more rigid line. In support of these claims, Wilfrid Ward refers to a letter from Wiseman directly contradicting the misrepresentations of those, probably Manning, Ward and possibly Vaughan, who attributed to him their own extreme version of Ultramontane opinion in attacking Montalembert's famous speech at the Malines Congress.[108]

Originally, in spite of reservations which Wiseman shared with Newman and with opinions expressed in the *Rambler*, the Cardinal urged the Holy See not to act against the *Association*. Later, however, with the agreement of the other bishops, Wiseman proposed to ask Rome for instructions and the Holy Office replied by forbidding Catholics to join the organization. Manning was considered to have been largely responsible for this negative reply and although the Catholic members of the *Association* submitted, they thought that Rome had been misinformed and Newman wrote that they themselves had been cruelly treated. After Wiseman's death, when some Anglicans appealed for a reconsideration of the case, a strong letter from Rome repeated the condemnation of the branch theory and firmly reasserted the essential *Roman* Unity of the Church. Yet even this strong statement disappointed both Talbot and Manning who had apparently hoped for a more uncompromising line. Manning also mentioned the existence of some of Wiseman's letters which manifested a greater tolerance of the *Association* 'than could be wished'.[109]

It might well be, therefore, that had Wiseman been at the height of his powers, he would have been more successful and positive in dealing with the situation. It is perhaps also significant that Manning's attitude, revealed in a pastoral letter of 1866, was remarkably similar to that adopted by Vaughan at the end of the century:

> So far as this movement shall lead to the submission of individuals to the truth, it is of God; so far as it leads to the suppression of individual convictions and individual responsibility, it is not of God . . . Thus far I have been constrained by the imperative law of truth to

lay bare the impossibility and the unlawfulness of all union except that which is based upon the only and infallible Church of God.[110]

Manning concluded by calling for prayers for the conversion of England, to be joined with the prayers of the Blessed Virgin and the English Martyrs.

Manning had the faults as well as the qualities of a man of conviction who found it impossible to compromise. He was a superb organizer and brilliant administrator, though his biographer believed that he 'was not the leader of the educated Catholic laity, but their master'.[111] Manning could be intransigent and even uncharitable. He was often unable to see another point of view and, according to Butler, was almost fanatical in his single-minded determination: the opposition of the Chapter to the Cardinal 'must displease God', while the fact that the Bishops drank wine or encouraged theatricals in convent schools were 'Hindrances to the Spread of the Catholic Church in England'.[112] Supported by other Ultramontanes like Faber and Ward, Talbot and Vaughan, Manning came to regard any opposition to his own or to Wiseman's policies as manifestations of a low, worldly, national, Gallican, anti-Roman or anti-papal form of Catholicism. They all used extreme language in condemning the laity for their disloyal and un-Catholic views, the clergy particularly Newman, and the Bishops especially Grant and Brown, Goss and Ullathorne. It was apparently impossible to expect any great progress in religion until all the bishops and most of the clergy had died out.

Bishop Grant who was regarded by most of his contemporaries as a saint was one of the victims of Talbot's hostility:

> The Bishop of Southwark from his long residence in Rome has learnt all the trickiness, and underhand intrigue practised by some persons here, but he has not imbibed the generous, noble Spirit, which I took upon as the great Characteristic of the Holy See. I have reason to suppose that by means of his letters he has been doing an immense deal of mischief at Propaganda, and especially lately when he has been the great supporter of the Archbishop of Trebizond against Cardinal Wiseman. Besides he is the sworn enemy of all the converts who are active and zealous, although he professes friendship towards them. He is the great supporter of the Old high and dry school.[113]

In 1860, Talbot recommended moving Grant to Beverley where presumably he would be far enough away from Wiseman.[114] Twelve months later, it was rumoured that Wiseman had suggested the removal of Grant and petitions were sent to Rome opposing this. Talbot first consoled the Cardinal and then had the gall to attack the Bishop: 'I don't know how such a report can have got abroad. I am afraid that poor Dr G. with all his sanctity is what they used to call at school a *sneak*, and works a great deal too much underhand.'[115]

All the Bishops and the older Clergy might not have shared the fulness of Wiseman's vision, several of them were certainly opposed to his Ultramontane policies, but all of them worked devotedly and industriously in almost impossible conditions to organize their dioceses and parishes, and to promote the religious life of their people. Bishop Ullathorne's achievement was not untypical. During his episcopate, 44 new missions were founded, 67 new churches were built and more than 100 new elementary schools provided for Catholic children. The number of priests increased from 86 to 200, and convents from 7 to 36. Originally the diocese had only one charitable institution, but at the time of Ullathorne's death, there were two Houses of Mercy, seven orphanages, two poor asylums, two hospitals for incurables and two homes for poor children. At the same time, Ullathorne also managed to consolidate the diocesan finances. When William Vaughan became Bishop of Plymouth in 1855, there were only 23 secular priests with a few regular clergy working in the three counties committed to his charge and within three years, he had lost 11 of these. Nevertheless, in spite of this unpromising beginning, he still managed to establish 40 new churches, 8 convents and 16 schools, and left 'not a mission with a debt'.[116]

The material expansion of Catholicism during Wiseman's lifetime was impressive. Towards the end of the first quarter of the nineteenth century, there were about 350 Catholic churches and chapels in England and Wales. By 1840, there were over 100 more in England, but only one more in Wales. Between 1840 and 1850, there was a further increase of over 100 in England and two more in Wales, while the number of priests during the same period increased from 542 to 788. The main increase, however, was in London, the Midlands and Lancashire. In other areas, growth was almost marginal. In 1820, there was not a single Catholic church or chapel in some English counties; by 1833, three counties had only one church, four counties had only two, and two counties had only three.

In 1851, there were 124 priests and 82 churches in the diocese of Birmingham, whereas Northampton, with a greater population, had only 27 priests and 26 churches, while there were only 22 priests and 18 churches in Newport and Menevia. At the same time, there was not one single priest, church or school in Cardiganshire and Radnorshire.

Meanwhile, according to Ward, in London alone between 1826 and 1863, the number of priests increased from 48 to 194, the number of churches from 24 to 102, while 15 religious houses of men and 34 charitable institutions were also established. In the country as a whole between 1851, 1870 and 1890, the number of priests increased from 826 to 1536 and 2478, the number of churches increased from 586 to 947 and 1335, so that by the end of the century there were just under 3000 priests and half that number of churches.[117]

The Catholic population had grown in numbers, influence and prestige, partly at least as a result of Wiseman's own encouragement of pastoral or missionary activity regardless of expense, and partly as a result of the respect which he himself had won and which can be seen in the many expressions of public esteem shown especially during his later years. But Wiseman's strengths and limitations were strangely combined. His own personality and policies played a large part in creating the problems as well as the conditions for progress which are both evident in the development of English Catholicism at this time. This curious combination of success and failure was manifested in private and public, and can be found in practical details of administration or in important matters of policy. There was then a certain ambiguity or confusion in Wiseman's attitudes and policies, and it is perhaps significant that he was not a good judge of men. He appointed both Errington and Talbot against their own wishes, and was engaged in lengthy conflicts with Grant, his own nominee. His relations with Newman, the leading Oxford convert, were at least awkward, and he found it difficult to work with Ullathorne, probably the best bishop of the restored hierarchy.

Wiseman was a man of wide vision and optimism who did more than anyone else to create the modern English Roman Catholic Church and to avoid the dangers of a native insularity. But he must also accept a large part of responsibility for the ultimate success of that Romanizing or Ultramontane policy which did not have entirely happy results. Wiseman and Manning apparently became convinced that when English Catholicism was 'assimilated to the . . . spirit of Rome', it would be better able to influence and share the life of the English people, or at least that these two operations were associated in some way.[118] But although English Catholics might gain support and a sense of confidence from the strength of Catholicism abroad, it is difficult to see how they could expect to identify themselves with England and things English by imitating Roman practices and adopting a foreign emphasis which in the event simply alienated Protestant Englishmen.

For some time, Wiseman suffered increasingly from diabetes. He grew fat and became lethargic, and was subject to repeated heart attacks so that his life was often in danger. After an illness in 1860, he was never the same. The disease which ended his life steadily advanced and made him almost incapable of active work. This illness coupled with the effect of his differences with the other bishops has led one of his biographers to describe him as 'a broken man'.[119] When he died in 1865, the press was sympathetic and the *Times* compared his funeral procession which was indeed remarkable for manifestations of respect and even affection, to that of the Duke of Wellington. On his death-bed, Wiseman had spoken of his funeral quite openly and had insisted that everything in the ceremonial should be 'done quite right' without a rubric being broken. Of the last rites, he said in a rather touching and very typical way, 'I want to have everything the Church gives me, down to the Holy Water. Do not leave out anything. I want everything'.[120] The office of the dead was said by representatives of eleven religious orders, nearly all of whom had been introduced into London by Wiseman; the congregations of secular priests were also represented, but not the Jesuits — according to Roman etiquette.

Notes

1. B. Fothergill, *Nicholas Wiseman* (London, 1963) 25; see also D. Gwynn, *Cardinal Wiseman* (London, 1929) 21-4; W. Ward, *The Life and Times of Cardinal Wiseman* (London, 1900) I: 126; N. Wiseman, *Recollections of the last four Popes* (London, n.d.) 195-6.
2. Wiseman, *Recollections* 251.
3. Ward, *Wiseman* I: 227, 233.
4. Ward, *Wiseman* I: 233-4; Fothergill, *Wiseman* 289.
5. A public letter of protest by Mr Eneas MacDonnell to Mr James Smith, secretary of the Institute, 26 June 1838, Archives of St Edmund's College, Ware.
6. Ward, *Wiseman* I: 310-11.
7. On 28 April 1840, it was proposed that the Roman Agent should be independent of the English College and that the clergy should contribute 'each a sum not exceeding *five shillings* per annum' to his support. Ushaw College Mss. (UCM) IV: 384; see also B. Ward, *The Sequel to Catholic Emancipation* (London, 1915) I: 142-51, 157, 165.
8. Ward, *Sequel to Emancipation* 137.
9. Nicholson to Ullathorne, 9 May 1843, Ware; see also Ward, *Sequel to Emancipation* I: 158, 160-2.

10. Wiseman to Ullathorne, 18 October 1848, Ware.
11. Ushaw, W. 883; see also Ward, *Sequel to Emancipation* I: 164-5; Briggs to Griffiths, 18 March 1840; Wiseman to Griffiths, 26 March 1840; letters from Baines to Griffiths at the same time, Archives of the Archbishop of Westminster (AAW).
12. Ward, *Sequel to Emancipation* I: 171; Walsh to Shrewsbury, 11 February 1840, Ushaw, W.S. 14.
13. Riddell to Wiseman, 7 August 1847, Ushaw, W. 504.
14. Grant to Wiseman, 15 September 1848, Ware; see also Ward, *Sequel to Emancipation* II: 221.
15. Spencer Northcote to Ullathorne [?] 21 May 1851, Ware.
16. Wiseman to Newsham, 19 December 1839, Ushaw, P.A. H5.
17. Ward, *Sequel to Emancipation* I: 108.
18. E.S. Purcell, *Life and Letters of Ambrose Phillipps de Lisle* (London, 1900) I: 50-1, 217.
19. Ward, *Sequel to* Emancipation II: 102-3.
20. Walsh to Shrewsbury, 26 December 1838, Ushaw, W.S.6. Shrewsbury was in Rome at the time.
21. Ward, *Wiseman* I: 345-6.
22. Fothergill, *Wiseman* 81.
23. Danson to Crowe, 15 September 1839, UCM IV: 377.
24. UCM unbound 407 (b).
25. Winstanley to Walsh, 6 September 1841, Letterbooks Lisbon College Archives (LCA) Ushaw.
26. Ward, *Wiseman* I: 346; see also J. Bowes Gwatkin, *Memor et Fidelis A Study of the Life and Role of Peter Le Page Renouf* (unpublished mss.) 15, 20-3; the principal sources for this mss. are the biographical essay by Professor E. Naville in the fourth volume of Renouf's works published in 1907 and Renouf's correspondence at Pembroke College, Oxford; R.J. Schiefen, 'The English Catholic Reaction to the Tractarian Movement' *Canadian Catholic Historical Association* (1974) 12-13, 26-7.
27. J.H. Newman, *Apologia Pro Vita Sua*, ed. M.J. Svaglic (Oxford, 1967) 111; see also 109-11, 121-2; *The Letters and Correspondence of John Henry Newman*, ed. Anne Mozley (London, 1891) II: 286; Ward, *Wiseman* I: 321, 327.
28. N. Wiseman, *A Letter on Catholic Unity, addressed to the Right Hon. The Earl of Shrewsbury* (London, 1841) 28, 32, 37; see also Ward, *Wiseman* I: 400-6.
29. 'Letters of Cardinal Wiseman: With a Commentary by Cardinal Gasquet' *Dublin Review* CLXIV (1919) 5.
30. Walsh to Shrewsbury, 21 December 1843, Ushaw, W.S. 27.
31. Ward, *Sequel to Catholic Emancipation* II: 92-3.
32. 1870, Birmingham Oratory Archives (BOA), B.2.9.
33. Winstanley to Wiseman, 9 January 1846, Letterbooks LCA; in an

editorial on 20 December 1845 entitled 'Prospects of the Church in England', *Tablet* IV: no. 294, pp. 801-2, the writer concluded with the words, 'Those who flatter themselves with notions of an easy course, and a sudden and speedy triumph, are, we fear, woefully mistaken'. At about the same time, Bishop Walsh remarked that it was important to keep reports of conversions out of the *Tablet* because members of the Oxford Movement had serious objections to their proceedings being published in that periodical; Walsh to Shrewsbury, 6 October 1845, Ushaw, W.S. 76. On a later occasion, Winstanley even had to encourage Wiseman when the latter was 'too despondent with respect to the effects of the Oxford Movement'; 8 November 1849, LCA.

34. Walsh to Shrewsbury, 'Sunday', Ushaw, W.S. 70.
35. Wiseman to Newsham, 24 November 1848, Ushaw, P.A. H19.
36. Wiseman to Newsham, 6 August 1856, Ushaw, P.A. H76.
37. *Catalogue of the Collection of Relics belonging to St Cuthbert's College, Ushaw* (Preston, 1881) 6-8.
38. Wiseman to Shrewsbury, 7 October 1843, Ushaw, W. 480; see also J. Fowler, *Richard Waldo Sibthorp* (London, 1880) 72-78.
39. Ward, *Wiseman* I: 448.
40. Newman, *Apologia* 117; see also Purcell, *Phillipps de Lisle* I: 205.
41. Ward, *Sequel to Emancipation* I: 182.
42. W. Ward, *William George Ward and the Catholic Revival* (London, 1893) 386; see also Gwynn, *Wiseman* 130; Pius, *Life of Father Ignatius* (Dublin, 1866) 276; Purcell, *Phillipps de Lisle* II: 221-2; M. Trappes-Lomax, *Pugin A Mediaeval Victorian* (London, 1932) 129-30; Ward, *Sequel to Emancipation* I: 116.
43. Ward, *Sequel to Emancipation* I: 94-5.
44. Purcell, *Phillipps de Lisle* II: 214.
45. Quoted by Schiefen, 'Catholic Reaction' 16.
46. Ward, *Sequel to Emancipation* II: 263, 272.
47. R. Chapman, *Father Faber* (London, 1961) 184; see also R. Addington, *Faber Poet and Priest* (Cowbridge and Bridgend, 1974) 178; Purcell, *Phillipps de Lisle* II: 218; *The Letters and Diaries of John Henry Newman*, ed. C.S. Dessain (London, 1961-) XII: 212-17, 220.
48. Winstanley to Wiseman, 19 October 1847, LCA.
49. Ushaw, W. 887; support for Briggs is also found in a petition dated 3 November 1847, W. 907; the Reverend Hardinge Ivers, one of Wiseman's opponents, signed one of the petitions sent to the Pope from the Chelsea clergy in favour of Wiseman, 20 October 1847, W. 903.
50. Ushaw, W. 887.
51. *Life and Letters of John Lingard 1771-1851*, ed. M. Haile and E. Bonney (London, n.d.) 353.

52. Ward, *Wiseman* I: 517.
53. Ward, *Wiseman* I: 516-17.
54. de Lisle to Wiseman, 18 March 1848, Ushaw, W. 524.
55. W.O. Chadwick, *The Victorian Church* (London, 1966) I: 287; C.R.H. Leetham, *Luigi Gentili* (London, 1965) 328.
56. C. Butler, *The Life and Times of Bishop Ullathorne* (London, 1926) I: 228; F.J. Cwiekowski, *The English Bishops and the First Vatican Council* (Louvain, 1971) 35.
57. Talbot to Wiseman, 22 December 1860, AAW; see also, E.S. Purcell, *Life of Cardinal Manning Archbishop of Westminster* (London, 1896) II: 164.
58. Butler, *Ullathorne* II: 159.
59. Talbot to Wiseman, 7 May 1859; Talbot to Patterson, 1 May 1860, AAW; see also Butler, *Ullathorne* I: 296.
60. Ward, *Sequel to Emancipation* I: 130.
61. Wiseman's pastoral is reprinted in Fothergill, *Wiseman* 293-7; Ward, *Sequel to Emancipation* II: 305-8; for the quotations from the *Times*, see Fothergill, *Wiseman* 158, 160-1; Ward, *Wiseman* I: 540, 544-5; II: 3-5.
62. Ward, *Sequel to Emancipation* II: 285.
63. Ward, *Wiseman* I: 550; see also *The New Cambridge Modern History*, ed. J.P.T. Bury (Cambridge, 1960) X: 85.
64. N. Wiseman, *An Appeal to the reason and good feeling of the English People on the subject of the Catholic Hierarchy* (London, 1850) 12-13; see also Fothergill, *Wiseman* 171-7; Ward, *Wiseman* I: 557-69; incidentally, it should not be forgotten that Disraeli among others argued that the condemnation of the Queen's Colleges by the Irish bishops at the Synod of Thurles, rather than Wiseman's pastoral was the real occasion of Russell's Ecclesiastical Titles Bill, V.A. McClelland, *English Roman Catholics and Higher Education 1830-1903* (Oxford, 1973) 91-2.
65. *Dublin Review* CLXIV (1919) 18; see also 11-15; Chadwick, *Victorian Church* I: 298-301; Fothergill, *Wiseman* 180; Purcell, *Manning* I: 632-3, 675; Lord Shrewsbury disagreed, Purcell, *Phillipps de Lisle* I: 336.
66. Winstanley to Brown, 28 October 1850, LCA.
67. Winstanley to Wiseman, 28 April 1851, LCA.
68. Ward, *Wiseman* II: 15; see also Purcell, *Manning* I: 673-4.
69. Tierney to Newsham, 28 November 1850, Ushaw, P.A. GI(a).
70. W.F. Finlayson, *Report of the Trial and Preliminary Proceedings in the case of the Queen on the prosecution of G. Achilli v. Dr Newman* (London, 1852) 204-8.
71. Anon., *The Life of Cornelia Connelly 1809-1879* (London, 1922) 185.
72. *Tablet* XXVI (1865) 107; Haile and Bonney, *Lingard* 361.

73. 'Church Government in England: Past, Present and Future' *Clergy Review* LX (1975) 420-8.
74. *Letters and Diaries* XXIII: 360; Ward, *Wiseman* I: 451; II: 152, 160-2.
75. Wiseman to Walker, 1843, Ushaw.
76. Dunn to Rigby, [8 ?] November 1790, Upholland College Archives.
77. *Catholicon* I (1836) 520.
78. Resolutions passed at the Conference of the Clergy of the Deanery of South Northumberland and North Durham in the Diocese of Hexham, held at the Presbytery, St Mary's Sunderland, Thursday 16 January 1851, AAW.
79. Ward, *Sequel to Emancipation* II: 289-90.
80. Fothergill, *Wiseman* 200.
81. W.B. Ullathorne, *The Autobiography of Archbishop Ullathorne* (London, 1891) 258-9; *From Cabin-boy to Archbishop* (London, 1941) 299.
82. *Dublin Review* CLXIV (1919) 18; see also D. Milburn 'Ushaw Papers XVI' *Ushaw Magazine* LXXI (1961) 39, 100.
83. Butler, *Ullathorne* I: 202-3; Purcell, *Manning* II: 56-7; incidentally, Grant was the bishop who often acted on behalf of the hierarchy in negotiations with the Government, K.O'Meara ['Grace Ramsay'] *Thomas Grant First Bishop of Southwark* (London, 1874) 104-6.
84. Wiseman to Newsham, 'Holy Saturday' 1855, Ushaw, P.A. H34; Ward, *Wiseman* II: 94-5.
85. *Tablet* XII (1851) 474.
86. Tierney to Newsham, 27 July 1851, Ushaw P.A. G1(b); J. Lingard, *The History of England* (London, 1855) I: 26; W.G. Roe, *Lamennais and England* (Oxford, 1966) 127-31.
87. Cwiekowski, *English Bishops and Vatican Council* 39-41.
88. Cwiekowski, *English Bishops and Vatican Council* 52-3, 58.
89. *Dublin Review* CLXIV (1919) 22-3.
90. Fothergill, *Wiseman* 230, 233-4; Ward, *Wiseman* II: 257-60.
91. Butler, *Ullathorne* I: 280-1.
92. The dedication of Oliver's *Collections illustrating the History of the Catholic Religion* (London, 1857) iii; G.A. Beck, ed., *The English Catholics 1850-1950* (London, 1950) 200-1.
93. Ward, *Wiseman* II: 370.
94. 'More Letters of Wiseman and Manning' *Dublin Review* CLXXII (1923) 110; J.G. Snead-Cox, *The Life of Cardinal Vaughan* (London, 1910) I: 82.
95. Ward, *Wiseman* II: 331, 341, 343; Wiseman had always enjoyed the support of the Pope, see also 70, 72-5, 79-80.
96. Talbot to Patterson, 12 November 1859, AAW; Ward, *Wiseman* II: 343-4.
97. Ward, *Wiseman* II: 335; see also Butler, *Ullathorne* I: 298.

98. Talbot to Wiseman, 21 March 1859, AAW.
99. Talbot to Patterson, 20 August 1859, AAW; omitted by Ward, *Wiseman* II: 340.
100. Butler, *Ullathorne* I: 306.
101. *Dublin Review* CLXXII (1923) 128; S. Leslie, *Henry Edward Manning* (London, 1921) 511.
102. Leslie, *Manning* 491, 512; see also Butler, *Ullathorne* I: 232-7.
103. 'Unpublished Letters of Cardinal Wiseman to Dr Manning', *Dublin Review* CLXIX (1921) 182.
104. Butler, *Ullathorne* I: 243.
105. *Letters and Diaries* XXII: 318.
106. Butler, *Ullathorne* I: 204-5, 228; II: 300.
107. *Tablet* XXVI (1865) 107.
108. Ward, *Wiseman* II: 460-2, 475, 477, 488-90.
109. 'Some Birmingham Bygones', *Dublin Review* CLXVI (1920) 210; Butler, *Ullathorne* I: 353; Leslie, *Manning* 177; Purcell, *Manning* II: 284.
110. H.E. Manning, *England and Christendom* (London, 1867) 222.
111. Purcell, *Manning* II: 810.
112. Butler, *Ullathorne* II: 303-5; Purcell, *Manning* II: 101, 793.
113. Talbot to Patterson, 20 August 1859, AAW; omitted by Ward, *Wiseman* II: 340; see also Purcell, *Manning* II: 85, 102, 144.
114. Talbot to Patterson, 29 September 1860, AAW.
115. Talbot to Wiseman, 7 December 1861, AAW.
116. Beck, *English Catholics* 198; Butler, *Ullathorne* I: 273-6; II: 192-3.
117. T. Murphy, *The Position of the Catholic Church in England and Wales during the last two centuries* (London, 1892) 62-4, 70, 98A, based on the figures given in the annual *Directory* and the statistics compiled by Richardson in 1853; see also Beck, *English Catholics* 19-20, 118, 422; Chadwick, *Victorian Church* II: 244, 251; Ward, *Wiseman* II: 459.
118. Snead-Cox, *Vaughan* I: 82.
119. Forthergill, *Wiseman* 260, 282-4.
120. Ward, *Wiseman* II: 513.

Augustus Pugin

Chapter III: Newman and the failure of Liberal Catholicism

Liberal Catholicism was a development of the Catholic revival at the beginning of the century. Liberal Catholics hoped to bridge the divisions between the Church and contemporary society, and to make a positive response to the intellectual, social or political revolutions of the nineteenth century. Developments in each country were largely determined by the national situation. French Liberal Catholics tended to concentrate on political problems and the Church's response to the principles of 1789. Liberal Catholics in Germany were also interested in problems of Church and State, but were more concerned with the need to reconcile traditional teaching with recent scientific and historical research, and the defence of intellectual freedom. In Italy, the *Risorgimento* became the crucial issue because the territorial possessions of the Pope prevented the unification of the country.

Originally, Liberal Catholics were also Ultramontanes, but the 'liberal' and the 'papal' aspects of the Catholic revival later diverged on both the political and the intellectual levels. In Italy, it became obvious that the Pope felt he could not support progress towards democracy or the unification of the country without jeopardizing his own secular authority and Pius IX not only refused to distinguish his spiritual from his temporal power, but even used the former to defend the latter. In fact, the temporal power of the Pope eventually became the essential issue within the Church and even the test of political conservatism outside.

The Ultramontanes increasingly emphasized the necessity of dependence on the Holy See and manifested a strong personal devotion to the Holy Father, seeking his guidance in practically every sphere of human activity on almost any possible occasion. In due course, they invoked papal supremacy in order to impose their own particular ecclesiological views on the Church at large. An antithesis between Liberalism and Ultramontanism replaced the earlier antithesis between the freedom of Ultramontanism and the subjection to the secular power which Gallicanism had too frequently involved. As a result, German Liberal Catholics ceased to be Ultramontane, while French Ultramontanes ceased to be liberal; Ultramontanism became clerical and anti-democratic rather than popular and anti-Gallican.

In general, the aim of the Liberal Catholics in England was to improve the social and political influence of their fellow Catholics by improving their intellectual standards. Newman, the leading Oxford convert, became the symbol of the hopes of the English Liberal Catholics. His career as Rector of the Irish University and his lectures both in Ireland and in England had revealed his conviction of the need for free Catholic thought and the important role which educated laymen should play in the life of the Church.

> I want a laity, not arrogant, not rash in speech, not disputatious, but men who know their religion, who enter into it, who know just where they stand, who know what they hold, and what they do not, who know their creed so well, that they can give an account of it, who know so much of history that they can defend it. I want an intelligent, well-instructed laity . . . In all times the laity have been the measure of the Catholic spirit . . . And one immediate effect of your being able to do all this will be your gaining that proper confidence in self which is so necessary for you. You will then not even have the temptation to rely on others, to court political parties or particular men; they will rather have to court you.[1]

The attempt to prevent the social or intellectual isolation of English Catholics or a divorce between the Church and educated opinion which will be discussed later in the struggle over higher education, first became evident in the controversial history of the most famous English Catholic magazine to be published during the nineteenth century. The *Rambler*, founded in 1848, was essentially the organ of those lay converts who tended to be critical of the attitudes and intellectual standards of the Old Catholics. J.M. Capes, the founder and first editor, wanted to improve the intellectual standards of English Catholics in order that they might become more influential in the country at large. The review also encouraged its readers by reporting the progress of the continental Catholic revival and it openly supported the more 'liberal' side.

During the 1840's, English Catholics shared a sense of unity and common purpose, but during the 1850's, controversies arose and divisions appeared. As Ultramontanes like Faber, Manning and Ward became more extravagant in their devotions and unquestioning in their belief or obedience, the *Rambler* reacted strongly and became involved in a series of conflicts with the bishops on education and the state of English Catholicism, as well as on the theological questions such as original sin. Wiseman himself was horrified at the prospect of divisions among Catholics and tended to be somewhat clerical in his attitude towards the opinion of the laity. The *Rambler*, however, continued to criticize and even ridicule its opponents; in politics, it moved closer to the position of continental Liberal Catholics like Montalembert and praised Döllinger in extravagent terms when dealing with academic freedom.

In 1857, Capes resigned and Richard Simpson became editor with Sir John Acton as his chief contributor and associate. Under Simpson and Acton, the *Rambler* assumed a more definite character and became an organ of the Liberal Catholic movement, particularly as this was developing in Germany. The magazine continued to criticize the intellectual and theological limitations of their fellow Catholics and to support the Liberal Montalembert against the Ultramontane Veuillot. Acton wanted to raise the level of English Catholic scholarship to that he had known in Germany where he had studied under Döllinger and come to share the same love of history and devotion to academic freedom. By 1859, it was clear that the *Rambler* represented a distinct minority party within the English Catholic community and was opposed by the *Dublin Review* which was then in the hands of the Ultramontanes.

Newman was convinced that the *Rambler* was too valuable to be able to afford the luxury of conflicting with the ecclesiastical authorities and he devoted himself to the unenviable task of preventing a final break when for a third time, the review became involved in a controversy with the bishops over the control of Catholic education. In an effort to save the magazine, Newman reluctantly became editor. He made every effort to preserve continuity for, as he himself said,

> I had no wish to damage the fair name of men who I believed were at bottom sincere Catholics and I thought it unfair, ungenerous, impertinent and cowardly to make in their behalf acts of confession and contrition, and to make a display of change of editorship.[2]

Simpson himself paid tribute to Newman's great generosity and kindness to the old editors who were welcomed as contributors. In submitting to the bishops' decision on the education controversy, Newman argued that their pastorals did not contain any particular reference to the *Rambler* and that the author of the articles in question had not opposed their decision since this was not known when he originally wrote on the subject. However, Newman himself went further and pleaded for greater consideration to be given to the opinion of the laity on the grounds that the faithful were consulted even in the preparation of dogmatic definitions.

Newman's statement was challenged and in his second and last issue as editor, he published his remarkable article 'On Consulting the Faithful in Matters of Doctrine'. Newman discussed the role of the laity in preserving dogmatic truth and pointed out that in the years following the Council of Nicaea, they had guarded the orthodox tradition, whereas the bishops had tolerated Arianism. Although the content of the article did not appeal to the Ultramontanes, they were also irritated by the explicit and conscious recognition of the theological significance of history. Extreme Ultramontanes were essentially unhistorical, English Catholics in general were not familiar with such historical discussions and the Roman authorities preferred loyalty to the Holy See to serious historical study. Almost predictably, Talbot wrote that the article was 'full of inaccuracies' and the spirit in which it was written was 'certainly detestable'.

> It is intended to encourage the laity to dogmatize, as they have been doing in the Rambler for years past, whereas the 'consensus fidelium' never meant their consensus in spight [sic] of the Clergy to whom alone Christ has given authority to teach, and has promised to be present with, all days, unto the Consummation of the World.[3]

Early in October, 1859, Simpson reported to Acton that there had been serious talk of condemning Newman's article at the Provincial Synod of Westminster which had met at Oscott during July. At about the same time, though without making a formal charge of heresy, Bishop Brown of Newport wrote to Rome and quoted those statements which seemed to be 'totally subversive of the essential authority of the Church in matters of faith'.[4] The Roman authorities demanded an explanation, but Wiseman, ill and absent minded, lost Newman's letter offering to provide whatever explanation might be needed. Meanwhile, Talbot and Manning who had apparently seen Newman's letter, never informed the authorities about it. Wiseman received from Propaganda a list of passages which ought to be explained, but this was never handed on to Newman. Instead Manning wrote to say that Wiseman himself would deal with the matter.

Manning did not actually suppress Newman's explanation, but he knew that Newman was suspected in Rome — the implication being that Newman had not been prepared to explain himself, and certainly Cardinal Barnabo presumed that Newman had refused to justify himself. Some months later, Manning informally told Newman that the affair had been settled. But as well as reassuring Newman, Manning could have removed the suspicions of the Roman authorities; he knew that

Newman was regarded as disobedient, though in fact the latter had never been asked for an explanation. Consequently, Newman's orthodoxy was under suspicion at Rome until 1867 when he first learned what had happened.

> Your letter to the late Cardinal W. quite thunder-struck him [Barnabo]. Why, he said, Cardinal Wiseman was in Propaganda and we never heard of this. He said, it quite cleared you (morally I suppose), but for Cardinal Wiseman he seemed not to know what to say, all he could say was , 'Well, he is dead now, requiescat in pace'. He said, A [mbrose] must take it to the Pope. He must go and show it to Mgr T [albot] and get another audience.[5]

In the meantime, Newman had resigned as editor of the *Rambler*. His policy had embarrassed the bishops in general and was opposed by his own bishop in particular. It was, incidentally, in this context that Ullathorne asked his famous question, 'Who are the laity?' and Newman replied that the Church would look rather foolish without them.[6] Acton and Simpson were allowed to resume the editorship apparently because the bishops were more afraid of Newman who enjoyed greater influence and prestige, while simply continuing their policy. Certainly Talbot reported that, 'Several persons have written to me about the *Rambler*. I am told that it is a more dangerous publication since its change of hands than it was before, and that it contains positive heresy'.[7]

In spite of the fact that Newman was out of sympathy with the tone rather than the views of the two editors, several events also brought about an increasing division between Newman on the one hand and Acton and Simpson on the other. Newman had not publicly revealed his resignation as editor and when the *Tablet* referred to him as an editor, he considered it necessary to clarify the situation. Acton and Simpson were annoyed at, what they interpreted as, an apparent dissociation from the *Rambler*, particularly when its circulation immediately declined.

In 1860, the magazine became involved in a controversy over seminary education. Oxenham, a former member of the staff of St Edmund's, denounced the Tridentine seminary system and used Newman's university lectures to support a more general and liberal education. This discussion irritated Newman because of the danger of repercussions on the magazine and because Oxenham seemed too simply secular in his approach. Since the controversy was conducted anonymously, an almost incredible situation resulted in which Newman used Oxenham's initials and Oxenham accused Newman of misunderstanding Newman!

When the two men realized what had happened, they both withdrew from the controversy which was then continued by Ward who defended the existing system, condemned the free reading of general literature as dangerous and objected to a public discussion of an ecclesiastical subject on the grounds that this amounted to an attack on the bishops.

There were personal differences as well as differences of attitude. Newman later wrote that he had never quite 'hit it off' with Acton, while Simpson was never at ease in Newman's presence though 'it was the awe of a superabundant admiration'.[8] As an undergraduate, Simpson devized all sorts of 'absurd' schemes to introduce himself to 'the venerable Noggs' which he eventually achieved by settling a discrepancy of a shilling in his account with Newman, the College bursar, rather than with the College butler. Acton himself wrote early in 1860, that for Newman the question was one of prudence rather than principle. Newman believed that the *Rambler* was a potential instrument for good and that no one could do more than Simpson in achieving this. Consequently Newman deplored anything which would hinder the good which the *Rambler* might achieve or reduce Simpson's authority; theological subjects were dangerous, not because Acton and Simpson were bad theologians, 'but because the better the doctrine the greater the offence to pious ears'.[9] Simpson for his part found it difficult to understand what could be discussed if the subject of religious toleration, for example, was regarded as too theological; the Irish bishops 'dictated' politics, the English bishops 'tabooed' education and Wiseman 'appropriated' science to himself.

Newman then wanted the *Rambler* to concentrate on politics and to avoid theological discussions which might occasion the intervention of ecclesiastical authority. Newman's advice, however, was easier to give than to act upon at a time when the Pope and the Ultramontanes were deliberately confusing the political with the theological, and when Acton and Simpson seemed determined to answer in kind. One of the two main problems facing Catholics at this time was intellectual — the rise of scientific and historical criticism, but the other was political — the temporal power of the Pope. The attitude of a Catholic towards the temporal power became the touchstone of his loyalty and orthodoxy on other issues and only a few individuals refused to be carried along by this strong current of Catholic opinion. The Roman Question united the majority of Catholics who increasingly adopted an attitude of fundamental opposition to the 'liberalism' of the age. According to Wilfrid Ward, between 1860 and 1870, the very word 'liberalism' was hated by most Catholics who used it only in a pejorative sense. The struggle between those who were anxious to influence the age and those who condemned it as alien to Christianity was decided in favour of the latter.[10]

English Catholics became emotionally involved in the trials of Pio Nono as they were urged by Manning to

> think with the Church; live with the Church; let your whole heart and soul, every thought of your intellect, every affection of your heart, every emotion of your will, be with the Church of God. The Church of God is the presence of God, and the mind of the Church is the mind of God, and the voice of the Church is the voice of God. Next, love the person of the Vicar of Christ — not as an abstract principle, not the Holy See, not an institution, but the living breathing man, who has upon him the dignity and the unction of the Great High Priest. Be filially devoted to him; for the time is come when, according to the prophecy, he is the sign which shall be spoken against; he is set for the fall and for the rising again of nations. He is the test of the world; Pius IX, that despised name to those who are not of his family, is sifting the nations. And there are voices coming up now as of old, Hail, King of the Jews!' and they would fain blindfold him, and buffet him, and spit upon his face. They mock him as a false king with a feeble reed, as an impotent king with a crown of thorns. They offer the mock loyalty of a revolting people, and they say, 'Away with him! we will not have this man to reign over us; we have no king but Caesar'. But he is Vicar of Him who will judge the world.[11]

Faber was another leading advocate of Ultramontane opinion at the time. As an Anglican, he had attended a Mass celebrated by the Pope on the feast of the Ascension in St John Lateran; even then, he wrote, 'I do not think I ever returned from any service so thoroughly Christianized in every joint and limb, or so right of heart'. As a Catholic, he declared,

> Ultramontanism is the only really converting thing, because it is the only really generous thing. Rome must not be merely our Court of Appeal from a national episcopate. Rome must really *govern*, animate and inform things with its own spirit. Bless us and save us! We don't want another dose of Anglicanism with Tridentine doctrine: we want to be sensibly and perceptively Roman. Then we can all go to work cheerfully and manfully, and work our hearts out for souls, and die in our harness.[12]

Speaking of the presence of Mary in the early Church, Faber argued,

Even the sublimities of apostolic holiness could not bear that both Jesus and Mary should be withdrawn at once. So in like manner now He has left us the Pope. The Sovereign Pontiff is a third visible presence of Jesus amongst us . . . He is the visible shadow cast by the Invisible Head of the Church in the Blessed Sacrament.[13]

In Faber's hymn, 'The Three Kings', Catholics were reminded that,

No Bibles and no books of God were in that eastern land,
No Pope, no blessed Pope, had they to guide them with his hand;
No Holy Roman Church was there, with its clear and strong sunshine,
With its voice of truth, its arm of power, its sacraments divine . . .

Let us ask these martyrs, then, these monarchs of the East,
Who are sitting now in heaven at their Saviour's endless feast,
To get us faith from Jesus, and hereafter faith's bright home,
And day and night to thank Him for the glorious faith of Rome![14]

Catholic devotion to the Pope was manifested in trivial as well as more extreme ways. Roman customs were introduced and became increasingly popular. Some English priests began to use Roman vestments or the buckled shoes and knee-breeches of Roman ecclesiastics as signs of the true Roman spirit, while those who did not were suspected of being lukewarm or disloyal. Every papal word or phrase became important and addresses were sent to him by every type of group on every possible occasion. It became customary to drink the health of the Pope at Catholic gatherings, while pilgrims to Rome treasured his slippers or pieces of his cassocks which were brought home as relics. In 1858, a group assembled at Ushaw heard an unrealistic and enthusiastic speech from Talbot 'upon the Pope as a model of the Priest, the Bishop and the Sovereign'.

According to Talbot, the Pope was the only ruler in the world who acted solely on the principles of justice and right, and not from the principle of expediency. The Pope merely tried to do his duty without seeking popular applause. At the same time, no sovereign was more loved or venerated by his people and respected by foreigners; on meeting the Pope, a Turk had exclaimed 'I have seen Mahomet', while a Jew remarked 'I have seen Father Abraham!' Talbot concluded by promising to tell the Pope

of the enthusiastic manner in which His Health had been drunk; and that in great St Cuthbert's College He had many children devoted to

Him and that he (Monsignor Talbot) had been present when 500 glasses were raised to drink His Health. (Loud cheers) He would tell His Holiness that even himself — humble individual as he was — had been received with the greatest kindness and hospitality, and was treated with the greatest honors merely because he came from Him and was there His humble representative. (Tremendous cheering).[15]

In 1867, the Chairman of the Broughton Catholic Charitable Society proposed the health of the Pope;

They all venerated the head placed over them, and might he occupy that position for many years to come. (Hear, hear). It was stated in the papers — and in the Catholic papers too — that at the liquifaction of the blood of St Januarius this year, there was seen a little black speck, and it was said also that that speck had been noticeable on other occasions previous to some great calamity happening to the Church. They must, however, pray and hope that this would not be the case now; but if it was, they must hope that His Holiness and all his spiritual subjects would patiently bear whatever Almighty God might send upon him and them. The Pope would, of course, go on in the same quiet manner which had drawn the admiration of the whole world to himself. (Hear, hear).[16]

Some years earlier, the press of the *Civilta Cattolica* had issued a series of volumes reprinting expressions of support which had been sent to the Pope from all parts of the world. Among these can be found the letters and pastorals of the bishops of the province of Westminster, the resolutions and protests of cathedral chapters, clerical conferences and lay confraternities, from parishes and convents, colleges and seminaries. The Catholics of London believed that the temporal power of the Pope had been 'the source of numerous blessings to mankind, by the extension of the catholic Faith, the diffusion of knowledge, and the promotion of the arts and sciences'. Catholics in Newcastle and Gateshead threw themselves at the feet of the Pope in expressing their deep sympathy and devoted loyalty. The Catholics of Wisbech in Cambridgeshire, though 'few in number, and removed from public notice', could no longer remain silent in assuring the Pope of their 'inviolable reverence' for his 'exalted authority', and of their 'deep sorrow and vehement indignation'.

Catholics in Clitheroe, Lancashire, 'learnt with sorrow that the paternal heart of Your Holiness has been afflicted by the ingratitude and rebellion of your subjects, who by the cunning designs and wicked

119

machinations of the enemies of the holy See have been instigated to subvert your sovereign authority'. They assured the Pope that 'every injury inflicted on our Head is felt by us: every insult offered to our Pastor falls upon us: every dishonour cast upon our Father is our dishonour'. The Duchess of Leeds sent a thousand pounds as a token of her 'respect and affection', while Virginia A. Millington wrote:

> Pardon me, oh, pardon me for the unprecedented freedom of addressing You, Holy Father. But hearing my Papa daily read from the newspapers of the many sorrows and political sufferings, which afflict Your Holiness and Rome, I could not resist the feeling, which stole over me to proffer my humble sympathies, knowing, Holy Father, that in your benevolence You would recept them, as most heartful and sincere even though they come from a shore, from whence have sprung all the anarchy and distress, which have afflicted our most holy mother Church.[17]

Nevertheless, not all English Catholics were Ultamontane supporters of the temporal power. M.J. Whitty was a former church student who became Head Constable of Liverpool, founder of the local Fire Brigade and the first daily penny newspaper. As editor of the *Liverpool Daily Post*, he maintained 'that the Ultramontanes did not represent the Roman Catholics of England and Ireland'. Whitty deeply regretted serious local disturbances which had resulted from differences over the 'Pope's miserable bit of land', and he accused those Catholic members of the Council who protested against the Mayor's invitation to Garibaldi of 'preferring the Pope to the Roman Catholic Church'. 'The Father of the Faithful', Whitty remarked, 'is obliged to surround himself with foreign troops, lest his people might force him to do them justice.[18]

Newman was the most famous English Catholic who eventually refused to support the temporal power; he declined to speak in its favour or to help its supporters. Newman suspected that the temporal power had an adverse effect on the spiritual life of the Church and in 1860, his opposition was even greater than Acton's who considered that territorial sovereignty was still necessary for the freedom and independence of the Church. In fact, Acton later wrote, 'Newman's influence made the *Rambler* anti-Roman'.[19] In 1860, both Acton and Newman declined to attend a public meeting in Birmingham Town Hall. Newman did not wish to attend a meeting the real purpose of which was to demonstrate in favour of the temporal power, but whose ostensible object was to express sympathy with the Pope.

In June, 1861, Wiseman established an 'Academy of the Catholic

Religion' as a means of enabling English Catholics to keep up to date with scientific and other intellectual developments. After some initial optimism, the Liberal Catholics became suspicious. Simpson accepted a place in the Academia 'with the intention of being Devil's advocate in a place where otherwise pious interests only would be represented'.[20] Newman told Manning that he would withdraw his name if Wiseman spoke about the temporal power in his inaugural address and 'From that day', Manning later wrote, 'a divergence began between us'.[21] Before the end of the year, Acton was complaining that it was 'disgraceful' that Manning and Ward should 'turn the academy into a field for disporting themselves on their peculiar hobbies'. [22]

Ward used the Academy to support his opposition to Catholic Liberalism, to lecture on the dangers of the uncontrolled intellect and the need for submission to ecclesiastical authority. Meanwhile, Manning was suggesting as subjects for future consideration,

> An examination of the principles of 1789, and especially of the pretended sovereignty of the people.
> The political aspect of the Temporal Power of the Pope; its foundations in political right, and the public order of nations.
> The office of the Temporal Power as the providential condition, not of the spiritual power, as some foolishly impute to us, but of the freedom of the spiritual office of the Pontiffs.[23]

The temporal power was the issue on which English Catholics finally divided. In 1861, Döllinger argued that the temporal power might be legitimate and useful, but that it was not essential to the Church which might even be strengthened by its loss. In the *Rambler* for May, 1861, Acton endorsed Döllinger's views and alluded to Newman's opinions in arguing that the time had come for Catholics to recognize that the loss of the temporal power would prove to be of benefit both to the Church and to the Papacy. In November of the same year, a reviewer of Manning's lectures on 'The Last Glories of the Holy See' complained that his logic was so remarkable that it almost defied analysis; the reviewer was particularly critical of Manning's association of papal sovereignty with the Immaculate Conception as a theological certainty if not a definition of the Church.

> The definition should be very precisely given, in order that we might know who are good Catholics and who bad, who orthodox and who heterodox. To leave the matter undefined, is to set a snare for the conscience. It is not for a moment to be supposed that

Dr Manning purposely abstained from making his meaning clear in order to make his readers think he meant more than he really intended, and to terrify them with obscurity and mystery. Yet there may be persons whom Dr Manning will make afraid that, in order to be good Catholics, they must believe something which in fact they need not, and which they cannot bring themselves to believe. These immediately suppose themselves bad Catholics; then they lose their fervour, and soon become what they suppose themselves. If this view of Dr Manning's were matter of faith, most Catholics would be heretics, for few believe it as of faith.[24]

The writer concluded by saying, 'When even Dr Manning places such stones in his brethen's path, what will reckless and imprudent disputants do?' and by asking whether the opinions of the laity as well as the clergy should not be taken into account when defining matters of faith. In any case, the reviewer argued, the problem of the temporal power was not one of faith, but of politics, prudence and foresight in which Catholics might differ without jeopardizing their orthodoxy; the divine right of temporal sovereignty was a theory to be judged by history and a theory which could do little good in practice, but might certainly do a great deal of harm.

Talbot now proposed that the English bishops should censure the *Rambler* and Manning told him that before long he hoped to be able to report that the magazine had come to an end. Talbot was particularly critical of the two articles on the temporal power and claimed that the *Rambler* had become one of the most offensive Catholic periodicals in Europe; its tone was detestable, it would do a great deal of harm. The Roman authorities also began to think that Irish Catholic M.P.s did not vote against a British Government which supported the Italian nationalists, because of the influence of the *Rambler*. Consequently, the periodical was required under pain of censure from Rome, to support the temporal power and to reject the Liberal Government. Before the end of 1861, Propaganda sent a rescript to the English bishops which was most critical of the magazine and the publisher refused to produce the next number unless it was issued under Manning's control. Acton's suggestion that Newman should resume the editorship was rejected by the publisher on the grounds that the Oratorian was so unpopular among Catholics that he would harm any chances of success. Acton, therefore, employed a Protestant publisher and the *Rambler* became the *Home and Foreign Review*, though policy and personnel, motto and spirit remained the same.

Newman's own attitude, as he himself appreciated, was not a simple one. Eventually, he felt unable to support either the *Dublin Review* or the *Home and Foreign* and ultimately he refused to write for either of the two magazines. But on one occasion, he wrote, 'I so dislike Ward's way of going on, that I can't get myself to read the Dublin',[25] whereas he always remained interested in the work of Simpson and Acton, and was most anxious that it should succeed. He was impressed by the high standard of the *Home and Foreign* which he hoped would win general support and become established. He described the bishops' opposition as 'imprudent and unhappy', and detested what he called 'the persecuting spirit' which pursued it. He denied that those who wrote for the magazine were rationalists, semi-infidels or the cause of apostasy; they were good Catholics attempting a necessary task in an age in which controversy was 'a sort of night battle, where each fights for himself, and friend and foe stand together'.[26] But if Newman was in sympathy with the principles and opinions of Simpson or Acton, he was often disappointed in the results or manifestations of their attitudes and with the tone or form of their writings.

Meanwhile, a circular letter listing offences was sent from the Prefect of Propaganda to the English bishops who were required to issue pastoral letters within three months warning the faithful against the review. Wiseman took the occasion of a false report about deliberations in Rome on the temporal power, to censure the *Home and Foreign*, while during September and October, 1862, all the English bishops except one issued pastorals strongly disapproving of the *Rambler* and its successor. The *Home and Foreign*, therefore, ceased to be a representative organ of English Catholicism and became a review on the same lines as the *Quarterly*, the *Edinburgh* or the *Westminster*. Although its scholarly integrity and ability won the admiration of many intellectuals such as Matthew Arnold or Max Müller English Catholics failed to support it. In general, English Catholics seem to have become completely exasperated with opinions expressed in the magazine about the Church or their fellow Catholics, while the bishops struggling with administrative problems were not very interested in academic discussions about the intellectual difficulties of the time; furthermore, the bishops did not see the point of alarming the majority of English Catholics by raising intellectual problems of which most of them were not even aware. As a result, the review's financial position was critical and its circulation falling when it finally came to an end as a result of events abroad.

In 1863, the Liberal Catholics organized an international congress at

Malines and Montalembert delivered his two famous speeches urging all Catholics to accept the principles of liberal democracy and religious toleration. Vaughan, who accompanied Wiseman to the congress, had earlier remarked that he would not be surprised if Montalembert 'put his foot into it when he speaks about liberty and liberty of conscience'.[27] Montalembert used Cavour's famous formula 'a free Church in a free State', 'which, though snatched from us and put into circulation by a very guilty man remains none the less the symbol of our convictions and our hopes'; Montalembert concluded by quoting Dupanloup's remark accepting the principles and claiming the liberties of 1789 — 'You made the revolution of 1789 without us and against us, but *for us,* God wishing it so in spite of you'.[28] Wiseman reported that Montalembert's doctrines 'made terrible, though silent confusion' and the inevitable critical letter from Rome, though courteous, confidential and friendly, was also a virtual condemnation of the cause to which the old man had given his life. Another line had been adopted in Rome and moves in the opposite direction were already being made.

Incidentally, Vaughan and perhaps even Wiseman himself apparently gave a misleading impression of events at Malines. Vaughan told Wilfrid Ward that Wiseman's speech on the state of Catholicism in England had been 'enthusiastically applauded' and he described the reception given to the Cardinal as 'most enthusiastic'. However, Professor Lamy of Louvain later gave a different impression to the future Bishop Casartelli of Salford:

> Wiseman's speech was a complete fiasco: he read from a paper an account of progress of Church in England; people couldn't hear him, were impatient to hear Montalembert and so tried to 'choke him off' with applause: in vain. Marvellous eloquence and power of Montalembert, although he *read* his speech *sitting*.[29]

In September, 1863, another congress was held at Munich. The main theme on this occasion was the necessity of academic freedom in scientific investigation and of recognizing the independent rights of reason in relations between science or history on the one hand and the authority or theology of the Church on the other. Döllinger offended Pio Nono by criticizing the quality of Italian scholarship and maintaining that the study of theology also involved an adequate knowledge of history or philosophy such as was found in Germany. The subsequent papal brief to the Archbishop of Munich did not condemn Döllinger but implicitly condemned his ideas on academic freedom by insisting that scholarly research should be conducted with respect and deference to ecclesiastical authorities. Catholic thought was to be guided by the ordinary *magisterium* of the Church, the decisions of Roman Congregations and the teaching of bishops and theologians, as well as by dogmatic definitions.

This was not an *ex cathedra* statement which condemned the opposite opinion as heretical, while the language and the censures of the Brief were vague and ill-defined. Nevertheless, the intentions of the Pope's letter were clear and its censures were capable of extending to the *Home and Foreign* which had endorsed Döllinger's views. Acton believed that the Munich Congress had been the most serious recent attempt to deal with contemporary intellectual difficulties, while recognizing the significance of ecclesiastical doctrines and authority. Both Simpson and Acton were unable to accept the Munich Brief and felt obliged to cease publishing the *Home and Foreign* lest they became subject to a more explicit and obvious condemnation. Ultimately, the Liberal Catholics were agreed on the practical need to be silent without surrendering their principles or their hopes for the future. As Acton wrote:

> If the spirit of the *Home and Foreign Review* really animates those whose sympathy it enjoyed, neither their principles, nor their confidence, nor their hopes will be shaken by its extinction. It was but a partial and temporary embodiment of an imperishable idea — the faint reflection of a light which still lives and burns in the hearts of the silent thinkers of the Church.[30]

However, the end of the magazine effectively ended the English Liberal Catholic Movement. From now on, the Liberal Catholics in England were forced to act simply as individuals. The circumstances of the time, rather than their ideas had proved fatal to their cause. The Ultramontane state of siege had denied to the Liberal Catholics the toleration and freedom which they needed.

At the moment of defeat, however, the English Liberal Catholics achieved a significant success. Privately, Newman had been most critical of the Ultramontanes and the Roman authorities. English Catholics, he claimed, were under the arbitrary, military power of Propaganda, which acted like a man of business with a civil service. Its attitude made any attempt to solve contemporary problems like fighting under the lash or with a chain on the arm. In 1864, as a result of the successful controversy with Kingsley, Newman had won the ear of the English nation. Acton urged him to use the opportunity to defend the Church as a whole as well as his own honesty, especially in the light of recent events involving the *Home and Foreign* and the Munich Brief which as

Newman himself admitted had tied his hands as an apologist.[31] Newman, whose own orthodoxy was so frequently questioned by the Ultramontanes, had every reason to show that they were not the true or exclusive representatives of Catholicism and he therefore followed Acton's advice.

The defence of the Catholic system with the discussion on ecclesiastical infallibility and intellectual freedom in the last chapter of the *Apologia* was an implicit attack on the Ultramontanes; so also was his criticism of foreign devotions as unsuitable for England as well as his praise and sympathy for the Church of England and things English. While affirming his loyalty and accepting the doctrine of infallibility, Newman emphasized its negative and limited nature, and he condemned the violent party which would turn opinions into dogmas or destroy every school of thought but its own. He defended the value and necessity of academic freedom or independent speculation and pointed out that the purpose of infallibility was to prevent extremes, not to reduce the freedom or vigour of human thought. In the event, Newman believed that there would be few infallible pronouncements which would be limited to faith and morals, statements of what was already believed and only made after long investigations into the actual beliefs of Catholics.

The English Ultramontanes did not welcome the favourable reception given to the *Apologia* and an attempt was made to criticize Newman's work at Rome. Manning told Talbot that the Anglicans 'look on the *Apologia* as a plea for remaining as they are'. Vaughan commented that there were 'views put forward which I abhor, and which fill me with pain and suspicion'. R.A. Coffin apparently maintained that all Newman's Catholic writings should be put on the Index.[32] Meanwhile, H.J. Coleridge who believed that Newman was 'perfectly and exactly right', suspected that W.G. Ward was preparing a counter-attack.[33] Coleridge was responsible for the review of reviews which appeared in the *Dublin* and he wanted to devote the whole section of the January issue to a defence of Newman and a refutation of misrepresentations of the *Apologia*. Ward and Manning, however, opposed this and in December, 1864, Thompson, the sub-editor who supported Coleridge, resigned in protest. Aubrey de Vere also found it incredible that the magazine was not allowed to defend Newman who was 'not only the greatest man in England, but one to whom Catholicity in England owes more than it has owed to any one else since the days of St Augustine of Canterbury'.[34] De Vere described himself as 'one of that large number who, (humanly speaking) would never have been

Catholics, but for Dr Newman', and he refused to write again for the *Dublin* while it remained under the control of Manning and Ward.

In 1865, Newman again criticized the Ultramontanes in his *Letter to Pusey* when he refused to identify their theological views or Marian devotions with those of Catholicism. Many English Catholics welcomed Newman's letter which naturally offended the Ultramontanes and those whom Ullathorne described as 'the Camarilla'. Talbot urged Manning to stand firm 'as the advocate of Roman views'. It would be necessary to fight 'because every Englishman is naturally anti-Roman. To be Roman is to an Englishman an effort. Dr Newman is more English than the English. His spirit must be crushed'. Manning replied that Newman

> has become the centre of those who hold low views about the Holy See, are anti-Roman, cold and silent, to say no more, about the Temporal Power, national, English, critical of Catholic devotions, and always on the lower side. I see no danger of a Cisalpine Club rising again, but I see much danger of an English Catholicism of which Newman is the highest type. It is the old Anglican, patristic, literary, Oxford tone transplanted into the Church. It takes the line of deprecating exaggerations, foreign devotions, Ultramontanism, anti-national sympathies. In one word, it is worldly Catholicism, and it will have the worldly on its side, and will deceive many.[35]

Ward wrote a reply to Newman's letter on the grounds that it was impossible to ignore the 'slur' which Newman had cast on foreign Catholics, and necessary to correct several anti-Catholic statements in his 'Protestant' letter. But both Ullathorne and Clifford refused to read Ward's article and this effectively stopped its publication. The same two bishops also wrote to defend Newman whose remarks had occasioned a controversial correspondence in the *Tablet* and the *Weekly Register* where the great majority of the correspondents took Newman's side and protested against attacks on him and on the Old Catholics.

Meanwhile, even more significant events were taking place abroad. In December, 1864, the *Syllabus of Errors* and the encyclical *Quanta Cura* had been sent to the bishops throughout the world. The encyclical itself might have occasioned a hostile reaction without causing a sensation; it condemned most of the opinions condemned in the *Syllabus*, but in more obscure and more moderate or conventional language. The *Syllabus*, on the other hand, was an index of condemnations torn from their contexts and simply referring to the relevant documents, listed those dangerous and perverse ideas which were in conflict with

Catholicism. Many of these ideas might be considered dangerous or destructive of the Church or civil society, but the following 'errors' were also condemned: that every man was free to embrace or profess the religion he believed to be true guided by the light of reason: that all those who were not at all in the true Church of Christ could hope for eternal salvation; that men might achieve eternal salvation in the practice of any religion whatever; that Catholics could dispute on the compatibility of the Pope's temporal with his spiritual rule; that the Church could not use force or any direct or indirect temporal power; that the Church should be separated from the State and *vice versa*; that it was no longer necessary that the Catholic religion should be held as the only religion of the State to the exclusion of all others; that the Pope could and should reconcile himself to and agree with progress, liberalism and modern civilization. The criticism of Montalembert and the publication of the Munich Brief had prepared the way for the *Syllabus of Errors* which was seen throughout Europe as a quixotic attempt to defend the *ancien régime* and the temporal power. Its publication was another victory for the Ultramontanes who were excessive in their lavish praise and a further defeat for the Liberal Catholics who were embittered or alienated, diverted into safer fields of activity or occasionally even driven out of the Church altogether.

Those who would defend Pius IX have pointed out that the *Syllabus* was obviously a technical document, enumerating previous condemnations which were to be understood in their original contexts and needed to be interpreted theologically, rather than discussed as subjects in a public debate. Yet the Pope allowed the use of value judgments and categorical language, and the adoption of a form which was unsuitable for even discussing, let alone condemning, 'errors' of such gravity. Furthermore, if the positive teaching of the *Syllabus* was difficult to determine, its context was hardly known outside Italy. But although the Italian situation prompted the *Syllabus* which had specific reference to Italy, publication was not restricted to Italy and the hostile reaction was universal.

Bishop Dupanloup quickly explained that only a *certain* type of progress and civilization was condemned and he distinguished between the ideal rule of the Church and the conditions of an imperfect world. Thus, the encyclical or the *Syllabus* were not meant to be outlines of practical policies and Protestants or atheists, for example, were to be tolerated without being approved. Dupanloup's approach was welcomed with a profound and widespread sense of relief. Eighteen English and Irish bishops wrote letters of congratulation and even Manning advised Gladstone to read it. But neither the Pope nor the Ultramon-tanes were completely satisfied with Dupanloup's interpretation. Veuillot and his friends claimed that it differed from the original pur-pose of the *Syllabus* and in this they were probably right because imme-diate and later interpretations such as Dupanloup's seem to have ob-scured the intentions of the Pope who could at any time simply have pointed out that he had been misunderstood. Simpson commented, 'I cannot see much duty in accepting a document, salaaming to it, and then explaining it away, as the French and Belgian liberal Catholics do'.[36]

The immediate English reaction to the *Syllabus* is to be found in the newspapers. In spite of the fact that it was mentioned in a few parlia-mentary speeches, it had practically no political impact and the dis-patches of the English representative in Rome merely aroused the interested curiosity of the Cabinet. Politically, the temporal power was the real issue and the encyclical was simply considered as an impotent fulmination vainly attempting to preserve the dwindling papal terri-tories. The intensity of the hostility in the newspapers varied. Criticism might be more objective in one case or simple sarcasm in another, but all of them were agreed that the encyclical was the most unreasonable fabrication that the Holy See in its nineteen hundred years of existence had attempted to foist on an astonished world. The Pope was a senile old woman, he was incompetent, imprudent, medieval, vindictive and bitter. Catholic publications failed to answer this hostile reaction partly because they appeared less frequently, but mostly because when they did appear, they simply greeted the papal statements with extravagant praise. Monsell told Newman that all the Catholic papers apparently maintained that eighty new propositions had been added to the creed. The *Tablet*'s Roman correspondent claimed that the Holy See was now committed to the principles of legitimate sovereignty; the *Dublin Review* maintained that the doctrinal declarations of the encyclical were infallible; and both of them used the papal condemnations of 'liberalism' as another weapon in their campaign against the Liberal Catholics.

In 1866, W.G. Ward published his *Authority of Doctrinal Decisions* which extended papal infallibility to most doctrinal instructions in the Pope's official public letters and even to private letters intended for general guidance. Incidental statements were not infallible, but minor censures were. Even Talbot thought that Ward might have gone too far, though he maintained that this was unimportant on the grounds that it was safer to believe too much than too little and impossible to be mistaken by always following the guidance of the Holy See:

> No one better than I can know the care with which all the Pope's Encyclicals and Allocutions are prepared, and as the Pope is no great theologian himself, I feel convinced that when he writes them he is inspired by God. As for myself, I have always read them on my knees and do all I can to assent internally with every word contained in them.[37]

Ignatius Ryder, a priest of the Birmingham Oratory and Manning's nephew, challenged Ward's opinions. Ward believed that any form of doctrinal instruction must be accepted as infallibly true under pain of mortal sin. Ryder maintained that such instructions only obliged in virtue of *pietas fidei* and must be shown directly and conclusively to be infallible in each individual case. Doctrinal instructions demanded obedience or assent, but were not necessarily infallible or binding under mortal sin. According to Ward, it was necessary to accept the teaching of the *Syllabus* under pain of mortal sin. According to Ryder, Catholics must accept the *Syllabus*, but its infallibility was only probable, at most. Although Ward himself never changed his personal belief in the infallibility of the *Syllabus*, he eventually allowed the possibility of another interpretation. In the last analysis, Ward's habit of imposing obligations where none certainly existed was perhaps the crucial point at issue, rather than the *Syllabus* itself.

Newman himself protested against what he called Ward's 'Novatian' tendencies and schismatical spirit; Newman accused Ward of *'dividing Christ'* by exalting his own opinions into dogmas, claiming that Catholics who refused to accept them were of a different religion and denouncing what the Church had never denounced.[38] On an earlier occasion, Newman had drawn a parallel between the Catholic Church in the nineteenth century and the rigorist schism in the early history of Christianity.

> We are sinking into a sort of Novatianism, the heresy which the early Popes so strenuously resisted. Instead of aiming at being a worldwide power, we are shrinking into ourselves, narrowing the lines of communion, trembling at freedom of thought, and using the language of dismay and despair at the prospect before us, instead of, with the high spirit of the warrior, going out conquering and to conquer.[39]

At the same time, Newman tended to be more critical of Ward's wife, rather than Ward himself who was always affectionate and honest in his somewhat eccentric opinion that Newman was 'an unmistakeable heretic'.[40] Their differences were theological not personal. According to Ward, Manning had the truth and Newman did not, but on the personal level, Ward was not particularly fond of Manning and was even reported to have expressed the opinion, 'As to Manning, it is quite wonderful what little ability he has'. Ward often expressed his affection for Newman with whom, he said, he should like to spend eternity, whereas Manning 'makes him creep'; a remark similar to Barnabo's comment, 'I know Manning best, but I love Newman'.

While Liberal Catholics like Acton simply rejected the *Syllabus* and Ultramontanes like Ward proclaimed that it was infallible, a moderate group including Ryder and Newman submitted to the *Syllabus*, but rejected its infallibility. The two Oratorians adopted very similar attitudes to the content and dogmatic value of the *Syllabus*. Newman was prepared to write to the *Register* refusing to accept its infallibility and Ryder used the *Apologia* in his controversy with Ward. Newman's attitude to the *Syllabus* was in line with his criticism of Propaganda and the Munich Brief. He was not so much concerned with the content, all of which he believed would have been condemned by Anglicans thirty years before, but with the spirit and methods of the Roman authorities which seemed calculated to make the position of English Catholics as difficult as possible. In fact, Newman did not even understand the condemnations since specific censures were not included and undefined terms like liberalism, progress and recent civilization were simply the newspaper 'cant' of the day.[41]

Newman's attitude to the *Syllabus* occasioned further criticisms from his Ultramontane opponents which were reflected in the pages of the *Old Hall Gazette* then edited by the younger Wards:

> We need not add that so loyally disposed a Catholic as Father Ryder really is, in spite of the extraordinary lukewarm jumble of theories he has formed for himself, would never for a moment put the matter before himself in so disrespectful a light. We only wish that his doctrinal position was on as high a level as his spiritual one, and indeed we by no means despair of seeing the day when so promising a mind will perceive its errors, and work as vigorously in God's cause as hitherto it has done, unconsciously against it. But that will not be, we fear, till the aged though majestic tree falls, which, while beautiful and venerable to look on, effectually checks the growth of the young and hopeful grass beneath its unhealthy shade.[42]

Between 1864 and 1870, the basic and fundamental issue was not so much the fact of papal infallibility, but the dogmatic significance of the *Syllabus* and the attempt to equate the necessity of the temporal power with dogmatic truth. Most theologians had already accepted papal infallibility and an interesting indication of the success of Ultramontanism and the decline of Gallicanism was that Dupanloup himself had defended 'The Infallibility of the Roman Pontiff' as his doctoral thesis in 1842. Twenty five years later, however, Newman spoke of efforts to introduce 'a new theory of Papal Infallibility, which would make it a mortal sin, to be visited by damnation, not to hold the Temporal Power necessary to the Papacy'.[43]

This close association between the *Syllabus* and the Vatican Council can be seen in the fact that the members of the doctrinal commission preparing for the Council were given various sections of the *Syllabus* to serve as the basis of a report. It is therefore hardly surprising that when Vaughan edited *The Year of Preparation for the Vatican Council*, he should have reprinted the text of the *Syllabus of Errors* and the encyclical *Quanta cura*. Acton thought that Döllinger would not have had any clear objection to the definition of infallibility, had it not been for the *Syllabus* and this would also seem to have been true of himself.[44]

The announcement of the first Vatican Council was originally welcomed by most Catholics including leading Liberal Catholics as well as by the inevitably enthusiastic Ultramontanes. But whereas the latter wanted the Council to reinforce papal authority by defining papal infallibility, the Liberal Catholics who were finding it increasingly difficult to reconcile their liberalism with their obedience to the Pope, hoped to end the exaggerations of Ultramontanism and to balance the growing papal autocracy. Liberal Catholics also hoped that the Council would make a positive contribution towards the solution of contemporary problems. As time went on, however, the Liberal Catholics were alienated by the activities of the Ultramontanes and began to oppose any moves which might strengthen their aims.

Although the ecumenical implications had not been ignored in calling the General Council, all opportunities for establishing better relations with the other Christian bodies were almost deliberately destroyed before the opening of the Council which in the event only succeeded in widening divisions. The Pope wrote to the eastern churches which 'are now, to our extreme grief, through the wicked arts and machinations of him who in heaven excited the first schism, separated and divided from the communion of the Holy Roman Church which is spread throughout the world'.[45] This letter was released prematurely in the press and the Patriarch of Constantinople returned it unopened suggesting that the contents were hardly less deplorable than the method of communication.

But if the Ultramontanes invited the Greek bishops 'to be reconciled to the Church from which they have gone away, and confess the supremacy of St Peter, and the lawful rule of his successor', the Protestant 'sheep of the Good Shepherd that have gone astray and lost themselves in the wilderness of sin' were reminded of the social and spiritual evils resulting from their errors and invited to reflect on their position and return to the Church. As a result of such attitudes, the story was told that when a Scottish Presbyterian asked on what conditions they might take part in the Council, Manning informed him that they should follow the example of the prodigal son, when they reached Rome, theologians would be waiting to convert them by argument.

During February, 1869, an inspired article appeared in *Civilta Cattolica*, the Jesuit review which maintained that when the Pope thought, it was God who was thinking in him! True or real Catholics were distinguished from those who called themselves Liberal Catholics; true Catholics hoped that the Council would be very short, that it would proclaim the doctrines of the *Syllabus* and that a unanimous manifestation of the Holy Spirit through the Fathers of the Council would result in a definition of papal infallibility by acclamation. As a result of indignant protests, the Holy See made it clear that this article was not an official opinion, though it had probably been officially inspired. Furthermore the fact remained that an ecclesiastical review had prejudged the issue and almost defined the terms and the extent of papal infallibility, while implying that Liberal Catholics were not true Catholics and that the Council would declare that the *Syllabus* was dogmatic. The attitude of the *Civilta* was widely applauded by Ultramontanes throughout the world and was echoed in other periodicals such as the *Tablet*.

Although at least one English Catholic review, the *Weekly Register*, took a moderate line during the Council, the attitude of Manning and Ward dominated the *Dublin Review* and through Herbert Vaughan, the *Tablet*. Manning and Ward were the leading representatives of the English Ultramontanes. Manning believed that there were,

> two things which the Council will certainly accomplish. First, it will bring out more visibly than ever the only alternative proposed to the human intellect, − namely, rationalism or faith; and next, it will show to the civil powers of the Christian world the inevitable future they are now preparing for themselves.[46]

Ward maintained that 'If we desire to know the extent of the Pope's infallibility we have only to inquire what extent of infallibility the Pope claims for himself in practice'.[47]

On the front page of Vaughan's first issue as editor of the *Tablet* in November, 1868, he had pledged himself 'to maintain, without compromise and without reserve, the great truths which have been so clearly declared to us by Pius the Ninth'.[48] Vaughan explicitly refused to tolerate any criticism of episcopal decisions in matters of doctrine, discipline or ecclesiastical government and during the Council, he refused to publish any letters which did not reflect the extreme Ultramontane position on the grounds that since papal infallibility was about to be defined, it would be immoral to provide arguments which might harden men's hearts against it. Vaughan also published a supplement to the *Tablet*, significantly entitled the *Vatican*, which reported events in an uncompromising Ultramontane way, unsympathetically criticizing opponents of the definition and enthusiastically welcoming every move made in its support. The point was quite simple:

> If the Bishops who are soliciting the definition, and praising the clergy and faithful who supplicate it, are obeying the Holy Spirit, and *'evidently striving'*, as the Brief of Pius IX lately assured the clergy of Chalons, *'for the glory of God and the honour of the Church'*; it seems to follow that the Bishops who are opposing it, with whatever purity of intention, are doing something else. We speak under correction, but this conclusion appears to us elementary.[49]

Vaughan's narrow policy had an unfortunate effect abroad where some of the publications which strongly opposed the definition of papal infallibility did so, at least in part, as a reaction against the views of Manning and Ward. The *Tablet* was described as 'very one-sided, silly and dictatorial', even in Rome.[50] A Professor from Bonn University who reported that not a tenth of the German clergy or laity were inclined to accept the definition, claimed that the *Tablet* was giving the impression that all English Catholics except a few eccentrics were enthusiastically in favour of the new dogma.[51] Montalembert wrote,

> How unfathomable are the designs of God in allowing such oracles as Dr Ward, Mr Vaughan, and others to be the representatives of Catholic intelligence in the eyes of that immense Anglo-Saxon race which is so evidently intended to cover the whole modern world![52]

Montalembert himself argued that the educated and theologically informed laity should have a voice in ecclesiastical decisions and that free and honest inquiry played an important part in the evolution of the authentic mind of the Church. Montalembert also believed that there could be nothing finer than a combination of the old English spirit with the Catholic faith and that there should be an 'Englishness' about the faith in England. He was therefore disheartened by the attitudes of Manning and Ward, and found both the *Tablet* and the *Weekly Register* 'un-English' in their Ultramontane views.

Yet the *Tablet* was not without its critics in England and these included at least two of the bishops. One priest pointed out that a considerable number of English Catholics had good reasons for opposing the definition of papal infallibility, whereas some of those who supported the definition did not know what they were doing or even pretended that the consequences would not be significant. The extreme attitudes of other Ultramontanes simply provoked opposition because of the way in which they condemned their opponents as semi-rationalists or disaffected Catholics. Another priest wrote,

> In the name of religion, of charity for those whom he is so sorely perplexing and driving to utterances which are actually a renunciation of Catholic faith – in the name of the Church upon which is brought, through the controversy among ourselves caused by the *Tablet*, ridicule and blasphemy on the part of its enemies, I adjure Dr Herbert Vaughan 'not to be more wise than it behoveth to be wise, but to be wise unto sobriety', and to turn his pen from pernicious endeavours to lower those of the Episcopacy who are discharging a solemn duty for which he ought to believe they are accountale to their consciences and in no manner to his notions.[53]

Newman, of course, was very conscious of the fact that the Ultramontanes could freely expound their extreme views, particularly after the silencing of the *Rambler* and the *Home and Foreign*, whereas moderate or Liberal Catholics could not oppose them without being accused of creating divisions. As he wrote on another occasion,

> I have felt much of late years, though I have said little about it, the great injustice of those who put out strongly their own views, and then accuse others as wanting in peace and charity, who, on this provocation, feel bound to show that there is another opinion on the point, and that there are good Catholics who hold it.[54]

Attacks and criticisms, however, simply reinforced Vaughan in his conviction that he was 'doing good'. The English *Januses*, he thought, were decidedly weak and he condemned his opponents as false brethren siding with the Church's enemies who fortunately would soon be unable to continue their attacks while remaining in the Church. Furthermore, the policy of the *Tablet* received a great deal of support, especially in the north of England. Consequently, Vaughan would continue to regard the *Tablet* and the *Vatican* as 'heralds and champions of the Truth', while Manning later expressed the opinion, 'the *Tablet* did good service in *The Vatican*. It was no time for "rose water".'[55]

The opinions of Catholics in England reflected those in the Church at large and within the Council itself where the bishops were roughly divided into three main groups. The majority were in favour of defining papal infallibility; a minority including many scholars, theologians and churchmen considered that a definition was inopportune; a small group was opposed to the doctrine itself. As a result of the attitudes of the Ultramontanes and their activities in Rome, these last two groups, the inopportunists and the opponents, were often in anguish and distress. The Bishop of Kerry, for example, was miserable at the loss of souls who were close to him and the prospect of open schism or secret heresy. 'A poor woman, a saintly woman, tried by all manner of misfortune — English, Catholic, fervent and well-informed — who has long been ill' was apparently 'beseeching God to let her die before the promulgation of the dogma, so that she could be saved'.[56]

The most important English representative of the moderate inopportunist group was, of course, Newman who was described by Ward as 'Our chief enemy' and who eventually condemned the aggressive insolent faction which would impose a definition of doctrine as a luxury of devotion rather than see it as a stern, painful necessity;[57]

> it is a new and most serious precedent in the Church that a dogma *de fide* should be passed *without definite and urgent cause*. This to my mind is the serious part of the matter. You put an enormous power into the hands of one man, without check, and at the very time, by your act, you declare that he may use it without special occasion.[58]

In Newman's opinion, support for the definition was unfortunate and ill-advised; a definition of papal infallibility was unnecessary and inexpedient, it was a practical danger and a theological over-emphasis which *'would unsettle men's minds'*,[59] increase indifferentism among Catholics and create apologetic difficulties while alienating other Christians.

By the end of 1867, Newman was urging Canon Walker of Scarborough whom he later described 'as one of the few remaining priests who kept up the tradition of Dr Lingard's generation of Catholics', to witness to those traditions in contrast to Manning's opinions on papal infallibility.[60] In 1869, Newman helped William Monsell to print and circulate for the bishops of the English speaking world, a translation of the confidential memorandum opposing the definition of papal infallibility addressed to the German hierarchy. In the following year, Newman refused to support Vaughan's petition in favour of the definition and Vaughan retaliated by criticizing Newman's attitude in the *Tablet*.

Although Archbishop Manning apparently attempted to exclude Newman from the Council, the Pope himself invited the Oratorian to attend as one of the consultors. Bishop Dupanloup also intended to invite Newman to join him at the Council — an invitation conveyed through Montalembert, and Newman was also invited by Bishop Clifford and by Bishop Brown who had delated his article on the laity which Newman now used as an excuse for declining. Ultimately, Newman felt that he would lose his independence by attending the Council without gaining any advantage and it is difficult not to conclude that Newman's presence in England where the voice of moderation was seldom heard, was more important than his attendance at the Council.

Incidentally, twelve of the fourteen English bishops were present at the Council as well as some 120 bishops from the British Empire and 47 from the United States. In fact, the English speaking bishops formed the largest single language group at the Council apart from the Italians. However, on the whole, the primary concerns of the English speaking bishops were pastoral and administrative, rather than theological. It is perhaps significant that none of the English bishops made any contribution to the discussions on the relations between faith and reason in spite of the obvious intellectual difficulties of the time which so concerned Newman and other English Catholics. It is perhaps also significant that three English speaking bishops headed the poll for the deputation on discipline.

Most of the Liberal Catholics in England were opposed to the actual definition or to exaggerated Ultramontane interpretations, rather than to a belief in papal infallibility as such. Renouf, for example, criticized the influential party which, dissatisfied with the present situation, was impatiently anticipating the definition of their favourite dogma as an article of faith. The Ultramontanes were the innovators. Catholic apologists had constantly denied that papal infallibility was an article of faith and Ultramontanism hardly existed among English secular priests during the first part of the nineteenth century. 'The impulse was first given by the 'Tablet' newspaper, under the editorship of two ardent converts, who were for a long time a terror to the ecclesiastical authorities'.

Interior of St George's Roman Catholic Cathedral as originally proposed by Pugin

Renouf associated the growth of Ultramontanism with the activities of converts who spread their opinions as priests or through the pages of Catholic periodicals; 'Time will show', he commented, 'whether or not it be wise to identify Christianity with a system of theology which is demonstrably untenable'.[61] During August, 1869, Renouf was informing Acton, the leading English opponent of the definition, of the opinions of the English clergy on the subject of papal infallibility. Renouf was in a good position to do this as he was an inspector of schools travelling up and down the country. In the following month, Acton went to Rome to prevent a definition which, he thought, would finally destroy Liberal Catholicism. He told Renouf, 'I am on my way, an unbidden guest, to the Council. I am afraid that before we meet again we shall be heretics'.

Acton tried to win over the educated laity and helped to organize the bishops who were opposed to the definition. His letters to Döllinger later appeared slightly modified in *Allgemeine Zeitung* under the name 'Quirinus' and when these were later published as a book, this was generally considered an accurate, if hostile, source of information. Newman, for example, was very critical of Döllinger's own letters when these appeared as *The Pope and the Council* by 'Janus', but he was told that the *Letters from Rome* by 'Quirinus' was the most accurate witness of what took place at the Council.[62] Acton's letters to Gladstone were also influential in his later attack on *The Vatican Decrees.*

At the time, the Council did not receive a favourable press, either in Europe or in England. But part of the reason for this lack of objectivity was the attempt to preserve the secrecy of the Council as well as the activities of the Ultramontanes. The Roman police censored communications with the bishops who were opposed to the definition, while Monsignor Nardi 'had the German Bishops in his house for their meetings, but they discovered that he had made a hole in the wall through which to listen to what they said!!'[63] Many of the English bishops were constantly critical of the *Times* as well as the *Tablet*. The *Times'* correspondent in Rome was Thomas Mozley, Newman's brother-in-law and an Anglican cleric. Unfortunately, Mozley did not speak French or Italian and depended on English gossip, while his contacts with Acton and the minority might well have been somewhat peripheral. However, Ullathorne believed that the reports in the *Times* became more sober and accurate after the first couple of months.[64]

In 1869, Acton had asked Renouf, 'Have you any idea how the English bishops stand towards the Dogma and towards Manning?' – a question which illustrated the close association of the Archbishop with support in favour of the definition.[65] Manning had attempted to insert the attribute 'infallible' in the bishops' address of congratulation following the Pope's original announcement of the Council, but this was carefully restricted largely as a result of the intervention of Dupanloup. On the eve of St Peter's Day, two days after the papal announcement, Manning and the Bishop of Ratisbon had vowed to do everything in their power to secure the definition of papal infallibility. Newman regarded Manning's pastoral on 'The Centenary of St Peter' published in 1867, as an expression of his extreme views and an attempt to influence and anticipate the decisions of the bishops in the forthcoming Council.

Manning's pastorals were clearly Ultramontane in tone and sentiment. Manning declared that the *Syllabus* and *Quanta cura* were among the greatest acts of Pio Nono's pontificate and part of the supreme and infallible teaching of the Church. He argued that the Roman Church had been regarded as the true seat of apostolic tradition, the doctrines of Rome as the form of truth, the Roman See as the pattern for judgments in faith, the judgments of Rome as equivalent to conciliar decrees.

> In a word, the Chair of Peter has been held to be the test of orthodoxy, the confirmer of Councils, the supreme tribunal of faith, the destroyer of heresies, the end of controversies, an authority which is subject to no appeal, to no reversal, to no revision, to no superior upon earth.[66]

Manning enjoyed an international influence among the Ultramontanes. His pastorals were translated into Italian, for example, and his theory of infallibility accepted as one of the standard presentations. In a pastoral on 'The Oecumenical Council', he expressed his opinion that the judgments of papal infallibility were 'in their essence . . . *apart* from the episcopal body'.[67] These comments were immediately translated into French by the *Univers* which implied that separation from the bishops might even include the idea of the opposition to the episcopal body. Manning later denied this, though without repudiating the French translation.

Originally, the *schema* on the Church did not deal with papal infallibility, but papal primacy. However, the special deputation *de fide* which was in charge of amendments to the *schemata* was not the neutral or mixed tribunal which it should and was expected to have been. Manning seems to have been largely, though not solely, responsible for the disingenuous trickery by which inopportunists were deliberately excluded. Manning secured a block vote for or against a list of names chosen by himself and his supporters, and was reported as saying that heretics came to a Council to be heard and condemned, not to take part in formulating doctrine. Ullathorne remarked,

> There has been much excitement and diplomacy amongst the Fathers about the election of the twenty-four for the special deputation on definitions of faith, and we English are not the only ones, though the chief ones, whose united wish, *one excepted*, has been outwitted by what everybody considers an intrigue.[68]

The *Vatican* saw things rather differently and reported to its readers:

> Without any shadow of constraint, with no guide but his own judgment and conscience, each Father gave his vote, of which God alone was the witness, in favour of those whom he deemed to bear the immense responsibility delegated to them by the Collective Episcopate. And what was the result? Not a single name identified with, or as we should prefer to say, compromised by Gallican or Liberal principles, was selected. And even this fact, significant as it is, does not suffice to indicate the almost unanimous spirit which animates the Council.[69]

There was in fact one inopportunist on the deputation, but he had changed his mind since arriving in Rome. In the event, however, the manoeuvring of the majority and the deliberate exclusion of representatives of the minority forced the latter into opposition, prevented fruitful discussion and contributed to the subsequent controversies both inside and outside the Council. The apparent willingness of the Curia to impose its views regardless of the Fathers' intentions was at least partly responsible for the later appeals to public opinion and government intervention.

Before the opening of the Council, the European governments decided not to intervene in its affairs and the British Government simply warned the Secretary of State of the grave dangers which might follow if the Council adopted the exaggerated views of the extreme party. European governments began to protest with the publication of the propositions on relations between Church and State in the *schema* on the Church and Acton tried to win the support of the British Government. However, only Gladstone, the Prime Minister, was inclined to intervene. The Foreign Secretary, Lord Clarendon, defined the Government's attitude as one of hostile neutrality. Although the British Government was not unwilling that the other European powers should express their opposition, a determination to preserve good relations with the Roman authorities and to avoid alienating Irish Catholics prevented a more direct or explicit statement of their hostility and concern.

Manning was inevitably closely involved in organizing the 'monster petition' that *the question* should be brought before the Council. His name was not among the first signatures since he was a member of the congregation to which the petition was addressed. However, the formula of the petition reflected Manning's own outlook and this harsh formula coupled with his personal inflexibility might have delayed the progress of the Ultramontanes. The substance of Manning's proposals became part of the final decree on the primacy and infallibility of the Pope, and he was at the centre of the debate with his theory of a personal, absolute and separate papal infallibility which became a focal point of the minority opposition.

Meanwhile, attempts to restrict, even by explanation, the extent of papal infallibility were strongly and insistently opposed by Manning and his supporters, and there is even a suggestion that Manning might have helped to reinforce the Pope when the latter might have been prepared to compromise. Manning's enthusiasm might well have injured his own cause and there was undoubtedly some tension between the Archbishop of Westminster and the other English bishops. His conduct occasioned a remark which he did not quickly forget — 'Non ita sunt tractandae res Ecclesiae'.[70] According to Renouf, Manning was regarded as being 'an imposter if not a hypocrite'[71] while Bishop Chadwick reported, 'He is not so esteemed here as he used to be. "Troppo Fanatico". He will not be made Cardinal yet awhile, and however zealous he is for the Pope, yet it would appear, that by over zeal, he has embittered the opposition'.[72]

Manning was undoubtedly the most prominent of the English bishops at the Vatican Council and certainly merited his title of 'Chief Whip'.[73] His manoeuvres contributed in no small way to the controversies surrounding the Council and his extreme views disguised for a time the comparative moderation of the final decrees. But the prominence of Manning has tended to obscure the fact that, with the possible exceptions of Chadwick and Cornthwaite, his attitudes and opinions were not shared by other English bishops. Bishop Goss, for example, accused the English Ultramontanes and particularly Manning of committing the unpardonable sin against the Holy Spirit whose decision they anticipated by denouncing their opponents as heretics or infidels. Goss believed that each local bishop was a witness of the traditions and teachings of his church in matters of faith. But neither Manning's learning nor his position — a thing to be ashamed of since he was standing in Errington's shoes — justified his opinions and his testimony was opposed to the traditional teaching of English Catholics: 'Truth, simple English truth, seems to have parted from the whole faction'.[74]

In Goss's opinion, the Pope had been so flattered that he imagined he could treat the bishops like children, while even the best of the Italian laity could never understand why bishops refused to give way when submission would result in honours and promotion.

> In case of disputes about property the Pope's altum dominium is used to cover every flaw in justice, and henceforth his Infallibility will be held to supply any defect of argument or revelation in matters of faith. My own opinion is that the Pope believes, feels himself now to be personally inspired . . . For years no one has dared to contradict him . . . The Pope is amiable and hence has now a sort of hysterical affection from ladies and young priests and he has unfortunately believed that he would be able to exercise the same fascination over the Bishops . . . With him the Infallibility is a personal affair and he works upon us who do not go in for it as enemies, personal enemies.

Bishop Clifford was the most active English bishop on the side of the minority. He questioned whether the doctrine could be defined and whether such a definition was opportune. His criticisms of the Council's procedure were regarded as almost sensational and certainly aroused the sympathy of many of the other bishops who had become dissatisfied. Clifford also played an important part in modifying the offensive language which the Fathers were prepared to use in describing Protestantism as the cause of all the errors of the day. Ullathorne regarded Manning's speech which turned out to be one of the major addresses of the Council as an attempt to anticipate Clifford, and in spite of the signs of disapproval which greeted Clifford's remarks, there can be little doubt that he was more ecumenical and accurate in his appraisal of the Protestant mind than Manning had been. Clifford also proposed that there should be an open discussion between the opposing sides as a means of restoring peace and tranquility to the Council. But according to the Pope, Clifford's opposition to papal infallibility was a result of his frustrated ambition; he had not been appointed Archbishop of Westminster. 'Quirinus', on the other hand, claimed that there was perhaps no other member of the Council 'whom every one credits with so entire an absence of any ambitious thought'.[75]

Only Grant and Cornthwaite joined Manning in signing the 'monster petition' in favour of the definition, while Errington joined Clifford in signing the opposing petition organized by the American bishops. Most of the English hierarchy, however, followed Ullathorne's example and avoided the various parties which were forming outside the Council. Ullathorne himself was significant as a leading supporter of a definition in more moderate terms than those which the Ultramontanes wanted; he was accused of Gallicanism as a result of his moderate views on infallibility and his criticism of the extreme Ultramontanes. With Goss and Brown who did not actually attend the Council, Ullathorne welcomed Newman's condemnation of the insolent and aggressive faction. William Vaughan, Bishop of Plymouth, thought that a definition would be inopportune, while Turner of Salford was concerned to avoid the adoption of extreme interpretations of infallibility. In the event, Manning, Chadwick and Cornthwaite voted in favour of *Pastor aeternus* and they were joined by Ullathorne and Vaughan who changed from their previous positions of *juxta modum* and *non placet* respectively. Clifford signed the letter to the Pope explaining the abstention of the minority from the final session.

The reactions of the English bishops to the definition of papal infallibility were as varied as their previous attitudes. Manning's exaggerated welcome and interpretation contributed to the hesitations of some English Catholics including some of the bishops, before they accepted the decrees, though there were other questions such as whether the Council was truly ecumenical, properly conducted or finally concluded. Ullathorne published the most balanced statement and his moderate interpretation could even be compared with the unofficial but authoritative work on the Council written by its secretary, Bishop Fessler. Although Clifford experienced the greatest difficulties, he was able to accept the decrees before the end of the year; Errington was the last English bishop to accept them formally. But in view of their continuing divisions, it is hardly surprising that the English bishops did not issue a joint pastoral letter on the first Vatican Council and the definition of papal infallibility.

The controversy over the extent of papal infallibility was not created by the first Vatican Council; Ryder and Ward had publicly debated the issue before 1870; neither did the Council settle the question. The minority did not succeed in preventing or delaying a definition of the doctrine, but did succeed in restricting infallibility to solemn universal official declarations of faith or morals. This was not the sweeping definition wanted by the Ultramontanes who extended the notion of infallibility to almost every papal speech or letter. Since 1870, it has become increasingly obvious that, doctrinally if not practically, the definition as actually promulgated represented nothing like the victory for the extreme party which it was commonly believed to represent at the time. As Newman himself pointed out, the Ultramontanes had hoped to secure a decree which would cover 'political principles' and the *Syllabus of Errors*, whereas only 'faith and morals', and that which Ryder had maintained against Ward, had been authoritatively defined.[76]

But Newman had also previously warned, 'Let us look to it lest a judgment come down upon us, if we do, *though we have a right to do*, what we ought not to do. We must not play with edged tools'. The definition was not only a mistake, but the way it had been passed was a scandal.

> I never expected to see so great a scandal in the Church . . . nothing had been passed, (as I think), but what I have ever held myself, about the Pope's Infallibility — but one's natural sense of justice, of loving kindness, of large forbearance and discretion, as Christian duties, is shocked by what has taken place at Rome'.[77]

Newman therefore continued to criticize the lack of tenderness or largeness of mind among some of the Church's officials and rulers, and he condemned extensions of the definition as cruel and tyrannical.

Manning, for example, tried to extend the province of infallibility, whereas Newman maintained that the Pope was not infallible beyond the Deposit of Faith, 'though there is a party of Catholics, who, I suppose to frighten away converts, wish to make out that he is giving forth infallible utterances every day'.[78] Manning claimed that papal infallibility extended to the limits of the doctrinal authority of the Church and was independent of the Church, but Newman argued that the active infallibility of Pope and bishops could not be divorced from the passive infallibility of the whole body of the faithful.

Newman also pointed out that 'ex cathedra' was not explained and that the definition itself would not have been passed if the formula had not been so vague. In any case,

> The dogma seems to me as mildly framed, as it could be — or nearly so. That the Pope was infallible in General Council, or when speaking *with* the Church, all admitted, even Gallicans. They admitted, I think I may say, that his word ex cathedra was infallible, if the Bishops did no more than keep silence — All that is passed last year, is, that in *some sense* he may speak per se, and his speech may be

infallible – I say in some sense, because a bishop who voted for the dogma tells me that at the time an explanation was given that in one sense the Pope spoke per se, and in another sense not per se.[79]

Newman himself believed that Pio Nono wanted the Council to say a great deal more than it did, 'but a greater Power hindered it'. A Pope was simply protected from saying what was untrue when speaking ex cathedra, he was not inspired and did not enjoy a gift of divine knowledge;

> I know you will find flatterers and partizani such as those whom St Francis de Sales calls 'the Pope's lackies', who say much more than this, but they may enjoy their own opinion, they cannot bind the faith of Catholics.[80]

The very idea of infallibility was negative. Ecclesiastical infallibility was a necessary inference from the Church's prerogative as divinely appointed teacher and guardian of revelation. The Church ascertained and taught the truth by human means, without the promise of invincible grace, but assisted by grace, like any other inquirer, and with the security that in order to fulfil its office, it could not ultimately *'go wrong'*; the *'outcome'* must always be true in matters of revelation.[81] The Church was not inspired; inspiration was positive, infallibility negative.

Furthermore, according to Newman, the history of the early Church seemed to show that it had moved towards the fulness of truth by successive statements which alternately moved in contrary directions, supplying or completing each other. Thus the definition of papal infallibility needed to be completed rather than reversed. Safeguards were necessary in order to explain the extent and matter of papal power. In spite of the violent or reckless party which would claim that no safeguards or explanations were needed, there was a limit to the triumph of the tyrannical. Faith and patience were necessary; a new Pope or a reassembled Council might well 'trim the boat'.[82]

Apart from some significant exceptions such as Döllinger, many Liberal Catholics eventually found that they were able to accept the decrees. Renouf, for example, told Döllinger that he had not changed his theological opinions and was as horrified as ever by the 'insolent and aggressive faction' which had been victorious during the Council. But it was now possible to see the limited extent of that victory. The Ultramontanes had imposed a formula on the Church, compelled some of the best and most learned Catholics to leave and completely destroyed the faith of many. Yet the cleverest Ultramontane in England felt that their success was infinitely less than Döllinger himself imagined.

Ward implied that the chief gain at the Council had been the expulsion of some disloyal Catholics from the Church, but he was also forced to admit that nothing had been decided on the basic issue between himself and his most dangerous opponent.

The term 'ex cathedra' in conjunction with 'infallible' was ambiguous and Ward had also conceded that it was perhaps impossible to define exactly when the Pope was speaking ex cathedra. Furthermore, when a formula was adopted by the Church, it was no longer the property of the 'framers' or of any particular party, but must be interpreted in accordance with the whole teaching of the Church. The language of the Council on other papal prerogatives had been given a more moderate interpretation than was originally given either by the supporters of the Roman curia or by their German opponents.

> Time is the great solvent of things, and though it operates *slowly*, it is the great interpreter of events And those who have faith in God and His guidance of the Church need not be disquieted, however fatally wrong events seem to fall out . . . I have not the shadow of a doubt that what I have been saying is the truth, and that the history of the Church in time to come will fully corroborate my view of things.[83]

Newman also continued to sympathize with Döllinger, writing to him and on one occasion even making preparations to meet him.

> Dr Döllinger has been treated very cruelly . . . Every consideration, the fullest time should be given to those who have to make up their minds to hold an article of faith which is new to them. To take up at once such an article may be the act of a vigorous faith; but it may also be the act of a man who will believe anything because he believes nothing, and is ready to profess whatever his ecclesiastical, that is, his political party requires of him. There are too many high ecclesiastics in Italy and England, who think that to believe is as easy as to obey − that is, they talk as if they did not know what an act of faith is. A German who hesitates may have more of the real spirit of faith than an Italian who swallows.[84]

In England, much of the confusion over the definition of papal infallibility disappeared after the controversy occasioned by Gladstone's attack on 'The Vatican Decrees' in 1874. Unlike earlier manifestations of anti-Catholic apologetic, the public reaction on this occasion was generally restrained and a newspaper like the *Times* was critical of Gladstone's argument that a belief in papal infallibility was incompatible with civil loyalty. But whatever criticisms might be made of Gladstone, it should not be forgotten that the actions and attitudes of the Ultramontanes had alienated one of the greatest statesmen of the age, while Newman's answer rather than their own was the approach ultimately adopted by the Church. Many Catholics of such different opinions as Acton and Manning had replied to Gladstone's attack, but the most famous reply was Newman's *Letter to the Duke of Norfolk* which emphasized the practical and psychological limits of papal political power and the fact and primacy of conscience.

In spite of the general welcome which Newman's pamphlet received from Catholics and non-Catholics alike, the reaction of some of the Ultramontanes was far from favourable. There was further talk of condemning Newman and hostile articles by Bottalla appeared in the Catholic press. The public was not unaware of these divisions and one reviewer praised Newman's *Letter*, but distinguished his 'personal' views from those of 'official' Catholics such as Manning who had been promoted while he had not.[85] Nevertheless, when the Prefect of Propaganda asked Manning whether anything should be done, the Archbishop gave no less than twelve reasons why no public action should be taken. Manning then received another letter informing him that the Pope wished some friend to let Newman know that there were objectionable passages in his pamphlet. Ullathorne was also given the unenviable task which he declined, of admonishing Newman on a suitable occasion.

Acton found himself in more serious trouble as a result of his famous letters to the *Times*. Manning asked him whether he had an heretical intention in writing them and whether he accepted the decrees of the Council. Acton felt unable simply to submit to the Vatican decrees without recognizing the need to reconcile and to interpret them in the light of ecclesiastical tradition and teaching. As he wrote to Newman,

> If therefore I am asked whether I accept the decrees with a definite understanding and inward conviction of their truth, I cannot say either yes or no. But this is the question which the Archbishop — taking his letter and his pastoral together — wants an answer to. I certainly cannot satisfy him. I hope you will understand that, in falling under his censures, I act from no spirit of revolt, from no indifference, and from no false shame. But I cannot accept his tests and canons of dogmatic development and interpretation, and must decline to give him the only answer that will content him, as it would, in my lips, be a lie.[86]

Fortunately Acton was not excommunicated, though other English Catholics were being refused the sacraments.

Yet in spite of these differences, there were signs that Newman's *Letter to Norfolk* was helping to heal the divisions which had been occasioned by the definition of papal infallibility. Newman himself thought that Gladstone's attack had 'thrown Catholics together in a most unexpected manner'; Acton thought that Newman's conditions made it technically possible to accept the Vatican decrees; and even W.G. Ward wrote that he would never have dreamed of describing Newman's *Letter* as 'minimistic'.[87] Ultimately, even Manning was too much of a statesman, or a politician, to continue to resist the general reaction. Following Gladstone's attack, the English hierarchy issued a joint pastoral letter during their Low Week Meeting of 1875. This pastoral was largely based on the declaration of the German hierarchy and the subsequent letter of approval from the Pope; very different in character from Manning's earlier pastorals. In 1890, Manning even joined Biship Hefele, an inopportunist, in sponsoring Salvatori di Bartolo's *I Criteri Theologii* which could almost be interpreted as surrendering any effective exercise of papal infallibility.

Far more serious in practice, however, was the fact that many Catholics as well as their opponents would in future exaggerate the theological significance of the definition. The aggressive policy adopted by Pio Nono and the Ultramontanes seemed to the outside world to have perpetually condemned the Catholic Church to an obscurantist position. As Newman himself pointed out, although the popes could not teach error ex cathedra, they could and had done a great deal of harm extra cathedram;

> As far as [the definition] is a tax upon faith it is, from its wording little enough — but considered in its effects both upon the Pope's mind and that of his people, and in the power of which it puts him in practical possession, it is nothing else than shooting Niagara.[88]

Notes

1. J.H. Newman, *The Present Position of Catholics in England* (London, 1903) 390-1; see also J.L. Altholz, *The Liberal Catholic Movement England The Rambler and its contributors 1848-1864* (London, 1962) 70, 213.

2. S.D. Femiano, *Infallibility of the Laity The Legacy of Newman* (New York, 1967) 86; see also Altholz, *Liberal Catholic Movement* 99-102; J.L. Altholz, D. McElrath and J.C. Holland, eds., *The Correspondence of Lord Acton and Richard Simpson* (Cambridge, 1971-1975) III: 12.

3. Talbot to Patterson, 12 November 1859, AAW.
4. Femiano, *Infallibility of the Laity* 108; *Acton Simpson Correspondence* I: 6.
5. *The Letters and Diaries of John Henry Newman*, ed. C.S. Dessain (London, 1961-) XXIII: 226; Femiano, *Infallibility of the Laity* 116.
6. *Letters and Diaries* XIX: 141; C. Butler, *The Life and Times of Bishop Ullathorne* (London, 1926) I: 315-21.
7. Talbot to Patterson, 22 October 1859, AAW; H.A. MacDougall, *The Acton-Newman Relations The Dilemma of Christian Liberalism* (New York, 1962) 43-5.
8. *Letters and Diaries* XXVI: 131; *Acton Simpson Correspondence* I: 136; III: 43, 46-7.
9. *Acton Simpson Correspondence* II: 31, 41-2.
10. W. Ward, *The Life of John Henry Cardinal Newman* (London, 1912) I: 526; *The Life and Times of Cardinal Wiseman* (London, 1900) II: 415-16.
11. H.E. Manning, *The Temporal Power of the Vicar of Jesus Christ* (London, 1880) 77-8.
12. R. Addington, *Faber Poet and Priest* (Cowbridge and Bridgend, 1974) 101, 313.
13. F.W. Faber, *Devotion to the Pope* (London, 1860) 16.
14. F.W. Faber, *Hymns* (London, 1862) 71, 73.
15. Ushaw, C.H. 110.
16. F.O. Blundell, *Broughton Catholic Charitable Society. History 1787 to 1922* (Preston, 1923) 104.
17. *La Sovranità Temporale dei Romani Pontefici* (Roma, 1864) Parte Quinta II: 19, 61, 78, 80, 88, 134, 142-4; these volumes contain frequent misprints and spelling mistakes. As a result of the general support for the Italian nationalists found in England, this country was considered to be especially responsible for the difficulties of the Pope; see e.g. the comments of F.A.P. Dupanloup, *The Papal Sovereignty* (London, 1860) 281-339.
18. T. Burke, *Catholic History of Liverpool* (Liverpool, 1910) 145, 155, 160.
19. MacDougall, *Acton-Newman Relations* 75.
20. *Acton Simpson Correspondence* II: 147.
21. E.S. Purcell, *Life of Cardinal Manning Archbishop of Westminster* (London, 1896) II: 349; S. Leslie, *Henry Edward Manning* (London, 1921) 272; Ward, *Newman* I: 525, 534-5; *Letters and Diaries* XXIII: 311; XXVI: 356.
22. *Acton Simpson Correspondence* II: 200; Altholz, *Liberal Catholic Movement* 152; D. Mathew, *Lord Acton and His times* (London, 1968) 122.
23. H.E. Manning, *Essays on Religion and Literature second series* (London, 1867) 3; Ward, *Wiseman* II: 421, 431-2.

24. 'Dr Manning on the Papal Sovereignty' *Rambler* VI (1861) 116-17.

25. *Letters and Diaries* XXII: 44.

26. J.H. Newman, *Fifteen Sermons preached before the University of Oxford* (London, 1906) 201; *Acton Simpson Correspondence* III: 117; *Letters and Diaries* XXIII: 227; Altholz, *Liberal Catholic Movement* 194-6; MacDougall, *Acton-Newman Relations* 85-7; Purcell, *Manning* II: 266; Ward, *Newman* I: 539, 547, 552-3.

27. B. Fothergill, *Nicholas Wiseman* (London, 1963) 267-8.

28. E.E.Y. Hales, *Pio Nono* (London, 1956) 267.

29. The Diaries of L.C. Casartelli, 7 March 1900, Ushaw; *Ushaw Magazine* LXXXV (1974) 36-7; Ward, *Wiseman* II: 457-8.

30. J.E.E.D. Acton, *Essays on Freedom and Power*, ed. G. Himmelfarb (London, 1956) 273-4; see also *Essays on Church and State*, ed. D. Woodruff (London, 1952) 159-99; *Acton Simpson Correspondence* III: 185-8; Altholz, *Liberal Catholic Movement* 230, 244.

31. Ward, *Newman* I: 585; see also 560, 584-9; *Autobiographical Writings*, ed. H. Tristram (London, 1956) 253-60; *Apologia pro Vita Sua*, ed. M.J. Svaglic (Oxford, 1967) 235-6; *Letters and Diaries* XX: 445-8; XXIV: 120; XXVI: 27; Altholz, *Liberal Catholic Movement* 230-1; MacDougall, *Acton-Newman Relations* 90-3; E. Kelly, 'The *Apologia* and the Ultramontanes', *Newman's Apologia: A Classic Reconsidered*, eds. V.F. Blehl and F.X. Connolly (New York, 1964) 26-46; Newman's own analysis of the Munich Brief can be found in Ward, *Newman* I: 640-2, and of the *Syllabus of Errors* in *Certain Difficulties felt by Anglicans* (London, 1907) II: 276-98.

32. Butler, *Ullathorne* II: 308; Purcell, *Manning* II: 206, 323, 326; J.G. Snead-Cox, *The Life of Cardinal Vaughan* (London, 1910) 1: 215.

33. Coleridge to Thompson, 13 October 1864, Catholic Record Society Archives now deposited in AAW.

34. Aubrey de Vere to Thompson, 6 December 1864; another correspondent criticized the *Dublin* and its editor for being completely one-sided in imagining that Wiseman and Manning were right in everything they did, Teebay to Thompson, January 1865.

35. Butler, *Ullathorne* I: 358, 363; Purcell, *Manning* II: 322-3; D. McElrath, *The Syllabus of Pius IX Some Reactions in England* (Louvain, 1964) 147.

36. *Acton Simpson Correspondence* III: 201; see also 'Liberal Catholicism and Newman's Letter to the Duke of Norfolk' *Clergy Review* LX (1975) 498-511.

37. McElrath, *Syllabus of Pius IX* 135-6.

38. *Letters and Diaries* XXIII: 217.

39. *Letters and Diaries* XXII: 314-5.

40. *Letters and Diaries* XXII: 57; XXIII: 202, 226; XXV: 445, 452.

41. MacDougall, *Acton-Newman Relations* 169; see also 97-8; McElrath, *Syllabus of Pius IX* 112-3, 127, 138-41, 204-5; Ward, *Newman* II: 81, 84.
42. M. Ward, *The Wilfrid Wards and the transition* (London, 1934) I: 32.
43. *Letters and Diaries* XXIII: 143.
44. MacDougall, *Acton-Newman Relations* 109; Mathew, *Acton and His times* 162, 165, 179, 218, 237.
45. H. Vaughan, *The Year of Preparation for the Vatican Council* (London, 1869) 10-11, 47, 55, 141-6; see also F.J. Cwiekowski, *The English Bishops and the First Vatican Council* (Louvain, 1971) 82-7.
46. H.E. Manning, *Petri Privilegium* (London, 1871) second pastoral 124.
47. W. Ward, *William George Ward and the Catholic Revival* (London, 1893) 255.
48. Snead-Cox, *Vaughan* I: 196; see also 198, 200-4; A. McCormack, *Cardinal Vaughan* (London, 1966) 116-17; Cwiekowski, *English Bishops* 161-3.
49. *Vatican*, 11 June 1870, 215; Cwiekowski, *English Bishops* 163.
50. *Ushaw Magazine* 212 (1961) 100; see also Cwiekowski, *English Bishops* 93.
51. Gwatkin, *Renouf* 88-9.
52. MacDougall, *Acton-Newman Relations* 110; B. Aspinwall, 'Montalembert and "Idolatry"' *Downside Review* 89 (1971) 158-64.
53. Snead-Cox, *Vaughan* I: 212; see also 210-11, 224-5; C. Butler, *The Vatican Council 1869-1870* (London, 1962) 106-7.
54. *Letters and Diaries* XXIII: 311; see also XXII: 85.
55. Purcell, *Manning* II: 454-5; *Letters of Herbert Cardinal Vaughan to Lady Herbert of Lea 1867 to 1903*, ed. S. Leslie (London, 1942) 137, 172, 176.
56. P. Spencer, *Politics of Belief in Nineteenth-Century France* (London, 1954) 231; Butler, *Vatican Council* 288.
57. *Letters and Diaries* XXV: 18-20; Butler, *Ullathorne* II: 60.
58. *Letters and Diaries* XXV: 175.
59. C.S. Dessain, 'What Newman taught in Manning's Church' *Infallibility in the Church* (London, 1968) 71; see also 'Newman's reaction to the definition of papal infallibility' *Spode House Review occasional papers* 3 (1976) 39-58.
60. *Letters and Diaries* XXVI: 331; see also 369; XXIII: 367; XXIV: 326-7, 335, 341; XXV: 20, 89; *Lea Letters* 176.
61. Gwatkin, *Renouf* 76, 81.
62. *Letters and Diaries* XXV: 47-8, 270; see also XXIV: 364; Cwiekowski, *English Bishops* 163-4, 253-4; MacDougall, *Acton-Newman Relations* 115-17; Mathew, *Acton and His times* 184-5, 199.
63. *Ushaw Magazine* 212 (1961) 96.

64. Cwiekowski, *English Bishops* 161-2; Hales, *Pio Nono* 294.
65. Gwatkin, *Renouf* 91; see also Cwiekowski, *English Bishops* 66-9; *Letters and Diaries* XXIII: 367.
66. Manning, *Petri Privilegium* first pastoral 26; see also 38; Cwiekowski, *English Bishops* 69-71.
67. Manning, *Petri Privilegium* second pastoral 142; Cwiekowski, *English Bishops* 93-8.
68. Butler, *Vatican Council* 142; see also 144-7; Cwiekowski, *English Bishops* 122-3, 126-7.
69. *Vatican,* 1 January 1870, 29; Cwiekowski, *English Bishops* 128, 162.
70. Cwiekowski, *English Bishops* 238; see also 156-8, 272.
71. *Acton Simpson Correspondence* III: 281, 286.
72. *Ushaw Magazine* 211 (1961) 38.
73. Leslie, *Manning* 219.
74. Cwiekowski, *English Bishops* 170-1.
75. Cwiekowski, *English Bishops* 250.
76. *Letters and Diaries* XXV: 224; see also 220, 278.
77. *Letters and Diaries* XXIV: 377; XXV: 283.
78. *Letters and Diaries* XXV: 297; see also 301, 420; compare Dessain, *Infallibility* 70 with Manning, *Petri Privilegium* third pastoral 57, 91.
79. *Letters and Diaries* XXV: 447; see also 297. 301, 420.
80. *Letters and Diaries* XXV: 299.
81. *Letters and Diaries* XXV: 309.
82. *Letters and Diaries* XXV: 310.
83. Gwatkin, *Renouf* 96-8; see also 'Döllinger, the Renoufs and Rome' *Tablet* 222 (1968) 54-5.
84. *Letters and Diaries* XXV: 430.
85. *Quarterly Review* 138 (1875) 459-98; see also, *Letters and Diaries* XXVII: 401-11; Butler, *Ullathorne* II: 100-6; McElrath, *Syllabus of Pius IX* 320-3.
86. MacDougall, *Acton-Newman Relations* 135; *Acton Simpson Correspondence* III: 331-33; Cwiekowski, *English Bishops* 307-14.
87. *Letters and Diaries* XXVII: 276; *Selections from the Correspondence of the First Lord Acton,* eds. J.N. Figgis and R.V. Laurence (London, 1917) 155; *Dublin Review* XXIV (1875) 454-5; but see also Purcell, *Manning* II: 480.
88. *Letters and Diaries* XXV: 262.

Cardinal Manning

Chapter IV: Manning and the establishment of Ultramontanism

Cardinal Wiseman had refused to nominate his own successor in spite of various suggestions which were made and the fact that Talbot in particular was afraid of a great 'scandal' unless this was done. Manning recommended Ullathorne, but for some time Wiseman had regarded the Bishop of Birmingham as one of his leading opponents and in any case he wanted to avoid any further trouble with the bishops and so the matter was dropped. Talbot himself suggested Manning and claimed that the other English bishops would recommend Errington, 'not from liking the man, but from an English feeling of triumphing over Cardinal Wiseman and gaining a victory over the Holy See'.[1] He therefore insisted that the appearance of Errington's name on the *terna* would be regarded by the Pope as a personal insult and threatened that if a certain name appeared — almost certainly Errington's — the canons would get a bishop they would not like! It was rumoured that the canons would prefer to elect Beelzebub than Manning and that Errington would prove 'a regular scourge to the Clergy'.[2] Nevertheless, the chapter over which Manning presided sent the names of Errington, Clifford and Grant to Rome. Apparently at Grant's suggestion, both Clifford and Grant withdrew their names in order to ensure that Errington 'who knows the details of Westminster better than any man living' should succeed Wiseman.[3] However, Newman later expressed the opinion that by doing this, the two bishops had ruined their own chances; the Pope was displeased and decided to choose someone else, either Manning or Ullathorne, though at one stage the Pope apparently suggested that Talbot might prove to be the best appointment!

Wilfrid Ward later recorded how even as a boy of only nine years old he shared the sense of tragedy on Wiseman's death and the subsequent excitement about his successor. There were two distinct bodies of opinion within English Catholicism. The 'wrong' side included Newman, Acton and all those guilty of the ecclesiastical 'liberalism' condemned by his father, as well as the President and Vice President of St Edmund's who also opposed the policies of Vaughan. Even the late Cardinal had only been a weak champion on the 'right' side. He apparently lacked a proper fighting spirit and was unable to recognize clearly the fundamental divisions of black and white; he had a sneaking sympathy for

Montalembert and was somewhat compromising on possible reunion between the churches of England and Rome. The two ideal leaders of the 'right' side were Manning and Vaughan and it was essential that the former should succeed Wiseman.

> They would bring in Roman vestments and cottas; they would make all the clergy like the Oblates; they would make the old-fashioned priests Roman and zealous – except perhaps a recalcitrant few whom they would excommunicate.

W.G. Ward himself, too anxious to sleep, was urgently writing to Rome and when the news was finally announced, he literally jumped for joy three times and his family sang the *Te Deum*. '*Te Deum laudamus*, good sleep by night, a good Archbishop by day and a good opera in the evening are adequate for human felicity'.[4]

Herbert Vaughan was equally apprehensive on Wiseman's death and similarly over-joyed at Manning's appointment:

> who is to sit in his vacant place? Who is to put on his armour? Who is to continue the work of which he laid the foundations? It seems to me that the future is more difficult than the past; it is a work more interior, more spiritual. It will require very delicate and prudent fingers to draw the threads which must bring into closer relationship the Church and the State; and, above all, it will need a very clear head and a very unfaltering hand, and the seven gifts of the Holy Ghost, to meet the disloyal Catholic intellect, which seems to be growing with a luxuriance and the strength of a weed. The only man I see is my Father Superior. What are his chances with all the Bishops and the Chapter and Barnabo against his appointment? The Holy Ghost has hard times of it with us English Catholics. I suspect Rome will choose '*Dignus*', or '*Dignior*'. Expediency and the Devil hate '*Dignissimus*'.[5]

Consequently when Manning preached Wiseman's panegyric, which he did at the late Cardinal's request, it must have seemed that any hopes of continuing Wiseman's policies might well be destroyed by the appointment of his successor. Manning could have been closing a chapter when he referred to 'a filial love to the Vicar of Jesus Christ' as one of Wiseman's bequests to English Catholicism, or when he pictured Wiseman,

> gazing upon the pattern in the Mount, on the outline and the splendour and the beauty of the Church of God in its unity, universality, and diversity, as it can be seen only in and around the Holy See.

In no other place is this lesson to be learned as in Rome. It is, under the new law, what Jerusalem was under the old – the city of the Incarnation, the home of the Word made flesh, the especial patrimony of the Son of God, who reigns by His Vicar in Rome, and from thence throughout the world. Rome is the last spot which is held by Christianity in its fulness, and in all the royalties of Jesus. Free, independent, and therefore sovereign, the Holy See owns no master upon earth. It is the exclusive throne of a Sovereign who is in heaven.[6]

Unfortunately, whereas Wiseman had originally hoped to unite the various groups of English Catholics by a common devotion to Rome, foreign or continental ideals were now replacing the theological and devotional attitudes which had developed as part of the English tradition. Miss Ward attributed this shift in policy to Manning himself, though it was already taking place before Wiseman's death as a result of the development of those Ultramontane opinions with which Manning firmly identified himself.[7] This identification probably explains Manning's appointment which he himself welcomed, not because he was personally ambitious, but in order to complete Wiseman's work. Manning's Ultramontanism also explains the fact that although he was moved and grateful for the loyal congratulations which he received from the Old Catholics, which incidentally he attributed to the Holy Ghost and the prayers of the Pope, he continued to suspect and condemn them.

By this time, Manning's theological views were simple and direct. Any church or communion which did not claim to be infallible automatically forfeited any authority over the consciences of its members. In 1862, he told one of his correspondents, 'the Voice of the Church is the Voice of God, and I submit myself to it as I should have submitted to Jesus himself'.[8] But if a church was infallible, its ruler must also be infallible. 'If the head on earth could err, how could he be the Vicar of the Divine Head, Who is the Truth?' Manning described papal infallibility 'as the only true and perfect form of the Infallibility of the Church, and therefore of all divine faith, unity, and obedience'.

According to Manning, Catholicism was identical with 'perfect Christianity' and Ultramontanism was identical with Catholicism. The essence of Ultramontanism was that the Church as an infallible divine institution was, within its own sphere, independent of all civil authority, and as the guardian or interpreter of the divine law, the judge of mankind in all matters of faith or morals affecting that law. The dangers of Manning's views did not result from his opposition to

Gallicanism, whatever that might mean in this context and by this time, or even in his claim that the Church alone had the right to define matters of faith and morals. The dangers lay in the implications of allowing the Church the sole right to determine the limits of its own jurisdiction and 'In the indissoluble union of the Church with, and submission to, the *universal jurisdiction* of the Holy See'.[9]

It is therefore fortunate that after the Vatican Council, Manning became less concerned with theological issues and increasingly involved in supplying the social and religious needs of his countrymen and fellow Catholics. Like other Ultramontanes, Manning showed a greater appreciation of the social problems of the time than some Liberal Catholics who were unduly influenced by liberal economic theories of *laissez faire*. This social concern was linked with the pastoral needs of the people, not only because Catholics in England were by now mostly Irish immigrants and from the poorer classes of society, but because Manning himself appreciated the impossibility of expecting religious or moral improvement without also securing improvements in the physical environment.

The existence of the Old Catholic community and a number of converts from the Oxford Movement cannot disguise the fact that the development of English Catholicism during the nineteenth century was more closely linked with the process of Irish immigration. Many English Catholics found it difficult to accept the Irish immigrants who were considered not only economically and socially poverty stricken, but politically disloyal and even criminally inclined. But although English and Irish Catholics were originally divided economically, socially and even occasionally linguistically, their divisions should not be exaggerated in view of the fact that both groups included people of very different incomes with a wide variety of occupations. Even at an early date, the inevitable processes of assimilation, intermarriage, common worship and schooling, were already rapidly operating. There were a few purely Irish committees, but these were on the whole a marginal phenomenon.

The English laity were sometimes bitterly accused of lacking concern for their Irish fellow Catholics particularly by the Ultramontanes. Talbot maintained that 'all the Catholics in England are bound in conscience to supply the means to the poor in the populous cities to fulfil their religious obligations'[10] and he recommended that rich Catholics should reduce their luxurious standards of living in order to build schools. But this accusation of lacking concern for the social and spiritual welfare of the Irish was often largely a polemical weapon used against the Old Catholics in much the same way as they were accused of being indifferent to the conversion of England or lacking in devotion to the Holy See. English Catholics frequently proved generous and self-sacrificing in collecting money, building chapels and finding priests for the Irish immigrants. On the whole, the English Catholic community did not shirk its responsibilities to Irish Catholics. There seems to have been a fairly general 'leakage' of about fifty per cent among the immigrants which would imply that in spite of the immense difficulties involved the mission of the English clergy to the Irish Catholics was also about fifty per cent successful.

The English Catholics were not uninfluenced by Catholic traditions or those of public service. Their devotions and spirtual practices were supported by the religious houses on the continent where their children were taught and their brothers and sisters, relations and friends were living. Before 1829, the Catholic gentry might be excluded from some occupations, but they moved easily among their Protestant relations, friends and clients, and many of them successfully managed their estates. As a result of their wealth and position, these were able to perform the duties associated with their class; some years later, the Earl of Shrewsbury, for example, was known 'as a good man who gives employment to many poor people in winter as well as in summer'.[11] Even before Catholic Emancipation, the Catholic gentry went up to London where the clergy organized charity dinners and balls to pay for chapels and schools. As a result of their involvement in the life of the capital, several leading Catholic families shared a sense of responsibility for various metropolitan charities, while Catholic tradesmen and their genteel Catholic customers established and supported several Catholic charitable societies.

Even during the eighteenth century, schools were built and supported with funds raised from bazaars and boat excursions, tea parties and tavern dinners, charity sermons and begging letters, subscription lists and circulars. There were Catholic societies to help the poor, the infirm and the aged. 'The Irish Charitable Society', for example, was founded as early as 1704 and survived into the twentieth century. These societies largely depended on the laity since the clergy were too few and uninfluential. The laity however tended to be rather paternalist, acting out of a sense of charity rather than justice and appealing to the snobbery of the charitable. The patronage of Catholic or even non-Catholic peers were guarantees of respectability and appeals to the general public emphasized the need to reform the poor, rather than the more specifically 'Catholic' task of saving the faith of the destitute.

This also was true even of 'clerical' appeals. In 1818, the Revd B. Barber launched an appeal to build a church for Irish labourers at

Blackwall, Limehouse and Poplar. This was endorsed by Bishop Poynter as 'most important to the cause of Religion, Morality, and good Order'. 'These poor people', the appeal read, 'are nearly three miles distant from any Catholic Chapel; the consequence is, that the Sundays, which should be spent in receiving religious and moral instruction, are devoted to drunkenness and dissipation; to the impoverishment of their families, to the annoyance of the peaceable Inhabitants, and to the propagation of vice'.[12] During the 1820's when the links between Catholics and the liberal Whigs were strongest, liberal Protestants could share the aims of philanthropic Catholics and the 'Benevolent Society' and 'Saint Patrick's Charity' enjoyed the patronage of the Duke of Sussex.

The development of Ultramontanism, however, alienated English Protestants, while the Ultramontanes themselves supported more 'Roman' forms of charity as opposed to 'Protestant' methods of raising money through appeals to snobbery or social engagements. Such methods were considered too indirect and class conscious, preventing that personal contact between rich and poor which was to be found for example in the St Vincent de Paul Society. One of the leading supporters of this new Ultramontane approach was Frederick Lucas who advocated his case in the pages of the *Tablet*. In due course, the St Vincent de Paul Society worked to supply the educational, social and moral needs of deprived Catholic families as well as finding employment for Irishmen, reclaiming prostitutes, assisting emigrants and delinquents. But it is also worth noting that even the Ultramontanes were later forced to make use of the despised dinners, dances and day excursions; lotteries raised money for Pio Nono who in turn sent gifts to be auctioned at Catholic bazaars.

Meanwhile, although the problems created by immigration were larger than the purses of the wealthiest Catholics, appeals for help did not go unanswered. The Huddlestons of Cambridge, for example, usually sent donations whenever they were asked and they received appeals from Ireland, Cambridge, the East End, Brixton, Tottenham, Kentish Town, Westminster, Somers Town, the Oratory, the Spanish Embassy Chapel, Moorfields, Spitalfields, Deptford, Stratford, Saffron Hill as well as from metropolitan agencies, former servants, relatives and friends. Some of the converts were also extremely generous, though when they opened chapels in rural areas where they were personally most influential, they were inevitably criticized for neglecting the greater needs of the Irish immigrants in the cities and the towns.

Many of the immigrants especially during the first half of the century, suffered from plague and fever, typhoid and cholera. In 1838,

Bishop Briggs lost 26 of his priests within 18 months and another vicar apostolic, Bishop Riddell, himself died of fever. Catholics and immigrants themselves worked hard to provide for their religious and social needs. Missions, churches and schools were built with the 'pennies of the poor'. When the foundation stone of a new Liverpool church was laid in 1856, Irish workers passed in single file, placing a day's wages on the stone, and within a year, the entire cost of the site was paid as a result of the efforts of weekly collectors. During the depression of 1862 in the Lancashire spinning trade, appeals for help from other Catholics in the north of England apparently met with a surprisingly generous response.

Yet in spite of all the considerable efforts which were made, there were never adequate resources, sufficient churches or priests to cope with the increasing population and new arrivals concentrating in London or the mining and manufacturing districts. In 1841, the small Catholic population of Merthyr Tydfil had no church and were forced to use the loft of the town slaughter-house 'whence issues the confused bellowing, bleating and screaming of pent-up and butchered oxen, sheep and swine, and . . . odours exceedingly offensive'.[13] At Abersychan, Catholics used a public house, while at Swansea, their chapel was in danger of collapse. In 1845, a priest in Manchester wrote that although the twelve priests in the city were working as hard as they could, about 40,000 Catholics had failed to make their Easter duties simply because there was no one to hear their confessions. It was estimated that a similar number of Catholics in Liverpool were unable to attend Mass because of the lack of accommodation. At Gateshead in 1851, there was only one priest with three thousand parishioners, saying Mass in a derelict warehouse which held three hundred.

The difficulty of estimating the increasing number of Catholics in England and Wales during the nineteenth century is complicated by the fact that it has proved impossible to adopt a uniform system of making returns even in the twentieth century. There are many isolated records in diocesan archives such as quinquennial returns, Lenten returns and even some national figures between 1850 and 1865, but a great deal of further research is needed before these can be properly evaluated. The figures given in the *Directory*, increasing from 700,000 in 1840 to a million and a half by the end of the century, were not based on accurate information. Similarly, the increased number of churches and chapels, from about 800 in 1861 to some 1,500 in 1901, might also be misleading if only because there was no weekly service in many places recorded as churches, while Catholic parishes tended to be fewer and larger than those of other denominations. In 1902, there were 15

Catholic parishes in North London with an average attendance of just over a 1,000, compared with 29 Wesleyan churches with an average of 541, 40 Congregationalist churches with 526, 50 Baptist churches with 442 and 180 Anglican churches with 400. The larger numbers attending Catholic churches might well have given a misleading impression, though they might also suggest that Roman Catholics were prepared to make a greater effort than other Christians to go to distant churches.

Towards the end of the eighteenth century, there might have been as few as fifty or a hundred thousand Catholics in England and Wales. The Catholic community increased as a result of the general facts of English rural demography, popular catechizing by the clergy, the conversion of members of the Oxford Movement and immigration especially from Ireland. The immigrants tended to concentrate in London, Birmingham and Liverpool; elsewhere, growth was most evident in Yorkshire and South Wales, whereas the fewest Catholics were to be found in the West country and East Anglia. Actual numbers are difficult to estimate and many of the Irish immigrants were of course Protestants. On the 30th of March, 1851, just over a quarter of a million Catholics attended Mass, nearly half of whom lived in London or Liverpool, yet by that time, over half a million Irish immigrants had already arrived in the country; Wiseman himself had once remarked that 'for every Puseyite gained two poor Irish are lost'.[14]

There was a rapid rise in the number of Catholic marriages during the 1840's which coincided with the arrival of the greatest number of Irish immigrants: in 1844, there were 17 Catholic marriages for every 1,000 in England and Wales; by 1854, there were 49 and then the number fell from 48 in 1864 to 40 in 1874 and 41 in 1904; there were 8,659 Catholic marriages in 1864, 7,231 in 1869 and 8,179 in 1874. Of course, not all Catholics could afford a Catholic ceremony, while the declining number of Catholic marriages might also be the result of assimilation or re-emigration. In short, the number of Catholics in England steadily increased during the second half of the nineteenth century, but much more slowly than in the twenty years before 1850. Towards the end of 1875, there was a total attendance of 116,504 at all the Sunday services in the diocese of Salford. In 1886 it was estimated that over 50,000 Catholics attended church in London and a further 40,000 by 1902.[15] By the end of the century, the shortage of priests, churches and schools was no longer as serious as it had been previously. The number of immigrants fell and the proportion of Catholics in the country rose with the general decline in church attendance and mainly as a result of the existence of large working class families.

Nevertheless, in spite of the 'leakage' of those who ceased to practise their religion, an important and immediate effect of Irish immigration was that the Catholic Church was the only Christian community in England which enjoyed a steady increase of support from the poor and the working classes. Catholics in England did not generally reject the 'Church' to the same extent as other socially deprived Christians. For this difficult achievement, a great deal of credit must be given to the priests, especially the Irish priests in the case of those immigrants who could not speak English and those who suspected the English clergy even when they could. The clergy received invaluable help from some of the laity, particularly the Irish publicans of Railway hotels or in small industrial towns who were said to give 'their parlours for Mass and their sons to the priesthood'.[16] Priests played a leading part in improving the social and economic conditions of their people, providing relief, improving sanitary conditions, encouraging temperance and even, on at least one occasion, establishing a Penny Bank. One local officer of health commented, 'I received very valuable aid and co-operation from the Catholic Clergy . . . whenever I have appealed to them'.[17] The Priest was always an important figure among the Irish and sometimes he was able to exert considerable influence. The clergy in Cardiff, for example, were almost entirely successful in destroying local support for Fenianism. This influence, however, should not be exaggerated and did not necessarily extend to attendance at Church or the practice of religion.

It is in fact possible to trace the variations in religious practice in Cardiff between 1841 and 1861, and to offer some explanation.[18] Less than 10% of the Catholic population made their Easter duties in 1841, but by 1847 the number had reached 50%. This was followed by a decline from about 22% in 1848 to less than 16% in 1853, before rising again to about 23% and reaching just over 25% in 1861. Before 1841, there was no resident priest in Cardiff, but in 1842 a chapel was opened and an apostolic missioner was appointed. Between 1847 and 1848, the Irish population more than doubled as a result of further immigration following the Famine and it became impossible for one priest to cope with the growing numbers which continued to increase until 1853. Furthermore, after 1849, the mission was served by several priests who only stayed for short periods of time until 1854 when a permanent priest was again appointed. But it is significant that in spite of this explanation and the undoubted influence of the clergy, the majority of Irish immigrants were apparently not practising their religion.

Although the pattern of the problem changed over the years, the danger of Catholics abandoning their religion in an hostile environment, the 'leakage', remained serious throughout the nineteenth century. It is doubtful if Protestant missionaries were very successful among the Irish because in spite of some occasional successes, they usually met with hostility. The Irish were sometimes married or buried in Protestant churches, but this was simply because these services were legally valid and financially cheaper. Far more serious was the fact that social or religious deprivation and the existence of merely nominal religious sentiment or affiliation existed among Catholics as well as Protestants, while Catholics were obliged to use Protestant schools, clubs or social services because they had none of their own.

It is therefore hardly surprising that Manning should have defined as his three main aims, providing a Catholic education for the young, saving Catholics from intemperance and improving the diocesan clergy. Manning believed that his first duty as a bishop was to educate poor Catholics and he used the money collected to build a cathedral in order to do this; 'could I leave 20,000 children without education, and drain my friends and my flock to pile up stones and bricks?'[19] Within twelve months of his consecration, he issued three pastorals on the need for education, the provision of reformatories and orphanages, and the importance of 'rescuing' Catholic children from the workhouses. After establishing the Westminster Diocesan Education Fund, Manning was able to open twenty day schools within a year and provide education for over a thousand children. During his years as archbishop, the number of children attending Catholic elementary schools increased by over 10,000. He also encouraged or established reformatories and orphanages, poor law and industrial schools for boys and girls, and later provided Homes for Destitute Boys and helped to organize schemes of emigration.

Manning's attempt to 'rescue' Catholic children from non-Catholic institutions was inevitably linked with the question of proselytism which became a burning issue during the century. In 1854, Catholics in Liverpool, for example, produced evidence of proselytism in the local workhouse where on an earlier occasion the children had been told that the wafer of bread shown to them was the God of the Papists and that every Catholic would go to hell with a copy of the Scriptures in his hand! Some Catholic children were sent out to Protestant families and employers, forced to attend Protestant religious services or even registered as non-Catholics. In 1856, the Bishop of Liverpool condemned the

Select Vestrymen, who have taken to persecuting in a small way. They are strong and valorous, and fiery with religious zeal against the poor children, but cowardly when they come face to face with men. If we are to have war, we ought to have it in the open, with persons who could stand persecution, and not on harmless and innocent children.[20]

A few years later, the local Catholic Club arranged that Catholic children would be sent to unprejudiced Protestant employers or to Catholic families, but before this was done, it was estimated that at least two-thirds of the Catholic children sent out previously had eventually left the Church. Originally, no register of religion was kept by the workhouse and in 1853, only 60 children out of a thousand heard Mass, whereas by 1865 when this information was readily available, 660 out of 1,200 children were receiving religious instruction.

Of course, Catholics could not expect Protestant philanthropists to refuse their social services, if they themselves did not make alternative arrangements, though it was by no means certain that Catholic children would in fact be handed over to Catholic institutions when accommodation was provided. These difficulties were exemplified in the relations between Dr Barnardo and the Catholic bishops. In 1887, Barnardo approached Manning's secretary and proposed to transfer all new Catholic applicants on condition that no further legal action was taken in the case of those Catholic children already in his care. This proposal failed because Fr Seddon, who had not actually promised to abstain from future proceedings, continued to give advice in legal actions against Barnardo, and also because Catholics could only provide for a couple of the sixteen or seventeen boys who had been sent to them; the rest who were under fourteen returned to Barnardo.

Barnardo himself openly and honestly explained his conditions to those Catholic parents who brought their children to him. But the agreement which they had to sign was illegal and gave Barnardo's Homes the right to detain the children until they were twenty-one, to move them without notice and even to send them to the colonies. Furthermore, Barnardo could afford the costs of a long trial, whereas his working-class opponents found the legal costs prohibitive, especially when the decision might not be put into operation even after they had won the case. Another relevant factor was that those parents who did secure the return of their children had to repay a maintenance charge of six shillings for each week of residence. This situation was obviously unsatisfactory, but until Catholics could provide accommodation in their own institutions, they were forced to choose between Protestant Homes or 'neutral' workhouses.

William Ward

Barnardo later told Lord Kinnaird:

I am as ready now as I have been at any time during the last fourteen years to send every Roman Catholic candidate for admission to these Homes to Cardinal Vaughan or to any person he may appoint; but I will only do this on condition that I receive a pledge, to be honourably kept, to the effect that if the Roman Catholics are unable or unwilling from any cause to assist a destitute case whom I send to them, they will not use any moral or spiritual influence to deter the candidate from applying to me again; for in the past this has been done. A Roman Catholic mother with three children applied to me for assistance. I sent all to Father Seddon. Three months after the woman and her children applied for a night's lodging at one of our all-night refuges, and then she told the matron that she had applied to me for the admission of the children, that I had referred her to Father Seddon, and that on some ground or other the latter had refused to admit the children; but before she left he solemnly warned her, under a threat of excommunication, that she should not apply to me again, or, under any circumstances, allow her children to be admitted to my Homes. I firmly believe that this sort of thing has been going on for years. Is it to be wondered at that I can be no party to any arrangement with the Roman Catholics while they deliberately and as a matter of conscience, as Cardinal Manning called it, break faith with me?'[21]

In 1894, Vaughan organized a census and appointed a Board of Inquiry which reported that many young people between the ages of fourteen and twenty-one had been lost to the Church and that the workhouses and police courts, non-Catholic benevolent homes and social or economic destitution were the main causes of this 'leakage'. Vaughan, thereupon, appointed Catholic agents to the courts and in 1899, he appealed for money and organized a Crusade of Rescue which was later amalgamated with an older society providing homes for children. In the same year, Vaughan also made a friendly arrangement with Barnardo who refused to surrender any children actually in his care without a legal struggle, but who promised to send any Catholic children who came in future on condition that they were received by Catholics and not returned to the workhouses or to the streets; children who were not received were to be returned to Barnardo without being subjected to moral or religious pressure in an effort to prevent this, while no further legal attempts were to be made to secure the return of children already in his Homes.

Throughout the nineteenth century, as many churchmen came to appreciate, alcohol was one of the most significant factors contributing to the demoralization and debasement of the poverty stricken masses. 'Talk about leakage!' said one Catholic of drunkenness, 'It is scuttling the ship'.[22] Catholics were already attempting to deal with the problem in the first half of the century:

> We the undersigned regretting the extent and deeply rooted habits of intemperance in this metropolis generally and anxiously solicitous for the good name and temporal welfare of this locality in particular and believing that abstinence from all intoxicating liquors is the only safe and satisfactory grounds which can be taken by the friends of temperance resolve to form a Society to be called the Lincolns Inn Fields auxiliary to the Metropolitan Catholic totle [sic] abstinence Association.[23]

Shortly afterwards this society was able to support Fr Mathew when he conducted a temperance campaign throughout the British Isles.

Manning himself became concerned with the problems of intemperance through the United Kingdom Alliance, of which he was later a vice president, and in 1872, he established the Total Abstinence League of the Cross. Manning associated total abstinence and the League of the Cross with religion, and he encouraged the temperance movement on every possible occasion. He once wrote to a priest who was organizing a retreat for girls working in a factory:

> By all means make them Total Abstainers. It is more necessary for young girls than for any. And if all our schools could be so reared, how many souls could be saved! I hope your League of the Cross is holding well together; and that your young men have not hindered it.[24]

This last remark illustrates the intractability of a problem which was not quickly or easily solved. Even the rallies of the League were not wholly abstemious and in 1891, regular 'scenes of drunken brawl and depravity' were reported among men returning home from the annual rally.[25]

Manning's support for the temperance movement was not universally popular among his fellow Catholics and not everyone was convinced that abstinence was the answer. Clerical and even episcopal opposition appeared in the *Tablet* and the *Month*, and he was even delated to Rome for heresy. A particularly unsympathetic and unjust critic commented when Manning was attending the Vatican Council:

at Rome they will know how to appreciate the ridiculously exaggerated ability of a man who has three hobbies, to make everyone a teetotaller, to build a Cathedral which would cost a million when he has not a million pennies, and to govern all England when he cannot keep his own priests in order, and has not the confidence of one third of the English Catholics.[26]

Manning was not content with voluntary efforts but he also appreciated the need for Government intervention. In 1871, he supported Bruce's Licensing Bill which would have restricted the opening of public houses. When this failed, he continued to demand Government action and in 1882, supported the idea of a Local Option which would have allowed the local population to veto the grant of a licence. Six years later, he wrote:

> The havoc and wreck by disease, madness, poverty, crime, and death, of body and of soul, spread without measure through every class. Of all this a little is known to police or to public opinion; but to God, Who reads all the hidden calamities and miseries of private life, one abyss of human sorrow calls to another in the shadow of death. Legislators are bound by the most strict responsibility to know the manifold evils of the drink trade. In this no ignorance can be pleaded in excuse. They can know all, and are therefore bound to know, or to cease to make our laws. Whatsoever be the financial or political interests at stake, we are bound to say, 'Salus populi suprema lex'. Let all Bills and clauses perish; the salvation of the people is the supreme law.[27]

Manning's third aim was to raise the religious, social and intellectual standards of the secular clergy so that they might influence the life of the nation. Manning fought strongly against the invidious distinction often made between the secular clergy and the religious orders. He encouraged the use of the title 'Father' instead of 'Mister', substituted the term 'pastoral' for 'secular' clergy, and encouraged them to accept responsibilities previously associated with the religious; to give missions and retreats in the streets and the open-air, not only to Catholics but to non-Catholics and even non-Christians. Manning expressed himself most forcefully in a work which curiously disappeared after his death:

> It is sometimes said that, with few exceptions, the canonized Saints are religious. I have a great devotion to the uncanonized Saints — the multitude which no man can number, whose names are not in the Calendar, but written in Heaven. Religious Orders can afford to canonize their Saints from time to time. The Church cannot. I love

all Orders, but I love most the Order of our Divine Master. I love the books of all Orders, but I love more the Pastoral Theology which can be found in no Order. The Regulars are under the vow of poverty, but we are under the reality.[28]

Manning's theme that the priesthood like the episcopate was a state of perfection was further developed in his most popular spiritual work, *The Eternal Priesthood*, which was translated into many languages.

The training and education of the English clergy during the nineteenth century dramatically reflected the spread and development of Ultramontanism which was frequently associated with the introduction of Roman practices or Italian devotions. Ullathorne reported that the introduction of a statue of our Lady into Prior Park had occasioned the comment, 'Let us have no Romanizing here. Take it away!'[29] But at Ushaw during the 1840s, new devotions to our lady spread rapidly and in 1852, a new statue of Mary was blessed personally by Pius IX who also granted three hundred days indulgence to those who recited the Litany of Loreto before it. A new form of public prayers mostly taken from a Roman prayer book was introduced into St Edmund's, while in the 1861 edition, unlike the 1844 edition, of the *Daily Prayers* for the use of the students of the English College, Lisbon, a prayer for the Pope was included as the first of the 'Prayers for Particular Occasions'.

At the same time, the theological teaching and opinion of English priests, as Ullathorne reported of himself, gradually moved in the same direction as those of their continental colleagues, from more or less Gallican notions to more or less Ultramontane ideas.[30] David Lewis recalled that in the 1840s, 'there was a good deal of Gallicanism in England, not to say Jansenism, and the English College in Rome was anything but Roman'.[31] Although this was undoubtedly a later Ultramontane reaction, the Gallican *Tractatus de ecclesia* by Louis Bailly was used at Ushaw during the first half of the century, whereas the professor of dogmatic theology after 1850 was John Gillow, the stern critic of Döllinger's letter on 'The Paternity of Jansenism', Newman's essay 'On Consulting the Faithful' and Ryder's views in his controversy with Ward. This transformation was, of course, a gradual development assisted by the ecclesiastical authorities, rather than a sudden, uniform and complete movement. At Oscott, for example, two members of the Staff supported Ryder in his opposition to Ward. But the general pattern was established and exemplified later at the English College Lisbon where the definition of papal infallibility was celebrated with High Mass and sermon in the morning, a *Te Deum*, sermon and Benediction in the afternoon, and a supper, bonfire and fireworks in the evening; and the cost to the College was under a pound!

In 1838, one of Wiseman's correspondents expressed the hope that the appointment of Edward Cox as professor of theology at Ware would 'Romanize that Gallican institution'.[32] However, Cox became one of the most prominent 'anti-Roman' priests in England as well as President of Ware and when he finally and *'cheerfully'* left St Edmund's in 1851, Wiseman reported to Talbot that the College was 'cleared of its terrible obstruction'; the whole system would be reformed and a 'sound, high-toned ecclesiastical spirit' introduced.[33] It was in this same year, that Wiseman appointed W.G. Ward to a lectureship at St Edmund's. Talbot's own opinion of many of the Old Catholic clergy was that the 'Sooner they die off the better; all we live to hope for, in the regeneration of the Church in England, is from the young'.[34] Frederick Rymer became President of Ware in 1868, but Manning relieved him of his post in September 1870 because of his sympathy for the inopportunists during the Vatican Council. He was replaced by James Patterson who significantly abolished Gothic and introduced Roman vestments.

Between 1851 and 1857, Robert Cornthwaite, an extreme Ultramontane, was Rector of the English College in Rome. A later rector, Frederick Neve, who to some extent sympathized with Newman and was regarded as a 'Newmanite', was replaced by Henry O'Callaghan, one of Manning's Oblates, in 1867. This was done without reference to the other English bishops and was resented by several of them especially by Ullathorne, Clifford and Brown. Neve himself asked Talbot for the reasons why he was being dismissed. He was told that the students complained that he had proved to be an unsuitable Rector because he was too recently at Eton and Oxford, and did not understand Catholic young men. Neve replied that Talbot himself 'was fresher from both places by many years than I was', at which Talbot offered him a present of fifty pounds if he was short of money![35]

Mere replacements of staff, however, were apparently not enough. One of the reasons why Manning supported the establishment of Tridentine seminaries in England was the fact that the existing seminaries were not sufficiently Ultramontane. In 1859, Rome had emphasized the importance of building seminaries in all those dioceses which could afford to do so. In the same year, the Third Provincial Council committed the English hierarchy to the establishment of diocesan seminaries wherever possible and Manning's views were reflected in the strong wording adopted. At the Fourth Provincial Synod in 1873, Manning's ideas dominated the legislation; the earlier undertaking was renewed and the adoption of this policy has been seen as a striking example of the extent of Manning's influence at the time.[36] The bishops had committed themselves to providing men and money which they could not afford for projects which were unlikely to succeed, particularly in view of the fact that the numbers of prospective students and qualified staff were both limited. It is perhaps significant that the first acts of the new Archbishops of Westminster and Birmingham who were both chosen by their predecessors, should have been to close their respective seminaries. A hostile contemporary later wrote:

> on the plea of more strictly carrying out the provisions of the Council of Trent, [Manning] determined ... to establish ... what the French call a *'grand seminaire'* ... It was situated in one of the noisiest, lowest, and most unhealthy suburbs of London, and consequently seemed but ill adapted for the purposes of education. Accordingly numerous remonstrances were addressed to the Archbishop, but remonstrance was in vain. Hundreds of pounds were spent on the old tumble down buildings in order to make them temporarily habitable, and when this was found insufficient the permanent structure, almost as it now stands, was erected at a cost of some forty to fifty thousand pounds. It is needless to dwell on the coldness, the dreariness, the poverty stricken air of this new seminary and its surroundings. It is sufficient to observe here that its discomforts were so great, the expenses of its maintenance so heavy that one of the first acts of the Cardinal's successor was to close it as a seminary, and sell the building for what it would fetch.[37]

Although Vaughan had originally supported the seminary at Hammersmith, he did not himself attempt to establish a diocesan seminary when he was Bishop of Salford and later closed Hammersmith when he became Archbishop of Westminster. The Salford clergy came from all parts of Europe. Vaughan's predecessor had established links with Belgium, while he himself also recruited priests from Holland and Germany as well as Ireland. In order to increase the number of candidates from the diocese, he established burses for the education of poor students and restricted the establishment of schools run by religious orders in case their students joined the regular rather than the secular clergy. Since Vaughan had not set up a diocesan seminary, he sent his students to be trained outside the diocese, both at home and abroad. As a result, many of his new priests were unfamiliar with their own diocese, unknown to their Bishop and strangers to each other. Furthermore, the urgent need for more priests resulted in young men being sent to unsuitable parishes simply because the need there happened to be the greatest. Consequently, Vaughan decided to establish a Seminary of Pastoral Theology close to the Cathedral for clerical students in the final year of training. There they would complete their studies, while living with the Bishop and could engage in parochial work before being appointed officially as curates. In this way, Vaughan hoped to provide an immediate solution for temporary emergencies in parishes, while enabling his young priests to make an easier transition from the seminaries to the industrial parishes of the diocese, but the costs involved and the continued shortage of priests eventually forced the Seminary of Pastoral Theology to close.

Meanwhile, attempts were made to establish Tridentine seminaries in most of the English dioceses, though they were ultimately successful only in Liverpool and Southwark. The diocese of Northampton had an establishment at Shefford which was described in the *Catholic Directory* of the time as the 'Diocesan Orphanage and Seminary', while the situation in the diocese of Nottingham was even more curious.[38] Bishop Bagshawe, a member of the London Oratory, had been suggested as coadjutor by Manning even before the chapter of canons had met to decide on the *terna*. Although Propaganda rejected Manning's proposal which would have circumvented the capitular procedure, his nominee became bishop in spite of the fact that he had not been nominated by the chapter. Bagshawe apparently first attempted to form a small major seminary at the Cathedral House, using the seminarians to teach in the Cathedral Grammar School. He later bought three houses in the area with a view to establishing a seminary.

The 'Diocesan College of Our Lady and Saint Hugh' was also a grammar school serving as a minor seminary which might have provided one or two students for the senior seminary. Financial difficulties brought the grammar school to an end in 1895, but the major seminary, which lasted for almost twenty years, survived with an average of eight or nine students. In all, forty-seven priests were ordained from the seminary; about twenty-five of these proved to be devoted and apostolic priests, but twelve left the priesthood and another nine earned public notoriety at some stage during their careers − figures which were certainly above the average 'failure' rate which might have been expected.

At one stage, there was a remarkably similar, if less significant, episode which paralleled the history of St Edmund's, when the 'Oblates of the Mother of Good Counsel' were appointed to the Nottingham seminary. This local congregation and two others were eventually dissolved by Rome in 1900 when there were three superiors with only one subject between them! These congregations were manifestations of a rather intense and simplistic religious devotion which was sometimes evident during this time and their devotional literature, pilgrimages and shrines were often very popular throughout the English speaking world. But not everyone was happy with such developments. In 1891, the canons commented on the scandal caused by advertisements for new shrines and they asked the Bishop to note the harm which had been caused by certain unworthy priests who had been allowed to join the diocese.

Bishop Bagshawe had undoubtedly encouraged a parochial expansion beyond the resources of the available clergy. He increased the number of priests by hasty ordinations and by accepting clergy from other dioceses or religious orders. In his attempt to alleviate a desperate shortage of priests, the Bishop sacrificed quality to quantity. By all accounts, the quality of the clergy was at the lowest point in 1900 when twenty-five of the eighty-two secular priests were unsatisfactory in one way or another; a quarter were mentally unstable, a few were guilty of early delinquencies later redeemed and eight of them left the priesthood; eleven of the twenty-five were hastily-ordained *alumni* of the diocesan seminary.

Canon Sweeney has calculated that at this time about 90% of the diocese was in the care of good and reliable priests, but that in Nottinghamshire itself, the figure scarcely exceeded 60%. It is therefore hardly surprising that in this particular county there was a correlation between the quality of the local clergy and the violent fluctuations of religious attendance. On the basis of the statistics available, Canon Sweeney estimates that in the diocese as a whole, besides the 31,295 who were known to be practising Catholics in 1901, at least another 10,000 baptized Catholics had left the Church. He concludes that apart from a small recovery between 1891 and 1896, a considerable progress between 1874 and 1886 had been followed by a continuous decline.

Clerical opposition to the Bishop's policies eventually centred on the seminary which not only suffered from financial difficulties, but disregarded almost every ecclesiastical regulation which had been made governing the education of priests. Most of the students never completed a full course and seem to have spent less than an average of two years in the college. After an initial caretaker rectorship, the seminary had two ordained students as rector and vice-rector. On three occasions, a student was appointed as rector immediately after his ordination, while the staff was exclusively recruited from newly-ordained priests or priests of doubtful reputation who had joined the diocese later.

In the meantime, the Bishops of Nottingham and Southwark had refused to support Vaughan's idea of establishing a common seminary for the South of England at Oscott. Vaughan, however, secured the approval of the Holy See and by 1897, Oscott became the Central Seminary for the dioceses of Westminster, Birmingham, Clifton, Newport, Portsmouth and also for Wales. But the ultimate failure of the Central Seminary was foreshadowed at its opening because Oscott never really became a common institution; all the old staff belonging to the diocese of Birmingham were re-employed which emphasized its 'old' character and defeated one of Vaughan's main aims of providing a better staff by calling on the resources of all the dioceses.

In providing for the pastoral needs of Catholics, Manning continued the policy, exemplified to a lesser extent in Wiseman, of attempting to improve the social conditions and political position of his fellow Catholics. Between 1866 and 1868, he tried to secure Catholic worship and education, and visits from their own priests for those Catholics in workhouses. In 1872, he directed attention to the condition of Catholic prisoners and pointed out that only sixteen out of 125 prisons had Catholic chaplains:

> I am told and taunted that, whereas we are only one-fifteenth of the population, we have one-fifth of the prisoners; that our prisoners are reconvicted again and again, if they are not reformed; and how shall they be reformed if they are deprived of the helps of their clergy and their Faith? This is hard-hearted and cruel as well as unjust . . . let us be allowed freely to bring the Sacraments to these poor souls.[39]

Manning's correspondence provides considerable evidence of his pastoral activity and social concern on the parochial level as well as of his personal generosity. In 1879, Manning contributed towards the cost of 'kitchen things' and later to repairs of a church in Poplar. In fact, his personal generosity later resulted in financial difficulties; he gave another fifty pounds in 1886, but was unable to act as surety for a loan because the demands of a dozen missions had left him in debt. In 1891, he referred to the missionaries who were being sent from Mill Hill to the negroes of America or to the natives of Borneo and he commented, 'Neither Priest nor Nun have we as yet sent to the millions of the East of London who are without the knowledge of God'.[40]

But Manning's remarkable manifestations of social concern and pastoral activity were far wider than his own 'parochial' interests. Although Bishop Grant of Southwark originally took the initiative when the *Times* asked, *'Why have we no Sisters of Charity?'*, Manning

175

was the driving force in securing nuns to care for Catholic soldiers fighting in the Crimean War and it was he who became the chief inter-mediary with the War Office.[41] Florence Nightingale herself was deeply impressed by Manning's social concern; at one stage, she almost became a Catholic and in spite of later difficulties, Manning's constant friendship proved to be of enormous importance to her.

In December, 1872, Manning publicly identified himself with the cause of the agricultural workers and he recommended concrete proposals such as the prohibition of child labour, the payment of wages in money, the regulation of housing conditions and the establishment of arbitration tribunals. Manning always remained interested in the conditions of the agricultural labourers and in 1878 and 1879, gave financial as well as practical help to their Union. Joseph Arch, the leader of the Union, paid tribute to Manning who 'spoke up nobly for us. The testimony at such a time and in such a place of a man so respected was of the greatest value to the Union'.[42]

In 1874, Manning delivered his famous lecture on 'The Dignity and Rights of Labour' in which he declared that:

If the great end of life were to multiply yards of cloth and cotton twist, and if the glory of England consists or consisted in multiplying, without stint or limit, these articles and the like at the lowest possible price, so as to undersell all the nations of the world, well, then, let us go on. But if the domestic life of the people be vital above all; if the peace, the purity of homes, the education of children, the duties of wives and mothers, the duties of husbands and of fathers, be written in the natural law of mankind, and if these things are sacred, far beyond anything that can be sold in the market, – then I say, if the hours of labour resulting from the unregulated sale of a man's strength and skill shall lead to the destruction of domestic life, to the neglect of children, to turning wives and mothers into living machines, and of fathers and husbands into – what shall I say? – creatures of burden – I will not use any other word – who rise up before the sun, and come back when it is set, wearied and able only to take food and to lie down to rest, – the domestic life of men exists no longer, and we dare not go on in this path.[43]

Ten years later, Manning was appointed to the Royal Commission on the Housing of the Working Classes. During 1886, he took part in a meeting of the National Association for Promoting State-Directed Colonization, and spoke at a meeting of the Shop Hours League and Trades Parliamentary Association. Between 1887 and 1888, he was a member of the Committee on Distress in London. He also wrote articles for magazines and letters to the press, and led deputations to secure Government grants for relief works during this period of economic depression. During one of the worst periods, he argued that a man's natural right to life and food prevailed over the laws of property and on one occasion wrote:

> The *Times* newspaper has stated that I have given countenance to the fallacy that under the Poor Law men have a natural right to work or to bread. It has also published a letter . . . stating that my words imply a censure upon the whole administration of the Poor Law, and would countenance the giving of relief to men in their own homes. I plead guilty to both of these impeachments, and in as few words as I can I will justify what I have said.[44]

Manning's greatest public achievement in the field of industrial relations, recognized both at home and abroad, was his intervention in the Dock Strike of 1889. This remarkable success was not simply a result of the fact that so many of the dockers in the Port of London were Irish, but illustrated the real respect which Manning had gained because of his genuine social concern and his ability to identify himself with the interests of the working classes with whom he became the most popular cleric in England. The dockers had demanded a minimum engagement of four hours, the abolition of contract or piece work, and wages of sixpence an hour or eightpence for overtime. Although the employers accepted the first demand, the others were refused and they insisted on a return to work before negotiating any wage increases. Manning intervened when the dockers issued an appeal, later withdrawn, for a general strike. The directors planned to introduce foreign labour and Manning feared that this move would provoke strife or even bloodshed. He became a member of the Committee of Conciliation which was set up at the Mansion House. When a compromise of sixpence an hour from 1 January failed, the Anglican Bishop of London withdrew from the Committee, but Manning remained and suggested 1 November as a further compromise. It took four hours of arguing with the strikers' leaders before they would agree and even longer to convince the employers, but eventually Manning was able to persuade both sides and the strike was over.

One of the dockers' leaders described Manning 'as the finest example of genuine devotion to the downtrodden'. The dockers themselves collected £160 which Manning used to endow a bed in the London Hospital and they also presented him with a touching address.

When we remember how your Eminence, unasked and unsolicited, under the weight of fourscore and two years, came forward to mediate between master and man; when we remember your prudent and wise counsels not to let any heat of passion or unreasonable view of the position beguile us or lead us away from the fair point of duty to our employers and ourselves; and when, in fine, we recall to mind your venerable figure in our midst for over four hours in the Wade Street School, listening to our complaints and giving us advice in our doubts and difficulties, we seem to see a father in the midst of a loving and well-loved family rather than the ordinary mediator or benefactor in the thick of a trade dispute.[45]

Another point of pastoral and social concern was the Irish Question, but this issue did not always result in a closer identification of Catholicism with the working classes or the life of the English nation. The immigrants' sympathies for Irish nationalism or Roman Catholicism were seldom shared by his English fellow workers and this divergence was reflected in social and political developments where the two groups might have been expected to unite most closely. The Irish were often welcomed by employers as unskilled labourers willing to accept employment which English workers found unattractive and wages or conditions which the latter considered intolerable. As a result, they 'enjoyed' a lower standard of living than the English which in turn reinforced their sense of social isolation. Occasionally, the Irish were also isolated geographically, living and working in particular areas where their solidarity was increased by such factors as class kinship or the lack of social mobility.

Many employers were able to use the Irish to reduce wages or resist strikers and this sometimes resulted in violence. In 1849, dockers in Cardiff were paid three pennies a ton for loading and two and a half pennies a ton for unloading; the Irish offered to work for one penny and a half penny, and when the local workers also accepted these lower rates, the Irish immediately offered to work for a farthing. Sometimes, the Irish opposed working class movements like Chartism in Manchester and South Wales or allowed themselves to be used to break strikes as in Preson during 1854. The attitudes of the Irish were formed by their poverty, mobility and lack of industrial experience as well as their need of regular money to send to their dependants at home and the conservative influence of Daniel O'Connell. Consequently, the Irish in general do not seem to have played a substantial part in the development of the labour movement or the trade unions, though there were some significant exceptions such as the Protestant Chartists John Doherty, Bronterre O'Brien or Fergus O'Connor and Ben Tillett or James Toomey in the Dock Strike of 1889.[46]

The political isolation of the Irish reinforced by the rise of the nationalist movement was not without its effect on the political development of the English Catholic community. At times, there had been a measure of effective political agreement between English and Irish Catholics. Catholics conducted successful local election campaigns and when voting was open, were quite capable of organizing their block vote if this was needed to defeat anti-Catholic candidates. As a result of the association of the Tories with the forces of 'no popery', Catholics usually supported the Liberal Party and as early as 1839, a Catholic Registration Society in Liverpool was described as 'really a *satanic* attempt to prevent the Conservative party having a majority at the ensuing November elections'.[47]

As their numbers and political influence increased, Catholics frequently, but not always, supported the Catholic interest with their votes. Consequently, when the Liberals introduced the Ecclesiastical Titles Bill, Catholics opposed them at the polls and in the second half of the century, the Catholic vote in the Scotland Ward of Liverpool was so strong that Irish or Catholic candidates were invariably returned. With the changing political scene, especially with the apparent threat to denominational schools from the Liberals which was occasionally supported by Orangemen, some Catholics began to support the Conservative Party. In 1861, the bells of two Liverpool churches were rung to celebrate a Conservative victory, while in 1870, the local Conservative leaders refused to support public meetings in favour of the Bill for inspecting convents.

Not all the Irish voters in Liverpool, however, were happy with this new political alignment especially since their interests diverged from those of English Catholics. This divorce became most obvious with the attempt to confuse Catholicism with Fenianism. A social reformer like Father Nugent found himself most unpopular with the Nationalist Party which wanted to cure the causes of emigration, while he was more concerned with curing its results. The Bishop of Liverpool had to adopt a position of political neutrality in order to avoid widening the divisions between Irish and English Catholics, Nationalists and Liberals. Bishop O'Reilly only once referred to politics and that was during the election of 1885 when the Catholic attitude to educational developments coincided with Parnell's policy of securing the return of a Conservative Government. In the following year, local divisions in Liverpool widened further when the Nationalists unsuccessfully challenged the re-election of an English Catholic who had a splendid record of working on behalf of the Irish and his fellow Catholics.

Irish Catholics became critical of English bishops like Ullathorne or Manning who actually sympathized with their cause, but who condemned the Fenians and refused to support Home Rule. In an effort to end the divisions between the Irish and English bishops, Manning supported Cardinal Cullen's aims of securing the disestablishment of the Irish Church and providing Catholic education at all levels for Irish children. The Irish Cardinal himself had condemned the Fenians, at least in part because they would alienate the English Government and make his task more difficult. During 1867 and 1868, Manning acted as an intermediary between the Irish hierarchy and the English Government which was willing to grant a charter, but not an endowment to the Catholic University. Manning informed Disraeli that Cullen was prepared to accept this, with some modifications, but the other Irish bishops did not in fact support Cullen and as a result the Government was defeated on the issue. Disraeli who had depended a great deal on Manning during the earlier negotiations, now accused him of having 'stabbed him in the back'.[48] This was unfair, though Manning apparently played an equivocal part in the later stages and certainly succeeded in embarrassing Disraeli, Gladstone and Cullen by giving unfounded assurances and suggesting that he had the complete confidence of others when he did not.

In 1868, Manning wrote a public letter to Earl Grey recommending a series of radical reforms including the disestablishment of the Irish Church and in the same month, Gladstone introduced his famous motion in the House of Commons. Although Manning's letter came too late actually to influence Gladstone, the latter kept in touch with Cullen through Manning and when the Church Act was finally passed, Gladstone thanked Manning for his 'firm, constant and discriminating support'.[49] In 1872, Manning issued a pastoral supporting the Irish on education and when Gladstone introduced a new Land Act in 1880, Manning again acted as an intermediary between the English Government and the Irish hierarchy. But in spite of Manning's constant sympathy with the Irish, he did not originally favour the policy of Home Rule. This is very obvious from the way in which he compared the English control over Ireland with the papal control of Italy, and he even claimed that 'the action of Italy upon Rome is like the action of America upon Ireland'.[50]

Manning told Ullathorne, 'We have an opportunity for showing that Mazzinianism and Fenianism are one in principle, and that our Government is reaping as it has sown'. He also dealt with the issue in his notebook; 'I have warned those who have praised, flattered, fostered, abetted, justified, glorified the Italian Revolution that the same principles would recoil upon themselves. They have *come!* The Church condemns them both in Italy and in Ireland'.[51] It is perhaps significant that Manning changed his opinions on the two issues at about the same time when incidentally he was strongly criticized by former friends in Rome. There were also practical difficulties for as Norman points out, Manning could not have openly supported Home Rule at one stage because of the danger of embarrassing both Cullen and Gladstone.[52] Nevertheless, in due course, Manning became increasingly aware that the grant of Home Rule was a necessary prerequisite for solving the Irish Question.

Manning's sympathy for Ireland was particularly important precisely because it was not universally shared and the divisions between Irish and English Catholics might have become even wider without him. During 1868, the *Tablet* was critical of the attitude of the Irish Catholic bishops to the Irish Protestant Church, but when Manning bought the magazine and Vaughan became editor, this policy was changed. Some years later, the *Tablet* was again critical of the Irish when Vaughan owned the journal which was then edited by Snead-Cox. During 1885 and 1886, Archbishop Walsh made several protests to Manning who promised to do, as he had always done, whatever he could to correct what was wrong. The point was that many English Catholics were less concerned with events in Ireland than the political reforms such as the acts of 1867 and 1872 which enabled the immigrants to play a greater part in English politics. The existence of the Irish vote and Irish M.P.s; was considered far more important than the existence of nationalist or local grievances. Thus, in spite of Vaughan's personal sympathy for the Irish, he later opposed Home Rule partly at least because it would, as in the event it did, reduce the political influence of Catholics at Westminster. Although Vaughan refused to support the Conservative opposition to Home Rule, he also refused to identify the Church with the 'political aspirations of one section of our flock'.[53]

The formation of Parnell's Irish Parliamentary Party united Irish support and by 1882, the Irish National League was able to organize the Irish vote and exert political pressure in an effort to secure Home Rule. During the General Election of 1885, Parnell urged the Irish to reject Gladstone and the Liberals, while Manning suggested that candidates should be questioned on their attitudes towards denominational schools – a move which also favoured the Conservatives. Some of the Liberals unacceptable to Parnell, however, were acceptable to the local clergy and some of them were Catholics. As a result, although this election demonstrated the effectiveness of the Irish votes where Parnell's instructions coincided with the advice of the local clergy, Irish voters elsewhere continued to support the Liberals. While the Irish Parliamentary Party held the balance of power in the House of Commons, the National League continued to organize the Irish vote outside, but Parnell's divorce threw everything into confusion. Although John Redmond reorganized the Home Rule movement, the Irish increasingly adopted a pragmatic policy of voting for Irish and occasionally for Catholic interests without at the time committing themselves to either British political party.

As well as national or political differences, social and economic divisions also appeared among Catholics in England. In some churches, there were notices designating the areas where the Irish might worship, other Catholic churches adopted the custom of charging for seats, while poorer Catholics in general found it embarrassing to attend Mass because of their shabby clothes; at Walsall, for example, there was a very early Sunday Mass for those who lacked decent clothing and did not want to be seen in Church later in the day. As a result, the upper class English Catholics were once again accused of neglecting their poorer co-religionists, of failing to assist the clergy in their social or pastoral work, and unfavourable comparisons were sometimes made with those non-Catholic laity who supported various Christian organizations which helped the working classes.

It is true that Manning usually found little support for his social attitudes and policies among his fellow Catholics. The *Tablet*, the *Month* and the *Dublin Review* which had often given such loyal support on other issues, did not always share his social or economic aims. Even the publication of *Rerum novarum* does not seem to have aroused the social conscience of English Catholics, though part of the reason for this was that the encyclical allowed of very different interpretations, condemned extremes and only defined the limits of controversy. Although Catholic periodicals loyally printed or paraphrased *Rerum novarum*, this would have been done in the case of any papal encyclical. Among the bishops, only Bagshawe of Nottingham manifested a similar social awareness, at a time when Vaughan associated Manning's concern with senile decay.[54]

Like Manning, Bagshawe rejected the theories of *laissez faire* and demanded state intervention in an effort to remedy the social injustices of the time — themes which were developed at length in two famous pastorals which he issued during 1883 and 1884. State intervention implied political action, but Bagshawe did not believe that Catholics could identify themselves with either of the two existing political parties. He therefore recommended the formation of an Association in each constituency to decide which political programme deserved the united Catholic vote. The Bishop's correspondence also reveals his suspicions of the Primrose League which he prohibited; a prohibition which he later had to withdraw as a result of the attitudes of the other English bishops and on instructions from Rome.[55] Bagshawe's rejection of the existing political parties was taken further in 1885 when he proposed that Catholics should support the Irish Parliamentary Party with a view to the formation of an English Catholic Parliamentary Party. This proposal occasioned a good deal of comment both at home and abroad, and a long correspondence in the Catholic press which revealed the deep divisions between English and Irish Catholics, but apparently little support for the Bishop's ideas.[56]

However, there were comparatively few wealthy English Catholics who were in any case unprepared for the type of social or political action being demanded by Manning and Bagshawe. English Catholics in general had neither the means nor the policies to cope with contemporary social and economic problems. Furthermore, the Catholic laity were still to some extent socially and politically isolated from the main life of the country, sometimes indeed as a result of the decisions of their own ecclesiastical authorities. It was after all at Oxford and Cambridge between 1875 and 1890 that many young men became conscious of their social obligations in the light of the economic and religious destitution of the masses. But Manning himself was primarily responsible for preventing English Catholics attending the older universities. Furthermore, upper-class English Catholics who had not been so involved in the social, economic and political development of the nation, seldom felt that sense of responsibility for contemporary problems which inspired some non-Catholic philanthropists.

Again, it would appear that increasing clericalism was one of the main factors why so few wealthy Catholic laymen were prepared to accept their social and pastoral responsibilities. The traditional organization of other Christian bodies often gave a greater role to the laity than was usually tolerated in the Catholic Church, especially with the development of Ultramontanism; was it not the province of the laity to hunt, to shoot and entertain? It was a common if clerical opinion that the task of the laity was to provide funds and that the layman, as belonging to the Church taught, should keep his place. One of the main faults of the new Ultramontane charitable associations such as the St Vincent de Paul Society was that they tended to be clerical and many of the best lay workers seem to have regarded this social and pastoral work as a test of their vocations before becoming priests.

Nevertheless, some success was achieved. In order to cater for the needs of 60,000 boys and girls between fourteen and twenty-one, Vaughan intended to establish youth clubs or Social Union Clubs in each parish with the headquarters at Archbishop's House, Westminster. This educational and recreational movement which eventually spread as far north as Sheffield, was intended to be a means of bridging the class distinctions between Catholics as well as enabling the rich to help the poor. The Catholic Social Union helped to provide settlements and missions, and to secure the support of the rich or the educated in helping priests to preserve the faith of the poor. But although the Catholic Social Union enjoyed some temporary success, it never received sufficient support and was eventually succeeded by the Catholic Social Guild, the aims of which were much wider. Incidentally by the end of the century, there were even Roman Catholic Socialist societies in Glasgow and Leeds.

Manning's appreciation of contemporary injustices or the inequalities of industrialism and his efforts to provide a positive social teaching to meet the economic needs of the time, had an influence far beyond England itself. Jules Lemire looked on the Archbishop of Westminster as in some sense his spiritual father. Manning was invited to address the Social Congress at Liege in 1890 and he corresponded with European Social Catholics like Bishop Von Ketteler and the Cardinals Mermillod and Capecelatro who spoke of him as a 'Catholic Socialist'.[57] Manning's most significant international influence was on the social encyclicals of Leo XIII and the Pope himself described his encyclical condemning slavery as Manning's encyclical. Nevertheless, although Manning's policies and social concern might be seen as part of a general movement in the Church associated with such names as von Ketteler in Germany, Capecelatro in Italy, Meyer in Austria, De Mun in France, Gibbons in America and Moran in Australia, they should also be seen as Manning's own response to English conditions. Manning was influenced by a genuine Christian compassion, but he was also aware that social or political action might enable Catholics to end their isolation from English society; a factor which had now become a point in their favour since unlike the Anglican or Nonconformist Churches, the Catholic Church in England was not identified with wealth or privilege, with the old establishment or the rising middle classes.

In spite of Manning's support for centralized authority within the Church — in the Catholic Church 'there is no House of Commons' —

there was no need for Huxley to tell him that it was by becoming a champion of democracy that the Catholic Church would find the great opportunity of achieving power in England.[58] Catholicism would spread by being identified with the interests of the working classes;

> God forbid that we should be looked upon by the people as Tories, or of the Party that obstructs the amelioration of their condition; or as the servants of the plutocracy, instead of the guides and guardians of the poor.[59]

At the same time, Manning was not uncritical or simplistic in his attitude to the rise of the working classes and the advent of democracy. In 1890, he wrote:

> You must be glad to see how the question of the people is becoming one, chief, dominant thought in all men who have heads – but then there is the motive power still to find; and that is God. 'Man without the Knowledge of God is Cattle'. Saint Jerome was right, and we must go back to him. This makes me thank God for my 300 Priests and 1,000 Nuns. They live and labour on this axiom of the Kingdom of God.[60]

The attempt to identify Roman Catholicism more closely with the life of the English nation might also explain the efforts which Manning made, often successfully, to establish friendly personal relations with leading public figures such as the Prince of Wales with whom he served on a Housing Commission. In view of this policy, it is, at first, somewhat surprising that he should have continually frustrated the establishment of diplomatic links with the Vatican, especially since in his relations with the British Government, he sometimes found it necessary to act as the representative of a sovereign independent foreign power. In 1870, for instance, at Manning's request, Gladstone ordered a British frigate to Civita Vecchia in order to guarantee the personal safety of the Pope and in spite of the fact that the British Government at the time undoubtedly sympathized with the Italian nationalists, rather than with their ruler.

Manning's approach, however, was far more realistic and consistent with an Ultramontane attitude and with his other policies than it would at first appear. He was afraid that the Church might seem to be divorced from the interests of the workers and he was very conscious of the dangers of Government intervention in such questions as Ireland or religious affairs like the appointment of bishops. As he told Cardinal Cullen,

I am afraid some attempt may be made in the direction of Nuncios. A Nuncio between the Episcopate of Ireland and the Castle or the Bishops of England and the Government would probably produce conflict between us and the Government, and greatly relax the close intimacy of the Bishops with the Holy See. In Rome they do not seem to realize that Nuncios belong to the period when Governments and the public laws of Europe were Catholic. At this day the Governments are powerless to help the Holy See. The real Governments are the people and the true Nuncios are the Bishops, who have real power and correct knowledge and are devoted to the Holy See.[61]

On the other hand, the possibility of appointing Nuncios to the British Isles might well have been one of the main issues which caused the former champion of papal infallibility to reflect on the limits of papal authority and the rights of the local bishops in relation to the papacy. As a nation became more democratic and with the separation of Church and State, the former would have to ally itself with the people which it could only do through local bishops and priests, and not by diplomatic contacts between papal envoys and government officials. Manning's correspondence with Bishop Keane of the United States illustrates their fundamental agreement on this basic point and some of the practical consequences involved.[62]

Manning also supported several of the other positions adopted by the 'Americanist' bishops as a result of a growing pessimism about the social and political future of Europe. Manning came to believe that the pattern of events in England and America were more likely to dictate future developments throughout the world; the future of the Church was jeopardized, not only by its isolation from these developments, but by the ignorance of the Roman authorities about the English speaking world. Manning, therefore, willingly responded when Cardinal Gibbons asked for his help in preventing a general condemnation of the Knights of Labour and when it was rumoured that Henry George's *Progress and Poverty* was about to be put on the Index.

Unfortunately, Manning did not always show such realism and some of his political interventions were even unhappy. When the atheist Charles Bradlaugh was elected to Parliament in 1880, he proposed to make an affirmation of allegiance rather than take the parliamentary oath. A select committee, however, voted against allowing him to do this and he therefore decided to take the oath in the ordinary way which several atheists had done previously. But on this occasion, a debate followed and an amendment was passed which prevented

Bradlaugh from either taking the oath or making an affirmation and in spite of being re-elected three times, Bradlaugh was not legally sure of his place in Parliament until 1886. This famous controversy has been seen as the last of the conflicts over religious restrictions on Members of Parliament and a recent writer has discussed the part played by the Catholic Church under Manning which was much more significant than its numbers justified.[63]

Many clerics regarded the issue as the last stand of religion and the Catholic Church became the driving force in a movement which Manning possibly used as another means of securing further recognition for the Church in England by making capital out of the popular emotion which had been aroused. Although the religious bodies in general and often officially tended to oppose Bradlaugh and any move by the Government which would satisfy the consciences of atheists, individual Christians sometimes appreciated that this was a mistaken policy. Newman, for example, eventually found himself at variance with other members of the Catholic Church, a Church which for historical reasons at least might have been expected to support the principle if not the personality involved.

In April, 1883, it was reported that Newman had refused to oppose an Affirmation Bill and a Catholic who intended to speak against it in Parliament wrote to ask him if this was true. In fact, Newman maintained that from the religious point of view, the Bill was so insignificant that it was not one of those social or political questions on which he felt it his duty to comment. The *Morning Post* and the *Tablet* quickly 'corrected' the earlier report, the Bill was defeated and Newman was told,

> Curiously enough the majority against the Government was just barely turned by a paragraph in the 'Morning Post' which said: 'We are authorized to state that Cardinal Newman approves, in no sense of the word, of the Affirmation Bill'.[64]

In order to correct this misinterpretation, Newman allowed one of his correspondents, who had asked if this later report was correct, to publish his reply:

> I feel myself to be so little of a judge on political or even social questions, and religious questions so seldom come before us, that I rarely feel it a duty to form and to express an opinion on any subject of a public nature. I cannot consider the Affirmation Bill involves religious principle; for, as I had occasion to observe in print more than thirty years ago, what the political and social world

187

means by the word 'God' is too often not the Christian God, the Jewish, or the Mohammedan, not a Personal God, but an unknown God, as little what Christians mean by God as the Fate, or Chance, or Anima Mundi of a Greek philosopher. Hence it as little concerns Religion whether Mr Bradlaugh swears by no God with the Government, or swears by an Impersonal, or Material, or abstract Ideal Something or other, which is all that is secured to us by the opposition. Neither Mr Gladstone nor Sir Stafford Northcote excluded from Parliament what Religion means by an 'Atheist'. Accordingly it is only half my meaning, if I am made to say that I 'do not approve, in any sense of the word, of the Affirmation Bill'. I neither approve nor disapprove. I express no opinion upon it; and that first because I do not commonly enter upon political questions, and next, because, looking at the Bill on its own merits, I think nothing is lost to Religion by its passing, and nothing gained by its being rejected.[65]

This letter provoked a very mixed reaction. Although Newman's correspondent was grateful for 'so clear and satisfactory an answer', the *Times* referred to Newman as 'an ambiguous Cardinal'.[66] On the other hand, the *Manchester Examiner* and *Manchester Weekly Times*, in identical comments, rejected the charge of ambiguity as typical of those who could not take the trouble to appreciate positions or attitudes with which they were unfamiliar. Far from being ambiguous, Newman had said something 'of a very decided character'. He had not agreed with thirteen thousand clergy that the interests of religion were at stake. He had not supported a protest signed by two archbishops and twenty bishops of the Anglican Church, two cardinals and twenty three other Catholic prelates, two archbishops and nine bishops of the Irish Protestant Church and seven hundred and sixty three nonconformist ministers. Unlike the rest, Newman had not simply supported or opposed the Bill. Having satisfied himself that it did not involve a religious principle, he was not prepared, as a religious man, to concern himself with politics, though had he been a politician, he would probably have adopted the same line as Gladstone:

In his views regarding the Affirmation Bill Cardinal Newman shines far apart from the other great ecclesiastical luminaries, and offers especially a striking contrast to his English colleague of the Sacred College. Cardinal Manning has had his eye fixed on Mr Bradlaugh ever since Northampton sent him to Parliament, and has two or three times made him the subject of a solemn appeal to the nation. In Cardinal Manning's eyes we are in an evil plight already. We have strayed from the true Church, and we have ceased to exact a recognition of Christianity as a passport to the Legislature, but we have still one virtue left. The oath still keeps out the atheist, and obliges him to pay toll in the shape of a hollow and worthless profession. Cardinal Manning has besought us again and again, with outstretched hands and fervent entreaties, to maintain intact this last bulwark of religion. Cardinal Newman, on the other hand, sees nothing in it. He regards the oath as useless for religious purposes, and cannot admit that the Affirmation Bill, against which the other Cardinal has been declaiming, involves any religious principle at all.[67]

When Newman's letter was published in the *Tablet*, the editor expressed regret that Newman's views differed from the policy which he had been advocating and suggested that Newman's long seclusion had led him astray on a question of practical politics; having lost touch with the feeling of the nation, Newman had discussed the question in too abstract a way.[68] But although Newman took a line of his own which was in opposition to the official policy and general attitude of his fellow Catholics, it did not lack support among them. Not all the Irish M.P.s, for example, supported Manning's campaign because they could hardly demand liberty for Catholic Irishmen while denying it to Bradlaugh. Catholic opinion was not as monolithic as Manning liked to think and shortly after Newman's intervention, he ended his active part in the struggle against Bradlaugh.

The reaction of the Manchester newspapers might well be seen as another example of what Manning meant when he commented:

almost every newspaper in England abused and ridiculed me. My name was never mentioned, but his was brought in to condemn me; his name was never mentioned, but mine was brought in to despite me. If only we had stood side by side and spoken the same thing, the dissension, division, and ill-will which we have had would never have been, and the unity of Catholic truth would have been irresistible.[69]

The contrast and conflict between Newman and Manning should not only be seen as the result of their different personal characters or temperaments, but, as Manning himself recognized, as a consequence of the more general ideological struggle over the development of Ultramontanism within the Catholic Church as a whole. As an Anglican, Manning once wrote of Newman, 'What do I not owe him? No living man has so powerfully affected me: and there is no mind I have so reverenced'.[70] But as a Catholic, Manning found that 'Newman was not in accordance with the Holy See' on the temporal power, the Oxford question and the infallibility of the Pope; 'If I have been opposed to him, it has only been that I must oppose either him or the Holy See'.

Butler believed that at least to some extent, W.G. Ward was responsible for Manning's more extreme intransigence and opposition. Originally, Manning did not seem hostile to the suggestion that Newman should return to Oxford, whereas Ward regarded it as his sacred duty to frustrate the project. When Manning wanted to establish happier relations with Newman, Ward warned him:

> is it not dangerous to speak of J.H.N. with *simple* sympathy? If it is true (and I for one have no doubt at all) that he is exercising a most powerful influence in favour of what is *in fact* (though he doesn't think so): (1) Disloyalty to the Vicar of Christ, and (2) worldliness – is not harm done by conveying the impression that there is no cause for distrust?[71]

Perhaps the most unhappy and unaccountable mistake in Manning's dealings with Newman occurred when the latter was offered the Red Hat in 1879. After being approached by the Duke of Norfolk and Lord Ripon, Manning himself wrote the petition to Rome asking that Newman should be made a Cardinal and, according to Lord Petre, Manning 'even said too much':

> The veneration for his powers, his learning, and his life of singular piety and integrity is almost as deeply felt by the non-Catholic population of this country as by the members of the Catholic Church. In the rise and revival of Catholic Faith in England there is no one whose name will stand out in history with so great a prominence.[72]

Ullathorne made it perfectly clear that Newman would accept the honour if he was excused from the obligation of residing in Rome which was impossible because of his age. Manning accepted Newman's letter at face value as declining and rumours to this effect began circulating in London. However, Manning's reply had aroused Ullathorne's suspicions. The Bishop, therefore, wrote to Rome himself, sending a copy of his own letter to Manning explaining Newman's attitude, which Manning had obviously not forwarded. When Newman's 'refusal' became public, a leak which could only be traced to Manning, *Punch* exclaimed:

> A Cardinal's Hat! Fancy Newman in *that*,
> For the crown o'er his grey temples spread!

'Tis the good and great head would honour the hat,
Not the hat that would honour the head.

There's many a priest craves it: no wonder *he* waives it,
Or that we, the soiled head-cover scanning,
Exclaim with one breath, *sans* distinction of faith,
Would they wish Newman ranked with old Manning?[73]

The Duke of Norfolk then wrote to Manning and the matter was finally settled, but Ullathorne who was undoubtedly in the best position to judge, maintained until the end of his life that Manning had tried to prevent Newman from becoming a Cardinal.[74]

If this was so, it was also probably true that policies rather than personalities were again the cause of this unfortunate misunderstanding. On one occasion, the Pope himself remarked:

My Cardinal! it was not easy, it was not easy. They said he was too liberal, but I had determined to honour the Church in honouring Newman. I always had a cult for him. I am proud that I was able to honour such a man.[75]

But Ultramontane suspicions of Newman's orthodoxy were not removed when Newman received the red hat. Although Vaughan had clearly distinguished between political and religious 'liberalism' in 1871, he remarked in 1874, that while Catholics would have supported Gladstone, they could not support Radicals who advocated the three condemned propositions in the *Syllabus* on popular education; it was therefore better for Catholics to suffer a little tyranny from the Tories.[76] Vaughan now reconciled himself to Newman's Cardinalate by interpreting Newman's attack on 'Liberalism' in his Biglietto Speech as an attempt to dissociate himself from 'Liberal Catholics':

The *Times* of this morning gives *in extenso* Cardinal Newman's address. I have read it with the greatest thankfulness and delight. His allusions to his own mistakes in the past, his public admission of such having existed, have entirely removed the apprehensions, which I admit I had felt, when I heard he was to be raised to the Cardinalate. It ought not to have been necessary for him to have done this, but certain persons had rendered it quite necessary and he has done it with his own peculiar skill and pointedness. Nothing could have been more opportune, either, or more forcible, than his remarks upon Liberalism and liberalistic ideas. I hope he will now cease to be quoted as the friend of Liberals in Religion and Faith. I think

J.H.N. will now have satisfied those Catholics who had felt uneasy as to the effect of the report which had been circulated, viz that his elevation was a recognition of all the points in his writings on which there has been and is difference with him.[77]

Vaughan, however, had further cause for concern a few days later:

Döllinger has written a letter which will do much harm, saying if J.H.N.'s writings had been *known* in Rome he would not have been created Cardinal. As a fact his errors and mistakes are well known. I hope he will do yet more to diminish the effect of these.

No doubt this lifetime of suspicion largely accounts for Vaughan's unsympathetic description of Newman as an old man; 'I hardly knew him again: doubled up like a shrimp and walking with a stick longer than his doubled body. His mind very much impaired and his memory for names curiously gone'.[78]

The fundamental cause of the difference between Newman on the one hand and Manning and Vaughan on the other probably resulted from the fact that the Oratorian was a great theologian always conscious of theological implications, whereas their concerns, their aims and ultimately, therefore, their success or failure must be judged by their activities in other fields. Newman showed a sensitive and sympathetic understanding of intellectual difficulties, but Manning and Vaughan simply swept them away. Manning was essentially a churchman, an administrator, a philanthropist. As a successful man of action, he was always respected for his clarity, courage and judgment, but his opinions were often extreme, unsubtle or even crude. Consequently, although at the time the Archbishop of Westminster was more influential than the Superior of the Birmingham Oratory, 'Catholic posterity has rated Newman's mind so high that it cannot think Manning even comparable'.[79]

Nevertheless, by his administrative ability and social concern, through his personal relations with public figures and his sympathy for the poor, Manning gained public recognition for the Catholic Church in the life of the English nation, contributed towards reducing the 'leakage' and gave the poverty-stricken Irish immigrants greater confidence in the English hierarchy. This social concern coupled with a radical sympathy for Ireland and a romantic view of the medieval church won for Manning the respect and affection of the working classes and the left wing which was manifested so clearly at his funeral. Yet Manning was never as successful in winning the masses to the Church as he had hoped, while his successor was more concerned with ending the 'leakage' than with attracting the working classes and made no attempt to continue his policy.

Notes

1. E.S. Purcell, *Life of Cardinal Manning Archbishop of Westminster* (London, 1896) II: 175; see also 174, 181-9, 203, 207, 213, 216; B. Fothergill, *Nicholas Wiseman* (London, 1963) 175-7; S. Leslie, *Henry Edward Manning His Life and Labours* (London, 1921) 142, 149.

2. J.L. Altholz, D. McElrath and J.C. Holland, eds., *The Correspondence of Lord Acton and Richard Simpson* (Cambridge, 1971-1975) III: 200.

3. F.J. Cwiekowski, *The English Bishops and the First Vatican Council* (Louvain, 1971) 34; *The Letters and Diaries of John Henry Newman*, ed. C.S. Dessain (London, 1961-) XXIV: 167; C. Butler, *The Life and Times of Bishop Ullathorne* (London, 1926) I: 266; Leslie, *Manning* 154.

4. M. Ward, *The Wilfrid Wards and the transition* (London, 1934) I: 20-23; Purcell, *Manning* II: 220.

5. J.G. Snead-Cox, *The Life of Cardinal Vaughan* (London, 1910) I: 141-2.

6. H.E. Manning, *Sermons on Ecclesiastical Subjects* (London, 1870-1873) II: 272-3, 286.

7. Ward, *Wards and Transition* I: 207; see also Butler, *Ullathorne* I: 269-70; Leslie, *Manning* 156-7; Purcell, *Manning* II: 224, 257-8.

8. Manning to Bradley, 12 December 1862. AAW: see also H.E. Manning, *Religio Viatoris* (London, 1888) 67; Purcell, *Manning* II: 160.

9. H.E. Manning, *Miscellanies* (London, 1877-1888) II: 140, 148, italics mine; see also Newman's earlier and more sober remarks in *Letters and Diaries* XV: 497.

10. Quoted by S. Gilley, 'English Catholic Charity and the Irish Poor in London' *Recusant History* II (1972) 180.

11. Walsh to Shrewsbury, 20 August 1842, Ushaw, W.S. 19; see also J. Bossy, *The English Catholic Community 1570-1850* (London, 1975) 309, 314-16.

12. Archives of St Edmund's College Ware.

13. G.A. Beck, ed., *The English Catholics 1850-1950* (London, 1950) 277; see also T. Burke, *Catholic History of Liverpool* (Liverpool, 1910) 71, 126-7; K.S. Inglis, *Churches and the Working Classes in Victorian England* (London, 1963) 16-17, 125; J.A. Jackson, *The Irish in Britain* (London, 1963) 115, 139.

14. W. Ward, *The Life and Times of Cardinal Wiseman* (London, 1900) II: 241.

15. The difficulties involved in estimating the Catholic population at the time can be seen by comparing the different accounts given in Beck, *English Catholics* 42-6, 52-3, 82-5, 411-12; W.O. Chadwick, *The Victorian Church* (London, 1966-1970) I: 272; II: 220-1, 225,

235, 240-1, 272, 401-2; D. Gwynn, *Cardinal Wiseman* (London, 1929) 153; B. Hemphill, *The Early Vicars Apostolic of England* (London, 1953) 102-4; J. Hickey, *Urban Catholics* (London, 1967) 11-13; Inglis, *Churches and Working Classes* 123, 141-2; Jackson, *Irish in Britain* 138-9; J. Morris, *Catholic England in Modern Times* (London, 1892) 71-3, 88-90; B. Ward, *The Dawn of the Catholic Revival* (London, 1909) I: 30-1; *The Eve of Catholic Emancipation* (London, 1911-1912) I: 18, 186; *The Sequel to Catholic Emancipation* (London, 1915) I: 177-8; II: 97.

16. D. Mathew, *Catholicism in England* (London, 1955) 185.
17. Hickey, *Urban Catholics* 102, 115.
18. Hickey, *Urban Catholics* 90-4.
19. Purcell, *Manning* II: 355, 683.
20. Burke, *History of Liverpool* 130; see also 77-8, 118, 149-50, 165-6.
21. Snead-Cox, *Vaughan* II: 265-6; it is revealing to compare E. St John, *Manning's Work for Children* (London, 1929) 122-5, 131-5 with the summary in V.A. McClelland, *Cardinal Manning His Public Life and Influence 1865-1892* (London, 1962) 48-9.
22. Inglis, *Churches and Working Classes* 127; Purcell, *Manning* II: 592.
23. Minute Book, 30 September 1840, Ware.
24. Manning to Lawless, 15 May 1883, LCA Ushaw; see also 'Cardinal Manning's Letters to Father Lawless and Mrs King' *Downside Review* 92 (1974) 19-24.
25. Inglis, *Churches and Working Classes* 127.
26. V.A. McClelland, *English Roman Catholics and Higher Education 1830-1903* (Oxford, 1973) 242.
27. Manning, *Miscellanies* III: 399.
28. Leslie, *Manning* 459; see also J. Fitzsimons, ed., *Manning: Anglican and Catholic* (London, 1951) 156-7; H.E. Manning, *The Eternal Priesthood* (London, n.d.) 3; Purcell, *Manning* II: 731.
29. W.B. Ullathorne, *From Cabin-boy to Archbishop* (London, 1941) 226.
30. Ullathorne, *Autobiography* (London, 1891) 46; *Cabin-boy to Archbishop* 40.
31. Purcell, *Manning* II: 307.
32. T. Chisholme Anstey to Wiseman, 14 April 1838, Ushaw W. 321.
33. 'Letters of Cardinal Wiseman' *Dublin Review* CLXIV (1919) 22.
34. Talbot to Wiseman, 7 December 1861, AAW.
35. Neve to Ullathorne, 24 October 1867, BOA.
36. Butler, *Ullathorne* II: 175; see also 180-7; Leslie, *Manning* 181-3; Snead-Cox, *Vaughan* II: 37-44.
37. Rymer, 'Memoir of the Right Reverend William Weathers', Ware; Rymer also noted that the building had been 'sold at an enormous sacrifice'.

38. I must express my deep gratitude to Canon G.D. Sweeney, former Master of St Edmund's House, Cambridge, who so generously allowed me to use his own unpublished work on the history of the diocese of Nottingham.

39. Leslie, *Manning* 173.

40. *Downside Review* 92 (1974) 19-20.

41. E. Bolster, *The Sisters of Mercy in the Crimean War* (Cork, 1964) 12-13, 49; see also Leslie, *Manning* 120; McClelland, *Manning* 16-17; C. Woodham-Smith, *Florence Nightingale* (London, 1952) 73-4, 144, 254.

42. Leslie, *Manning* 350; see also 348; Fitzsimons, *Manning* 140-1; McClelland, *Manning* 132-4; Purcell, *Manning* II: 640-1.

43. Manning, *Miscellanies* II: 94; see also, Fitzsimons, *Manning* 145-7; McClelland, *Manning* 134-6; Purcell, *Manning* II: 643-8.

44. Manning, *Miscellanies* III: 371.

45. Leslie, *Manning* 368-9, 373.

46. Hickey, *Urban Catholics* 40-2, 46-7, 53, 124-33, 137-48; Jackson, *Irish in Britain* 115-19; Hickey quotes Faulkner in support of the claim that a Father O'Malley was elected as a Nottingham delegate to the Chartist Assembly in 1848, *Urban Catholics*, 148; unfortunately no Father O'Malley is to be found in Canon Sweeney's lists of the Nottingham clergy.

47. Burke, *History of Liverpool* 59; see also 65-7, 77, 91-2, 97-8, 119, 134-5, 147-8, 167, 179-82, 188-9, 199-200, 209-19, 240-3; Butler, *Ullathorne* II: 168.

48. E.R. Norman, *The Catholic Church and Ireland in the Age of Rebellion* (London, 1965) 281; see also 219, 242-5; Butler, *Ullathorne* II: 139-44; McClelland, *Manning* 164, 168-9; Purcell, *Manning* II: 516-19.

49. W.E. Gladstone, *Correspondence on Church and Religion*, ed. D.C. Lathbury (London, 1910) I: 163; Manning, *Miscellanies* I: 213-55; Fitzsimons, *Manning* 123-5; McClelland, *Manning* 169-71; Norman, *Catholic Church and Ireland* 335-44, 382.

50. Leslie, *Manning* 206; McClelland, *Manning* 176.

51. Leslie, *Manning* 196-7, 203; Purcell, *Manning* II: 614-5.

52. Norman, *Catholic Church and Ireland* 419.

53. Snead-Cox, *Vaughan* I: 473; A. McCormack, *Cardinal Vaughan* (London, 1966) 215-16; see also Jackson, *Irish in Britain* 120-1; McClelland, *Manning* 187-92; Norman, *Catholic Church and Ireland* 330-1.

54. Inglis, *Churches and Working Classes* 308; see also 129-30, 311-17; Vaughan's reference to 'senile decay' was simply the result of an unhappy use of language according to Snead-Cox, *Vaughan* II: 377; Lytton Strachey, *Five Victorians* (London, 1942) 429, referred to a 'kind of frenzy' of the 'demagogue'; the 'frenzy' is most unjust,

Manning himself might have accepted the 'demagogue', Leslie, *Manning* 347.

55. Leslie, *Manning* 446-7.

56. See the comments and letters in the *Tablet* for 1, 22, 29 August, and 12 September 1885. Bagshawe's recommendations were not entirely new; the *Tablet* had published a letter on the 19 April 1873 suggesting the formation of a Catholic Party, while the foundation of a Catholic Registration Society in Manchester had been discussed in the *Tablet* on 28 December 1872 and on the 4, 11, 18, 29 January 1873; see also the *Tablet* 29 March and 26 April 1873 for other examples of correspondence on social issues and political attitudes.

57. McClelland, *Manning* 149; see also 158-60; Inglis, *Churches and Working Classes* 309-11; Leslie, *Manning* 366-7.

58. Leslie, *Manning* 188; Ward, *Wards and Transition* I: 223-4, 392.

59. Purcell, *Manning* II: 637; see also McClelland, *Manning* 10, 19-21, 129.

60. Manning to King, 2 October 1890, LCA.

61. Leslie, *Manning* 464; see also 235, 463-71; Purcell, *Manning* II: 740-2.

62. T. Wrangler, 'Emergence of John J. Keane as a Liberal Catholic and Americanist (1878-1887)' *American Ecclesiastical Review* 166 (1972) 457-78; see also Leslie, *Manning* 262-3, 295-6, 343, 352-67, 429, 464, 467; McClelland, *Manning* 152-8; Purcell, *Manning* II: 580, 625-6, 648-51, 743; *Tablet* 69 (1887) 683-5.

63. W.L. Arnstein, *The Bradlaugh Case* (Oxford, 1965) 5-6, 323-5; Manning had previously supported state neutrality in matters of religion, equating 'liberalism' with Gallicanism or erastianism, *Miscellanies* I: 265-6; for his articles demanding a continued 'public recognition of God', see *Miscellanies* III: 97-166.

64. MacColl to Newman, 4 May 1883, BOA.

65. *Letters and Diaries* XXX: 216; see also 'Cardinal Newman and the Affirmation Bill' *Historical Magazine of the Protestant Episcopal Church* XXXVI (1967) 87-97.

66. Chesson to Newman, 9 May 1883, BOA.

67. *Manchester Examiner*, 21 May 1883, Newspaper clippings BOA.

68. *Tablet* 61 (1883) 761-2; see also Arnstein, *Bradlaugh Case* 204-5, 229-31.

69. Leslie, *Manning* 270-1; Purcell, *Manning* II: 350-1; see also Butler, *Ullathorne* II: 315.

70. Fitzsimons, *Manning* 17.

71. Butler, *Ullathorne* II: 305, 307; Purcell, *Manning* II: 231, 309.

72. Purcell, *Manning* II: 555, 557, 570.

73. Quoted by Butler, *Ullathorne* II: 118.

74. Butler, *Ullathorne* II: 121, 158-60.

75. *Letters and Diaries* XXIX: 426; Butler, *Ullathorne* II: 110.

76. Vaughan to Thompson, 22 April 1871, AAW; *Letters of Herbert Cardinal Vaughan to Lady Herbert of Lea 1867-1903*, ed. S. Leslie (London, 1942) 243-5.

77. Vaughan, *Lea Letters* 306-8; see also, Chadwick, *Victorian Church* II: 422; J.H. Newman, *My Campaign in Ireland* (Aberdeen, 1896) 393-400; *Addresses to Cardinal Newman with His Replies*, ed. W.P. Neville (London, 1905) 61-70; W. Ward, *The Life of John Henry Cardinal Newman* (London, 1912) II: 459-62, 437.

78. M. Trevor, *Newman Light in Winter* (London, 1962) 639.

79. Chadwick, *Victorian Church* I: 300; see also Fothergill, *Wiseman 284.*

Cardinal Vaughan

Chapter V: Vaughan and the rise of Triumphalism

When Manning was dying, Vaughan was at his bedside and unlike the situation in 1865, there was never any doubt who would succeed him. In fact the appointment was announced several times before it was actually made. Vaughan apparently first met Manning on returning to Rome with him in 1852 when he found the former Archdeacon's concern about the safety of a silk hat so exasperating that with one of his companions, he 'lost' Manning at Lyons and continued without him. However, at the Accademia Ecclesiastica, Vaughan almost immediately fell under Manning's influence and the two men became close colleagues and intimate friends. When the see of Salford fell vacant in 1872, Manning persuaded the canons of the chapter to nominate Vaughan as one of the *terna* and Manning himself would then have commented on the three names with the other bishops before sending them on to Rome. The result could hardly have been in doubt since by this time all appointments to the English hierarchy had effectively become Manning's appointments.[1] Vaughan reflected Manning's opinions in many ways, but especially in supporting the devotional, theological and practical manifestations of Ultramontanism. As Bishop of Salford, he issued a copy of de Montfort's work on the Blessed Virgin to all his priests and ordered 'Prayers in every Church to St Peter on all the Sundays of Petertide and the usual Peterpence Collection'.[2]

But although Vaughan often originally agreed with Manning even when he later changed his mind, as in the case of the diocesan seminary at Hammersmith, he did not always identify himself with Manning's policies. There might seem, for example, to be more than a difference of tone in their references to democracy:

> The Archbishop, who is better, has been at a great Temperance meeting at Manchester, six thousand people present: *The Times* in a leader has spoken of him as 'the representation of public benevolence and common sense'. We are making a way into public life by degrees. This is a great work before us, but neither Bishops, Clergy nor Laity seem to see the importance of it. And yet if the people are going to rule, or to stir up rebellion, equally it is vital that we should not be strangers to them or bear a hostile name.[3]

Although Vaughan was not unconscious of social issues, he was less willing than Manning to become involved in public or political activities. The two men also disagreed on such issues as the establishment of diplomatic relations with the Holy See, vivisection and temperance, contacts with the Salvation Army, while as owner of the *Tablet*, Vaughan had been associated with its anti-Irish sentiments. There were occasionally more personal differences. In 1881, Vaughan was 'unable to reconcile the Cardinal's letters to me with his acts' when as owner of the *Tablet*, Vaughan was anxious about the possible rivalry of the *Weekly Register*.[4]

Yet in spite of their differences — after one argument Manning deleted Vaughan's name as an executor of his will, Manning always apparently hoped that Vaughan would succeed him — Vaughan himself, however, was not unaware of his own limitations and almost prophetically appreciated that the qualities needed by a Bishop of Salford were very different from those demanded of a Cardinal Archbishop:

> The See of Westminster ought to be occupied by a Bishop distinguished for some gift of superior learning or by remarkable sanctity, for he ought to be commended to the Church and to the people of England (for whose conversion he may be able to do more than any one else) by some manifest superiority or excellence. Holy Father, it is no mock modesty or fashion of speech which makes the confession that I have no qualification of learning for such a post. I do not excel as a preacher, an author, a theologian, a philosopher, or even as a classical scholar. Whatever I may be in these matters, in none am I above a poor mediocrity. It will be very easy in such a position as the See of Westminster to compromise the interests of religion in England by errors of judgment — and the very quality of a certain tenacity and determination would make these errors still more serious.[5]

Nevertheless, in 1892, Vaughan was appointed to the archbishopric and early in the following year he received the cardinalate. Somewhat typically, he chose to receive the *pallium* in London rather than in Rome in order to take the opportunity of making a controversial point in favour of the Roman claims; it was 'too good a trump-card against the Anglican to throw away'.[6] The splendid ceremony took place in the crowded Church of the Oratory and in the presence of the other English bishops, the heads of religious orders, four hundred priests, members of the diplomatic corps and of the Catholic nobility and gentry. In view of later events, it was perhaps fitting that the sermon should have been preached by Abbot Gasquet. At the feet of the papal delegate, Vaughan renewed the traditional act of homage of the English Church to the Holy See. The *Daily Chronicle* recognized that the ceremony was 'a palpable triumph' for the Catholic Church, while the *Times* appreciated the significance of the direct intervention of Rome and saw the occasion as an important stage in the development of a more tolerant public attitude towards Roman Catholicism.[7]

Vaughan's efforts to secure recognition for the Catholic Church in England differed fundamentally from those of his predecessor and the building of Westminster Cathedral was both symbolic of his general attitude as well as an example of his administrative ability. The possibility of building a Catholic cathedral had been suggested in Wiseman's time and on his death it was decided that the Metropolitan Cathedral should be his permanent memorial. But although Manning made some initial moves and later with his customary shrewdness secured and extended a splendid site, he postponed the actual construction until he had made better provision for the education of Catholic children. When Vaughan became archbishop, he immediately decided as his major project, to build a cathedral which would be a liturgical, pastoral and intellectual centre for English Catholicism. His attitude, however, was not a simple return to the demonstrative grandeur associated with Wiseman. Vaughan was always a realistic administrator and he succeeded in building and paying for the Cathedral within eight years. The architect was asked to design the cathedral in the style of the old Byzantine basilicas because this would be less expensive and more suitable for a large congregation, and would avoid the danger of occasioning invidious comparisons by pretending to rival the great English churches of the past. Vaughan successfully raised the £200,000 needed, met the costs of upkeep from other sources and left the work of completing the cathedral to future generations.

In general, as Snead-Cox has pointed out, Vaughan's administration of the Archdiocese of Westminster was a continuation or development of his work in Salford.[8] This northern diocese was the smallest in area, but its almost entirely working-class population was increasing rapidly and was already estimated at almost 200,000. In spite of the cotton famine in the early sixties, the previous bishop had more than doubled the number of missions in the diocese, built a couple of grammar schools and attempted to establish a system of elementary education. The organization of the diocese, however, remained inadequate and its social and pastoral problems were serious. Vaughan, therefore, immediately took steps to improve the administration of the diocese. Synods were held annually instead of every seven years, while the local deans were instructed to visit the parishes in their areas every three years. Vaughan standardized and centralized the diocesan finances. A Board of Temporal Administration advised him on financial matters and with him was solely responsible for contracting diocesan or parochial debts. The Board was a direct result of Vaughan's constant preoccupation with the difficulties of raising money from a predominantly working class population.

Vaughan had noted in his Diary, 'Dr Newsham used to say "the Bishops are Bankers" — Please God, I will not be a Banker'.[9] Nevertheless, Vaughan appreciated that if a mill or a colliery was closed, the local population might decline and leave a parish unable to pay even the interest of a debt contracted during earlier and more prosperous times. Consequently, he refused to adopt a policy of going into debt and simply paying off the interest, but always attempted to pay off the capital. In 1877, he paid £6,000 off the general debt without reducing the programme of expansion. At his personal request, money collected to build a tower for a church was used instead to redeem part of the debt and it soon became general practice to use fifteen or twenty per cent of collections for building improvements to reduce parochial debts. Vaughan himself actually succeeded in paying off the cathedral debt and reducing the diocesan debt in spite of continued expansion. Within six years, he paid off over £30,000 from a diocesan debt of about £100,000 and paid off almost £65,000 in fourteen years.

Neither as Bishop nor as Archbishop was Vaughan universally popular with the priests who had to find the money which his policies demanded. Furthermore, he himself had no personal experience of parochial life and as a result of his involvement in other concerns, was almost a stranger to some of his priests from whom he certainly demanded a great deal. As Bishop of Salford, he closely defined the size of clerical salaries. The normal salary of a curate was £40 and that of a parish priest £50. But although Vaughan fixed the minimum salary for a curate at £25 which was usual in many dioceses at the time, the normal salary could not be paid before all current liabilities had been discharged and until the Bishop himself had considered the size of the parochial debt. When a parish was in debt, 'stole fees' or voluntary offerings had to be used to make up the priests' incomes.

Vaughan was equally demanding in his attitude towards the pastoral work of his priests, emphasizing the importance of visiting homes and schools, the need for adequate preparation of sermons and the value of catechetical training. He was even delated to Rome for encouraging the use of devotions in the vernacular; 'though the people may pray in a tongue which is unknown', he remarked, 'it is far better, especially under all the circumstances of the present day, that they should pray in a language they understand'.[10] In 1875, with the help of the religious orders, he organized a mission in all the churches of Salford and Manchester. Masses began at half past five or six in the morning, priests visited during the day and heard confessions at evening services. This mission to the lapsed and the sick was extraordinarily successful. The early masses were crowded and some priests were still hearing confessions in the early hours of the morning.

In an effort to increase the number of possible candidates for ordination, Vaughan restricted the number of schools run by the religious orders and when he refused to allow the Jesuits to open a grammar school in Manchester, he became involved in a long and complicated controversy. The Jesuits claimed to possess certain privileges which allowed them to establish schools without episcopal approval — a claim which once again raised the wider issue of relations between the hierarchy and the regular clergy. In 1875, the Jesuits actually opened a school and Vaughan retaliated by threatening to suspend the staff if it was not closed within two days. This brief period was later extended and the school was closed only to re-open four days later! Episcopal authority was clearly the point at issue and Vaughan left for Rome, determined to stay until the question was decided and to resign if the decision went against him. Vaughan rejected any compromise which would bring about the closure of the school while implying a recognition of the Jesuits' alleged privileges and he eventually succeeded in closing the school on his own terms. Both sides, however, recognized the fact that the real issue, the definition of relations between bishops and orders, was still to be decided.

The point was that the ecclesiastical administration of the Catholic community remained unsatisfactory. Apart from the privileges of the Jesuits, there were other controversies over episcopal control or inspections of the schools and parishes of religious orders. At the annual Low Week meeting of the bishops in 1877, Manning proposed that Ullathorne and Clifford should petition Rome for a new constitution determining relations between the hierarchy and the orders, and twelve specific points were raised on which decisions were asked. By 1880, Clifford and Vaughan who were representing their colleagues in Rome, felt that they were opposed by an organized policy of delay. They again determined to stay until their case was decided and were later joined by Manning whom the Roman cardinals referred to as the 'diplomat';

Clifford was the 'lawyer' and Vaughan was the 'devil'.[11] In fact, Manning's help seems to have been somewhat doubtful; it was suggested that he talked and revealed too much and he was therefore persuaded to return home.

The orders, however, also suffered from the behaviour of their allies and their own advocate alienated support by his procrastinations and delays. The religious were also divided and prepared for compromise, whereas the bishops were united and enjoyed the support of the Scottish and American episcopates. It was therefore not surprising that the Bull *Romanos Pontifices* of 1881 was a victory for the bishops and made only minor concessions to the regulars. Ullathorne commented,

> The Papal Constitution is admirable; I read and re-read it with increased delight . . . there is nothing left to be desired. The episcopal office is strengthened all through the document, and it gives a complete reply to the objection raised in the Vatican Council, that the infallibility would weaken the episcopate . . . If it tends to bring our brethren of the Religious Orders, and especially those of the Society, to a more modest estimation of their position it will be to them a great blessing . . . One valuable result will be to rectify certain vague and misty notions which prevailed quite as much in Rome as in England, if not more so.[12]

Another reason for Vaughan's reluctance to allow the Jesuits to open a grammar school in Manchester was his own intention of establishing a Catholic Commercial College in an area which was increasingly becoming one of the main centres of commercial life. Vaughan had become familiar with the idea of commercial schools in Europe and America, and now wished to provide a business training for the boys who would find employment in the commercial city of Manchester. St Bede's began not far from Owen's College, but was soon moved to two houses near Alexandra Park. When a neighbouring Aquarium Company was on the verge of collapse, the Bishop bought it in order to prevent it from being turned into a music hall and in spite of opposition based on the claims of Science and Protestantism! The Aquarium was kept open for a time in an effort to silence the critics, but public interest continued to decline and the building eventually became part of the College.

As St Bede's expanded, Vaughan appealed for support but only from the wealthier Catholics who might be expected to benefit from the courses being offered. And the College did not survive without difficulty. The first rector had to be replaced by a more efficient successor who did not prove to be entirely satisfactory. An attempt was made to establish a subsidiary college in Germany where the students might more easily learn the German language. Originally, 'St Bede's on the Rhine' was to consist of a professor and a class of ten attending a German gymnasium. But the 'Bedians' only made moderate progress and so the scheme was extended to establishing a school in which German students would be in a majority and German the language used. The experiment, however, proved too expensive and was abandoned after a few years.

A far greater and more pressing need was to provide elementary education for the increasing number of working-class children. The Catholic Relief Act of 1778 did not allow Catholics to open schools, but since this Act was applied in a relaxed and permissive way, Catholics had established both private and charity schools by the end of the eighteenth century. At the beginning of the nineteenth century, wealthier Catholics found it possible to provide for the education of their children and advertisements in the *Laity's Directory* during the 1820's illustrate the development of Catholic schools for the sons and daughters of the well-to-do. At this time, there was a substantial body of prosperous Catholics who were able and willing to support a fairly exclusive type of Catholic education such as schools for young ladies where they might be taught English and French, history and geography, plain and ornamental needlework. Other Catholic children might be able to attend one of the few parochial Charity or Free Schools which were being established at about the same time. There were five Catholic schools in Blackburn, for example, by 1839; four of these were described as of mixed denomination where, no doubt, the fees of the non-Catholic students helped to pay the schools' expenses.

Incidentally, the many non-Catholic pupils who attended Catholic schools at the time were not compelled to attend either Catholic services or Catholic instructions. During 1840, Bishop Briggs wrote in one of his pastorals:

> Let not your schools be exclusive, but open to children of all religious denominations; and when Protestant children attend let them not share in the duties of prayer or religious instruction, unless at their own desire, expressly sanctioned by their parents or guardians.[13]

It was in such a spirit of conciliation that Catholics at the turn of the century had been working with other Christians in promoting Sunday Schools. However, during the first half of the nineteenth century, the main obstacle preventing Catholics from joining in school projects with other Christians was a result of the long-established Catholic tradition objecting to the use of non-Catholic versions of the Scriptures. In the second half of the century, Catholics became preoccupied with the dangers of proselytism, by which time, they also had to face the problem of financing schools for a predominantly poor population.

The impact of Irish immigration transformed the character and the scale of the problem as an ever-increasing proportion of Catholics found it impossible to pay for the education of their children. Foreign religious orders might obtain staff and financial help from abroad and many Catholic parishes solved their problems with the arrival of a group of nuns, but the difficulties elsewhere seemed insoluble. In London, for example, 1,600 children were attending Catholic schools in 1816 and by 1841, 6,000 children were attending school, but by then there were more Catholic children without schooling than ever before. Furthermore, the quality of the teaching was often poor and conditions in the schools sometimes deplorable. In an effort to remedy these deficiencies, the Catholic Institute of Great Britain was founded in 1838 and during 1847 this was merged with the Catholic Poor School Committee which had been established to collect money on a national level.

During the first twenty years of the century, the number of Catholic elementary schools had increased from ten to fourteen; the number doubled during the next decade, more than doubled between 1831 and 1841, and then increased from 69 to 166 so that there were just over 300 Catholic elementary schools by 1851. In the following year, however, the first Provincial Synod of Westminster emphasized the priority of building more poor schools which might also serve as chapels or meeting places:

> prefer the establishment of good schools to every other work. Indeed, wherever there may seem to be an opening for a new mission, we should prefer the erection of a school, so arranged as to serve temporarily for a chapel, to that of a church without one ... it is the good school that secures the virtuous and edifying congregation.[14]

Following the Factory Act of 1844, poorer Catholics who could not afford the fees charged at the parochial schools sometimes attended the new Factory Schools. There were only a few Catholic factory owners so that most Catholic children went to the schools of the non-Catholic owners and then attended Night Schools or Sunday Schools in the parish. However, by respecting the religious convictions of their Protestant employees, some Catholic employers secured similar concessions from Protestant employers. In 1850, a Catholic mill-owner in Blackburn opened a Factory School and 'as the school was open to all, irrespective of religion, Catholic children were given Catechetical Instruction in a separate room'.[15] Catholic children might also go to the parochial school on a part time basis and by 1867, the Catholic and Protestant mill-owners in Blackburn allowed 'half-timers' to attend their own denominational schools. There were, however, many difficulties with part time students, not least their tendency to play truant especially during periods of unemployment or short time working. Yet in spite of the obvious evils of the system, it was not officially abolished until 1918 and in 1909, one teacher recorded, 'Sent a half-timer in the little room to have a sleep. The poor boy fell asleep during the drawing lesson. He had to be up at a quarter past five to go to work'.

The British Government first recognized its financial responsibility for education by giving annual grants to Anglican and Nonconformist societies. The Newcastle Commission of 1858 recommended extending this financial support which would then include Catholic schools. Every school which achieved the standards laid down in the Education Code of 1862 became eligible for a grant depending on the number of students and their achievements – a system of 'Payment by Results', and those schools which applied for a grant became subject to Government inspection. The maximum grant was twelve shillings for each child: four shillings for a minimum of two hundred attendances and eight shillings for passes in all three basic subjects of reading, writing and arithmetic; there was a deduction of two shillings and eight pence for each failure.

Obviously, the poverty of Catholics had a direct effect on the finances of their schools; they received less from the Government than other Nonconformists and less than their own efforts justified. In 1886, over 50% of Catholic children paid only a penny a week, whereas the national average was just over 26%; only 8% of the Catholic population could afford to pay three or four pence a week, whereas the national average was just over 17%; few Catholics could afford higher contributions. Furthermore, one school inspector reported that many Protestant mill-owners in the north of England obliged their Catholic employees to contribute to the support of 'Protestant school mills' and these parents were then unable to afford a second contribution to the costs of the Catholic schools.[16] Nevertheless between 1850 and 1870, there was further, if insufficient, progress in building Catholic schools and training Catholic teachers.

According to a report issued in 1868, less than 6,000 Catholic children in Liverpool regularly attended school and by 1870, the average attendance was only about 6,000 out of a possible 20,000. At least one commentator believed that this was a major cause of the 'leakage', whereas compulsory education had proved to be 'the handmaid of religion in Catholic Liverpool since 1870'.[17] Forster's Education Act of 1870 created a national but dual system of education. The denominational schools were to be supported by voluntary subscriptions and assisted by Government grants which were doubled, but the non-denominational or Board Schools were to be maintained by an education rate. This placed a heavy financial burden on the churches in general and Catholics in particular and was originally seen as a threat to the very existence of Voluntary Schools. The Catholics of Liverpool, for example, of all classes and political opinions, united in their opposition and at a public meeting inaugurating a campaign to raise funds for Catholic schools, wealthy Catholics contributed generously towards the cost of providing education for poor Catholics.

Although Manning himself naturally defended the denominational system and 'a true, full, unimpeded, Catholic education', he did not oppose Government intervention in the field of education.[18] When Manning failed to obtain more favourable terms from the Government and in spite of the oppostion of other Catholics and their bishops who feared that Government grants might jeopardize their independence, Manning persuaded them to accept the grants and to co-operate with the Government and the Boards. The laity collected £40,000 to help those schools which rejected the Government's terms, but Manning accepted the money and then gave it to those schools which co-operated with the Government. Manning explained to Ullathorne:

> The Boards may destroy our lesser schools by reporting them to be insufficient or inefficient. The effect of this in London would be to destroy one half of our schools. By opening negotiations with the Board, as I have with the Privy Council, I hope to save these.[19]

Forster's Act created competition between the Board and the Voluntary Schools which the latter, unable to draw upon the rates, could only lose. Only the Anglican and Roman Catholic Churches attempted to compete and between 1878 and 1885, the number of Anglican schools increased by 9% and Catholic schools by just over 22%, from almost 700 to 850. Between 1870 and 1890, the number of Catholic elementary schools increased from 350 to 946 and accommodation from just over 100,000 to almost 350,000 places. It is revealing to compare the proportion of voluntary subscriptions with Government grants; the former rose from just over £22,000 to over £70,000 and the latter from just over £30,000 to over £160,000. Nevertheless the denominational or Voluntary Schools inevitably compared unfavourably with the Board Schools. The former had less equipment and fewer teachers who were also underpaid. The average salaries of principal teachers in 1886 were £111 in Catholic schools, £120 in Anglican schools and £148 in Board Schools. In 1887, it was estimated that the Catholic School of St Patrick's in Huddersfield had only 0.52 square yards for each child, the denominational schools had an average of one square yard and the Board Schools 4.8 square yeards. Yet the standards demanded from all schools were constantly raised so that the Voluntary Schools began to close and were replaced by Board Schools. Before 1884, more than 1,000 Voluntary Schools had disappeared, but none of these was a Catholic School in spite of the fact that as a result of the poverty of Catholics, these had the highest proportion of free admission and received the smallest contributions.

Some of the difficulties resulting from the conflict of interest between the Board Schools and the Voluntary Schools were occasionally settled peacefully on the local level. One country parish in Yorkshire gave the rate collected from Roman Catholics to the Catholic school, while other School Boards paid the fees of poor children attending Voluntary Schools. The School Board elections, with a system of transferable votes, ensured that minority interests would be represented; a Catholic priest in Rochdale once headed the first poll for the local School Board and in 1886, a Catholic priest, a Baptist minister and two Anglican clergymen were on the Board at Burnley. But national grievances remained and in 1884, the Voluntary Schools Association was founded in order to secure the four specific reforms and increased Government grants.

By that time, it was impossible to give more than a total annual grant of seventeen shillings and six pence for each student, unless the school had an independent parallel income of the same amount; a provision which in effect penalized poverty. Secondly, although teachers or education boards could remit the fees of poor children attending Board Schools, those parents who sent their children to denominational schools had to suffer the indignity of apppearing before the workhouse authorities. Thirdly, no other school could receive a Government grant in an area where a Board School already had sufficient accommodation for local children. Consequently, Catholic children often had to travel long distances simply because the local Board considered that another Catholic school was not needed. The final grievance was the rating of Voluntary Schools.

The support of Archbishop Manning and the English hierarchy gave the Association an official character in its effort to secure the appointment of a Royal Commission which would examine the four grievances and what changes were needed in the Act of 1870.[20] Before the 1885 election, Manning instructed Catholics to ask their local candidates whether they would support the policy of treating Voluntary and Board Schools equally, and the appointment of a Royal Commission to review the contemporary state of education resulting from the Act of 1870 and its administration by the Boards. Catholics put continuous pressure on parliamentary candidates especially in Lancashire and Sir Richard Cross pledged the Conservatives to appoint such a commission and to adopt any remedies which might be needed. Although the Liberals soon returned to power, a Commission was appointed with Cross as chairman and with Manning as one of its members. After two years, the Commission issued a majority report which favoured the Voluntary Schools by recommending a limited payment from the rates, but there was also a minority report which provided the Government with an excuse for further delay.

Adequate relief from the financial burdens incurred by the voluntary organizations could only come when the principle of free education was generally accepted, but Catholics had previously opposed this under the impression that the abolition of fees would either only apply to the Board Schools and thus destroy their own, or alternatively threaten their independent control. Meanwhile, an Act passed in 1891 provided an annual grant of ten shillings for every non-paying pupil under fifteen years of age and supplemented fees up to that amount; Catholic schools as the poorest gained most from this grant. However, the costs of education continued to rise as improvements were demanded in buildings, staffing and equipment. Furthermore, none of the original grievances had yet been settled so that some Catholics were still paying for the Board Schools while financing their own. The possibility of conducting a joint campaign with both Anglicans and Catholics, the leading supporters of the voluntary principle, was destroyed as a result of interdenominational controversy, particulary the dispute over Anglican Orders, and Catholics were left to campaign on their own.

The fact that supporters of the Voluntary Schools had to contribute through the rates towards the costs of Board Schools was interpreted by Vaughan as a religious disability and a restriction on freedom of conscience. Although the Anglicans apparently wished to make the financial sacrifices involved, Vaughan maintained that Catholics were too poor to do so. The Board Schools received nineteen shillings from the rates for each child, whereas denominational schools depended on voluntary subscriptions averaging just over six shillings; in twenty-four years, the School Boards had spent some £43,000,000 on capital charges and administration, while the supporters of the voluntary principle had spent the equivalent, teaching more children without there being any charge on the ratepayers. Although the attitude adopted by the Anglicans ensured that equality for elementary schools would not yet be adopted, an Act of 1897 gave a further grant of five shillings for each child, abolished the limit of seventeen shillings and six pence as well as the rating of Voluntary Schools.

In 1899, the *Tablet* came out in support of Lord Salisbury who publicly declared himself to be in favour of 'free schools' and 'assisted education'.[21] During the General Election of the following year, this support was extended to the Conservative Party which published a leaflet on the inequalities between Board and Voluntary Schools. Two years later, a Bill was introduced which placed public elementary schools under the control of the local authorities and recognized that both Board and Voluntary Schools had the same claims to financial support for maintenance and ordinary working expenses. This Bill left the supporters of the voluntary principle at least to some extent, at the mercy of local prejudice, while they still had to finance the interest on existing debts, and the costs of repairs and new buildings, but, on the whole, Vaughan considered that it was a just and permanent settlement.

Providing Catholic schools for Catholic children was only one means of alleviating complex social and religious problems. Towards the end of the century, Catholics became increasingly conscious, as had Anglicans and Nonconformists before them, of a widespread decline in religious practice and the problem of the 'leakage' was discussed more frequently in the Catholic press. Catholic priests became increasingly concerned with the problems resulting from 'mixed' marriages, particularly when the courts declared that promises to educate children in the Catholic faith were not legally binding. Catholic children who attended non-Catholic schools were reported to be unfamiliar with the sign of the Cross, the 'Hail Mary' or the Catholic version of the Lord's Prayer. On one occasion, Catholic children apparently commemorated St Patrick's Day by singing Protestant hymns to their local priest.[22] In 1889, Manning wrote to one of his priests:

> Year after year, and often in the year, I have to warn Catholic parents that in sending their Children to Non-Catholic Schools, such as the Board-Schools, they not only rob them of education

211

in the Catholic Faith but expose them to the danger of losing both faith and morals. In doing this they sin against God, and their children. If our Forefathers had done this where would be the Catholic religion in England at this day? It was the fidelity of Catholic Fathers and Mothers in Ireland that has kept the Faith of the Irish people pure to this day. If therefore you have any Parents in your parish who send their children to Board Schools, read to them this warning: and bid them from me to obey the voice of the Holy See.[23]

Vaughan had already become increasingly worried at the extent of the possible 'leakage' particularly among children by the end of 1884 and he established a Board of Inquiry to investigate the number of children who ceased to practise their religion and eventually left the Church as a result of the neglect or death of their parents, the work-house system and proselytism. This was followed by a census, not only of regular congregations, but also of those Catholics who had contracted mixed marriages or moved to other towns, of children left on the streets or living in workhouses, attending non-Catholic schools or philanthropic institutions, working as 'hands' in mills or as servants in Protestant households. The results were inevitably inaccurate and incomplete, but they were still revealing. The Catholic population of Manchester and Salford was estimated to be about 100,000. 74,000 names had been registered and all but 10,000 carefully analyzed. About 8,500 children under the age of sixteen were considered to be in unusual danger to faith and morals, and over a quarter of these in extreme danger, as a result of never attending a Catholic church or school, or because of the influence of their careless or hopelessly bad parents. Yet only 196 youths between sixteen and twenty-one were known to be in danger which suggested that there were many in this age group who were no longer considered to be even nominal Catholics.[24]

The problem of the 'leakage' now dominated Vaughan's attitude and actions. In 1886, he issued his pamphlet on 'The Loss of our Children' announcing the formation of a 'Catholic Protection and Resuce Society' which was followed by the establishment of committees which eventually covered the whole diocese. He appealed for the manpower and financial resources needed to set up Catholic Homes, night shelters and refuges, industrial schools and schemes of emigration. City missions, ragged schools and soup kitchens were means of proselytizing Catholic children who were also offered coal, clog or breakfast tickets in winter and tickets for pleasure trips during the summer. According to the

Board of Inquiry, half the institutions which had been visited proved to be 'hotbeds' of proselytism and over 150 Catholic children were in five of the most prominent.[25] Representatives of these institutions were often found in the police courts and by the beds of sick or dying parents. Sometimes an illegal form of contract was used which obliged parents who later reclaimed their children to pay the costs of their residence, while many parents, under the impression they had forfeited their rights over their children, felt unable to challenge the situation.

Vaughan offered to fight the legal cases of these parents at his own expense. He also publicly offered to send any Protestant child who came to a Catholic Home to the non-Catholic institutions if these would return those Catholic children for whom he could provide. This disingenuous offer obviously worked in favour of the Catholics, but it would also seem to have been a genuine attempt to prevent the waste of charitable funds on long court cases. Some Protestant philanthropists changed the names of children, moved them from one institution to another or even sent them to North America in an effort to prevent them from being returned to the care of Catholics. However, Vaughan succeeded in winning the support of public opinion and the courts usually upheld the claims of Catholic parents so that within about three years and following some twenty lawsuits, open resistance, at least, came to an end.

The workhouse system was another occasion of a serious 'leakage' among Catholics. Over 1,000 Catholic children were in workhouses throughout the Salford Diocese and in the Manchester area alone about 100 left annually, of whom 80 had also ceased to practise their religion. By this time, the Boards of Guardians usually proved to be considerate in providing Catholics with their own priests and teachers, but isolated from a Catholic environment and subjected to anti-Catholic prejudices, at least when they began to work, many of them still left the Church. In Middlesex, Manning had succeeded in making an arrangement whereby Catholic children were sent to Catholic Homes which received an agreed sum for maintenance. Although most of the Boards in the Salford diocese refused to adopt the practice immediately, Vaughan was ultimately successful by appealing to their sense of economy or generosity and after persuading the Brothers and Sisters of Charity to establish homes for boys and girls in his diocese.

But whereas the loss of children from proselytizing or the workhouse system was estimated at less than 1,000 a year, almost 4,000 children were lost as a result of parental neglect and just over 1,500 children of mixed marriages. Vaughan therefore set out to find homes for the children of mixed marriages and the victims of parental neglect. He had to provide food, clothing and education for children, night refuges and clubs for young people, and to secure the attendance of officers of his Rescue Society at the courts of law. Before Vaughan left Salford, more than 2,000 people were engaged in rescue work, ensuring that Catholic children attended Catholic schools and their religious duties. The annual report of the Society for 1890 revealed that 536 destitute children were being supported in two Poor Law Schools and five other homes. The Central Committee had dealt with just over 1,500 cases, while 234 children had been adopted by Catholic families in Canada. Expenses were running at about £160 a week. Vaughan himself gave the original subscription of £1,000 and the whole of his salary of £500 while he remained in Salford. Wealthy Catholics in different parts of the country were also generous, but most of the money came through appeals and collections from a diocese of working class Catholics.[26]

In the course of this rescue work, Vaughan had been advised by public officials as well as his priests and guided by the local police, he made a series of visits during the night into the worst urban areas in order to see for himself the conditions in which people were forced to live. These visits to the Salford slums aroused a real sense of social concern. Vaughan supported sanitary improvements, housing redevelopments and the condemnation of slum properties without compensation. He produced the facts and figures which demanded Government action; the number of deaths in Salford each year was over 1,000 above the national average, while within Salford itself, the death rate in Regent Road was 16, whereas it was 47 in Greengate; even in Regent Road one child in five died as a result of infectious diseases resulting from insanitary conditions. The proportion of deaths from typhoid fever was 37 to the 1,000 in the nation as a whole, 33 to the 1,000 in London, but 93 to the 1,000 in Salford; the death rate from scarlet fever in Salford was 100 in the 1,000, whereas elsewhere the figure was as low as 28 in the 1,000.[27]

Vaughan also discovered that there was a 'drinking-shop' for every two hundred men, women and children in Salford. In an effort to deal with the pastoral and social problems caused by drunkenness, Vaughan organized another 'Crusade of Rescue' and tried to establish branches in every parish. This was an organized form of Catholic action whose members visited other Catholics, persuading them to fulfil their religious obligations to send their children to Catholic schools, while at the same time encouraging temperance. Vaughan himself did not believe that total abstinence was a permanent remedy. Instead, he advocated a reduction in the number of licences granted and a prohibition on public houses in the slums; he recommended the introduction of light lager beers coupled with increased taxes on stronger varieties and the provision of alternative entertainment.

This social or pastoral concern inevitably led to public recognition and some involvement in local affairs. Vaughan attended a Licensed Victuallers' dinner in order to outline his views on temperance. He took an active part in the campaign against slavery and publicly condemned the trade in opium; 'We are forming our revenue out of the bodies and souls of the Chinese', he declared, 'and we are far worse than the cannibals, for the cannibals are not enlightened, they only destroy and feed upon the body'.[28] As Bishop of Salford, he frequently attended the discussions of the local Chamber of Commerce, sometimes inviting his own missionaries to speak about the countries which they were opening up to civilization and the cotton goods of Manchester as well as to Christianity.

But unlike Manning who was a genuine social reformer, Vaughan's social concern was essentially pastoral. Certainly he preached on social justice and strongly denounced contemporary abuses; he supported such measures as old age pensions, graduated income tax and the establishment of settlements. But in spite of Manning's constant advice to take an active part in social and political questions, Vaughan does not seem to have considered that this was a proper task for a Cardinal Archbishop. After Manning's intervention in the Dock Strike, it was Newman, not Vaughan, who sent a note of congratulation. Vaughan only engaged in social action out of a sense of Christian duty; on the natural level, he apparently had no love for the world – an attitude to which Manning could make the stinging reply, 'God so loved the world that He sent His only begotten Son – but that is a detail'.[29]

Nevertheless, Vaughan's pastoral concern was not narrowly parochial; in 1877, for example, he published a pastoral on 'The Indian Famine and the Apostacy in Europe'. Furthermore, he himself always had a sense of vocation to the foreign missions which was reinforced by the example of the Protestant missionary societies and his own consciousness of the imperial power and influence of England:

Nation is dependent upon nation, and we have to carry on the light. In less than a thousand years Africa may be as civilized as Europe or America. The mission of the English-speaking races is to the unconverted, especially to the uncivilized, nations of the world. God calls upon you for co-operation: His plans are prepared from afar.[30]

215

Vaughan's own intentions fluctuated between a personal sense of vocation to the missions and a desire to establish a permanent source of missionary priests. Initially, Vaughan found Wiseman most encouraging and although Manning was less enthusiastic, he eventually allowed the Oblates to commit themselves in principle to the idea of establishing a seminary for the training of foreign missionaries. Vaughan himself finally settled on the idea of building a missionary college with endowments and in 1863, decided to go to the Americas in order to raise the necessary funds. He won the approval of the English hierarchy, secured a favourable resolution from the Malines Congress, drew up a formal petition to Propaganda and obtained the blessing of Pio Nono. By the end of December, he was sailing for the Caribbean.

The Archbishop of San Francisco who had his own financial problems originally gave permission for a single sermon on behalf of the missions in the country areas of his archdiocese, but this was later extended to a sermon and collection in each church. Eventually, Vaughan collected between six and seven thousand pounds with promises of more and he reported that his visit to San Francisco had provided four or five and possibly six or seven burses for students. Vaughan then moved on to Lima where he was so successful that the Government passed a decree prohibiting him from collecting any more money. But as Vaughan himself reported, laws were of little consequence in this part of the world; the President himself apologized for the decree and his wife contributed a further 250 dollars to the fund. After collecting about 15,000 dollars in Peru, Vaughan travelled to Chile where he collected 25,000 dollars and received promises of another thirty three or thirty five thousand. He then went on to Brazil where he met a similar generosity. It now seemed that he had sufficient financial resources to justify beginning his project, having received ten burses or about £11,000 with promises of more and in the event, for some years after returning to England, Vaughan continued to receive substantial sums of money for his Missionary College from California and South America.

In 1866, Vaughan issued 'A Statement on behalf of the College for Foreign Missions', calling on English Catholics for help in his work and appealing to their sense of responsibility as members of the British Empire. In the same year, Vaughan purchased Holcombe House and the new missionary college began with one student and one professor, Herbert Vaughan. Life in the new college was far from easy. The Rector was determined to establish a sound financial basis and had no intention of wasting money which he had so labouriously collected; fuel, cooks or even beds were considered unnecessary luxuries.

Two years later, Manning spoke at a packed public meeting in St James' Hall which included ten bishops and many distinguished laymen on the platform. Manning referred to the two centres from which the light of faith should be diffused throughout the world — the spiritual centre of Rome and London, the centre of the greatest empire in the world. This meeting was so successful that Vaughan issued a second pamphlet on 'Our Duty to the Heathen' which was translated and distributed throughout the continent, and which led to an increase in foreign vocations as well as further financial support for the new society.

By this time, there were three priests and twelve students. The foundation stone of the present college was laid in June, 1869 and in March, 1871, it was opened free from debt with a community of thirty four. In November, 1871, Vaughan accompanied his first four missionaries to Baltimore where they were assigned to care for the local negro population. During a tour of the southern states when incidentally Vaughan had called on Jefferson Davis, he had been horrified by the conditions of the negroes and the divisions between white and coloured Catholics even where the latter had made substantial financial contributions to the Church. Although the American mission later separated from the English society, Vaughan and the Mill Hill Fathers through the work of the Josephites were instrumental in training the first coloured priest to be ordained in the United States.

Both as Bishop of Salford and Archbishop of Westminster, Vaughan remained Superior General of the Society, continued to direct the college at Mill Hill and remained responsible for its financial arrangements. It was perhaps fitting that he should have chosen Mill Hill as his place of rest and retreat, and the place of his death and burial. Vaughan always showed a constant and fatherly care for his missionaries, advising them on financial or pastoral questions and frequently corresponding with them. The Society expanded rapidly and its priests would eventually be found in Uganda and the Congo, in Madras, the Punjab and Kashmir, in Borneo and Sarawak, in New Zealand and the Philippines. The need for men and money was partly met by building minor and major seminaries in Lancashire, Holland and the Tyrol and establishing local agents among the laity to collect donations for the Society. Vaughan also established a new Religious order of women, the Franciscan Missionary Sisters of St Joseph, to assist in the work of his various institutions and in 1875 he admitted the first four lay-brothers into his Society.

The original spirit of Vaughan's foundation was thoroughly Ultramontane and manifested his determination to establish a papal and

Roman Catholicism, not only in England, but throughout the world.

> Next our oath contains a special clause obliging each student who takes it in a particular manner to maintain the authority and to defend the rights of the Holy See wherever he may be sent. Our missioners will go out as Roman as any Roman and as specially devoted to the Pope. It seems to me that the times and the character of England, and her position in the world make it clear that the woof must be laid upon papal warp. In England a strong papal adherence is growing up. The same must be weaved into all our work in pagan lands and in the Colonies. This is part of our work here, and you need not doubt our clear perception of its necessity. Humanly speaking it is the safeguard against national tyranny and spiritually it is the building of the Religion of Christ upon the Rock which He has set in Himself.[31]

But if Vaughan's work for the missions provided a successful outlet for his enthusiaastic Ultramontanism, his Ultramontane convictions did not always have such happy results.

Between 1894 and 1897, Vaughan became involved in the controversy over Corporate Reunion and Anglican Orders which he originally regarded with amusement, then with impatience and finally with obvious dislike. In 1894, he commented, 'Benson is going to get himself declared a Patriarch within the next two years! So I hear from certain well-informed Anglicans'.[32] But irony aside, Vaughan had neither the character nor the history to sympathize with the efforts of a Lord Halifax or an Abbé Portal. Vaughan's attitude to the Reunion Movement which he crudely saw as a threat to the faith of Catholicism or a means of saving Anglicanism from collapse, was similar to his Ultramontane approach at the time of the Vatican Council when he confidently ignored or intolerantly discredited the arguments of his opponents. Vaughan was undoubtedly a conscientious and attractive character as Halifax himself recognized:

> I have a great regard and affection for your Eminence. It has come to me for many reasons, I feel it, and feeling it I like to say it for this once because, however unequal the contest, Your Eminence compels me to fight, instead as I had hoped and prayed helping us to peace.[33]

But Vaughan's vision was simple and straightforward. He thought he was being sympathetic to Anglicans when he was injuring their deepest convictions and thought he was simply establishing the truth when he was becoming involved in the use of rather disreputable methods.

The apologetic considerations which dominated Vaughan's thinking were clearly revealed when Lord Halifax wrote a letter of protest to the Cardinal Archbishop of Toledo after the Protestant Archbishop of Dublin had consecrated a bishop of the Reformed Church in Spain. On reading Halifax's letter, Vaughan feared that the Spanish prelate might imagine that these 'Catholics' were in communion with Rome and so he himself wrote to clarify the position. A badly translated version of Vaughan's letter suggested that Halifax was deceiving the Spanish Cardinal and this was reprinted in the *Times*. Although the misunderstanding was publicly and privately corrected, Vaughan made a revealing comment in a letter to the Duke of Norfolk:

> I have come to the conclusion that Providence overrules our actions and often directs them in spite of ourselves to a wise end. I believe that it is supremely important for me to be perfectly clear and explicit on the points which were put, brutally of course, in the Toledo letter. It will not be necessary to insist very much more on them — they are at last understood: so also as to Anglican Orders *at last!*[34]

Public attention centred on Anglican Orders when the historian Louis Duchesne supported their validity in a review of a book by Portal. Portal's own enthusiasm for reunion was greatly influenced by his friendship with Lord Halifax and his acquaintance with High Churchmen. Pope Leo XIII's pontificate had already been marked by efforts to end political and religious quarrels, and when the Pope and the Secretary of State welcomed Portal in audience, this was interpreted as a sign, however limited, of papal approval. On the other hand, both the Archbishop of Canterbury and the Archbishop of Westminster were less than enthusiastic and felt that the particular individuals concerned could not adequately represent the two churches and did not fully appreciate the situation. Vaughan believed that Portal had been unduly influenced by his High Church friends who held a minority opinion within Anglicanism which was incomplete compared with the fulness of Roman Catholicism. High Churchmen talked of reunion without being prepared to accept the decrees of the Vatican Council, whereas in Vaughan's opinion, the so-called 'Catholic' members of the Church of England were simply and unconsciously preparing their fellow Anglicans for an easier submission to Roman Catholicism.

According to Vaughan, corporate reunion could only mean corporate submission and individual conversions must not be delayed in a futile anticipation of such an impossible hope. In the event of corporate reunion, the heretical or schismatical church must, like the individual, reject the past as well as particular beliefs, but the Anglican Church did not have the teaching authority needed in order to make a collective submission. Once Vaughan felt that the reunion movement might be preventing or delaying individual conversions, he became openly hostile; as he wrote in 1896:

> Reunion means submission to a Divine Teacher. When men have found the Divine Teacher and determined, at whatever cost, to submit to Him, there will be Reunion. And Reunion with the Catholic Church can never take place on any other terms. This was well known. The question of Anglican Orders, therefore, was never in it ... [Anglican Orders] stand alone, shivering in their insular isolation − and worse; for they are disowned within their own Communion as well as by the immense majority of the English people.[35]

Vaughan, therefore, denied the validity of Anglican Orders not only because of liturgical or historical difficulties, but because the sacramental powers of the Catholic priesthood were also denied by most Anglicans. He opposed efforts being made in Rome to secure the recognition of Anglican Orders and when attempts were also made to delay or to prevent the conversion of individuals, he supported the idea of a thorough investigation, the outcome of which, he never seems to have doubted. The *Tablet* was equally hostile to the Anglican claims and when Wilfrid Ward suggested that it might be prudent to take a less categorical line, Vaughan confidently told the editor that an investigation involving English history would obviously have to include English experts and that he himself would undoubtedly be consulted in selecting them![36] Vaughan also had the support of the Irish, Scottish and other English bishops in his opposition to Anglican Orders and would also be aware that his efforts to defeat the supporters of the reunion movement and to secure the condemnation of Anglican Orders would enjoy the invaluable support of Monsignor Raphael Merry del Val.

Merry del Val frequently offered advice on almost every subject in his letters to Vaughan and was always critical of that 'spirit of liberalism and revolt' which he considered to be prevalent in England.[37] He therefore 'encouraged' Vaughan in his later dealings with Mivart, made no secret of his low opinion of Tyrrell and even advised the Cardinal on etiquette and his public appearances.[38] In 1893, Acton informed Vaughan that the Prince of Wales had expressed his fears, in the most friendly way, that 'the striking colours in which his Eminence occasionally appears . . .

in general society' might be imprudent and lead to protests or demonstrations.[39] Vaughan modified his dress to the satisfaction of the Prince of Wales and Lord Acton, but Merry del Val thought that he had made too many concessions to English practice for a Roman Cardinal!

Merry del Val's attitude to the Anglicans and their Catholic friends was openly hostile. He referred to 'the poisoning of men's minds' by Portal and company who 'have done and are doing much harm. They are practically picking faith and principle to pieces by preaching Liberalism in religion'.[40] Convinced of his own orthodoxy, he was highly suspicious of those who disagreed with him. 'Gasparri is simply an emissary of Portal's, full of Portal's ideas and I must say honestly at times hardly orthodox. I don't know where he has learnt or unlearnt his theology'.[41] Most revealing of all, perhaps, was Merry del Val's presumptuous conclusion: 'Great harm was done and continues in consequence of the imprudent way in which Portal and those Anglicans were encouraged here, and had not God been there to help us I think worse and irremediable mistakes might have been made'.[42]

In January, 1895, Vaughan himself went to Rome where he maintained that there was no possibility of corporate reunion and advised the Pope against making any move which might be used as an excuse for delaying or preventing individual conversions. This warning was repeated by Gasquet shortly afterwards and supported by Merry del Val. It is now clear that the Pope's letter *Ad Anglos* − an invitation to the English people to pray for the light to know the truth in all its fulness, was undoubtedly influenced by Gasquet and Bishop, Vaughan and Merry del Val. The facts that the Pope did not address the Anglicans, said nothing on the question of orders and granted indulgence to those who recited the rosary for the conversion of England, were all considered significant.

When the question of Anglican orders was formally re-opened in 1895, Vaughan established a committee to consider the evidence, and when the Pope established an International Commission in 1896, the English members were the leading members of Vaughan's committee, Moyes, Gasquet and Fleming who was later secretary of the Pontifical Biblical Commission. The three foreign members, Augustinis, Duchesne and Gasparri, who favoured the Anglican claims were later reinforced by an English representative, Scannell, and the English group was reinforced by the Spanish theologian, Llevaneras. Both the president of the Commission, Mazzella, and its secretary, Merry del Val, supported and advised the English group.

The Pope himself was also hostile to the Anglican claims, possibly as a result of the influence of Merry del Val and his friends. Leo XIII apparently shared Vaughan's fears that good Catholics would be shocked or scandalized by a decision in favour of Anglican orders as well as his confidence that many Anglican clergymen would immediately join the Church, if they could but afford it, because he constantly recommended that relief funds should be established for them. On one occasion, to the evident satisfaction of Moyes, the Pope referred to Anglican bishops as the employees or creatures of the state,[43] and on another occasion, 'emphatically said that he regarded this movement of Portal in France as "a continuation of Gallicanism and a danger to the Church" '.[44]

The hostility of Leo XIII was clearly revealed on this second occasion: 'certain Frenchmen have been interfering *(se sont entremêlés)* in this matter. They are *des têtes légères* and act without sufficient knowledge ... Lord Halifax *est un homme qui va* – (a series of curved gestures to express crooked or slippery ways)'. Moyes and his friends emphasized that Anglicans were heretics who were not interested in reunion and the Pope agreed; he revealed that with his decision, he would publish an encyclical on the Church and the primacy of St Peter. When Fleming pointed out that Anglicans would not join the Church as long as their orders were recognized in any way, the Pope again agreed and commented:

> I have placed these conferences under the presidence of one of the most distinguished and learned of the Cardinals in whom I have absolute confidence – the Cardinal Mazella. He added smilingly 'He is my creature! He was almost unknown, and when I raised him to the Sacred College people made remarks, and said 'we do not know him'. I said 'never mind. You *will* know him'.

The task of the Commission was to consider the evidence and to present a series of reports on which the Cardinals of the Holy Office presided over by the Pope might make a final decision; and the work did not take long. Only the four members who had been appointed precisely because they opposed the Anglican claims positively voted against the validity of Anglican orders. The statement outlining the findings of the Commission was prepared by two of the officials who sympathized with the opponents of the Anglican claims, while the Pope and the hostile party were both confident that the Commission of Cardinals would refuse to recognize the validity of Anglican orders. In July, 1896, the Cardinals of the Holy Office unanimously declared that Anglican orders were invalid. Merry del Val, assisted by Gasquet, then drafted the Bull *Apostolicae curae* which was published in September and which declared that Anglican orders were null and void, defective in form and intention.

The unfortunate letter which Vaughan wrote to Halifax on the condemnation of the Anglican orders speaks for itself:

> I should have thought that, from the point of view of piety and devotion to Our Lord, you and I ought to rejoice to think that men have not had the power to profane and dishonour Our Lord in the B. Eucharist during the last three centuries which they would have had were their Orders valid. Think of how the bread and wine have been treated, not only by clergymen but by sacristans and the people generally, who disbelieved in any real presence. Think of how shocking it would be if men were actually producing Our Lord − not to be honoured and adored, but in truth to be disowned and dishonoured by themselves and the people. This is a consideration which cannot fail to suggest itself to a devout mind like your own. But is it not good and useful that, instead of groping in the mist of uncertainty, we should be brought face to face with test questions? Such a question is, the Supremacy of the Pope and the necessity of submission to the Church − the Church of which the Pope is the legitimate Head. No doubt such submission requires humility, for human nature is filled with that spirit of pride and independence which has been the ruin of an angelic as well as of a human race . . . the real question between us is, where is the Divine Teacher to be found? In a small but respectable section of the Church of England or in the Church of which the Pope is the Head. This is the question to which I hope all your attention will be given, with constant earnest and humble prayer for guidance.[45]

Not all English Catholics, however, were able to associate themselves with Merry del Val, Gasquet, Moyes and Fleming when they celebrated their victory over the Anglicans with a private dinner party in London. Men like William Barry and George Tyrrell, Bishop Brownlow, Baron Friedrich von Hügel and the Duke of Norfolk deplored the controversial attitudes and policies, the polemical tone and 'jubilant crowing' sometimes adopted by Vaughan and his supporters.[46] Vaughan always tended to be narrow and dogmatic when he considered that the faith of the Church was being discussed. In 1897, a book entitled *Steps Towards Reunion* by Fr James Duggan was refused an *imprimatur* and Vaughan was also prepared to condemn Fr W.R. Carson's later work, *Reunion Essays*. Vaughan could not have sympathized with the author's deliberately moderate or 'minimising' attitude towards theological doctrines like infallibility or papal encyclicals such as *Apostolicae curae*.

But in spite of the obvious fact that Vaughan himself was certainly not an intellectual, he appreciated the pastoral, social or even political importance of being on good terms with leading Catholic figures. As Archbishop of Westminster, he established friendly links with Lord Acton in spite of the fact that as Bishop of Salford, he had refused the sacraments to another Catholic who, like Acton, had apparently written to the *Times* in terms which seemed incompatible with the definition of papal infallibility. When Acton became Regius Professor of History at Cambridge, Vaughan wrote a friendly letter which contained the astonishing admission:

> I know and understand something of the awful trials you must have gone through in years past, and I cannot but thank God that you are what I believe you to be — faithful and loyal to God and to His Church, though, perhaps, by your great learning and knowledge of the human in this same Church, tried beyond other men.[47]

Vaughan also finally ended the impasse into which Catholics had forced themselves on the provision of higher education. When Newman had returned disappointed from Dublin, the Liberal Catholics were divided on the best means of realizing their hopes of providing Catholics with higher education. Acton dreamed of a new Catholic university and offered the means to establish such a university at Bridgnorth. Renouf, on the other hand, preferred the idea of founding a Catholic Hall at Oxford. Both men, however, were convinced that something must be done and in 1863, Acton asked Renouf to write an article on the necessity of providing a university education for English Catholics. Acton referred to the 'leakage' among the Oxford converts; 'You must know how much scepticism has spread (among them) and how many apostasies of priests, and even religious, we bury in silence'.[48] This was itself, he felt, sufficient reason for ensuring that Catholics had the education to deal with the religious issues raised by contemporary intellectual developments.

Ultramontanes like Manning and Ward, however, were opposed on theoretical and practical grounds to the attendance of English Catholics at the two older universities. They believed that mixed education of Catholics and non-Catholics was undesirable in itself, condemned in principle by the Holy See and dangerous to faith and morals. Manning and Ward as well as a number of their supporters had been particularly successful Oxford graduates, but other English Catholics and especially the bishops were not at all familiar with Oxford or Cambridge and feared what they imagined. The Roman authorities knew even less about the place of the universities in English society and their ignorance was vividly illustrated later when Lord Braye had to explain to Leo XIII that the Queen's Colleges were in Ireland and that the Irish education question was not connected with Oxford.

In 1863 Manning wrote an article in the *Dublin Review* which was, on the whole, a fair and balanced account of the needs and problems of the time, and which also revealed his own awareness of the need to provide higher education. But the article also revealed Manning's uncompromising Ultramontanism and his conviction of the necessity of ecclesiastical control in view of the 'Rationalism' and 'Wordliness' which he attributed to English society. Manning did not want 'a tame, diluted, timid, or worldly Catholicism', but 'Downright, masculine, and decided Catholics – more Roman than Rome, and more ultramontane than the Pope himself':

> There is but one safety for us: *'Sentire cum Ecclesia'*, in the whole extent of faith, discipline, worship, custom, and instincts – the most intimate and filial fidelity of intellect, heart, and will to the living voice of the Church of God.[49]

As a result of the appearance of this article, Acton recommended Renouf to postpone his own which eventually appeared during 1864 in the form of a *Letter from a Catholic Layman to the Very Reverend J.H. Newman, D.D.*, which Manning interpreted as an attack on himself and his own article.

The issue was never really an 'open' one. When in 1864, a questionnaire was sent to the leading Oxford converts on the advisability of Catholics attending the university, it was not sent to Newman or any of those who agreed with him and the questions were so phrased that it was difficult to give an affirmative answer; 'In other words: Do you think Catholics should be prohibited from attending the Universities, or are you an enemy of God and Man?'[50] Almost ten years later, when Manning sent a report to Rome outlining the arguments in favour and against reopening the question, the President of Oscott commented:

> I never read a document which so much disgusted me, from its palpable injustice, and even occasional falsehood; and that it goes very far in my mind towards justifying the hardest things that Newman has ever said of its author. I suppose it arises from sheer inability to take in any view of a subject which differs from his own.[51]

In 1864, a majority of the English bishops decided, probably as a result of the known wishes of the Pope and Propaganda which later confirmed the decision, to discourage without prohibiting the attendance of Catholics at the older universities. Most of the bishops, in varying degrees, were opposed to the establishment of a Catholic College at Oxford and Propaganda also refused to approve of such an establishment. Clifford's opposition to this policy coupled with his support for Errington apparently showed that he was 'very weak in principle' and was later held against him when he was suggested as Wiseman's successor.[52] Once Manning himself became Archbishop, the university question, at least in so far as Oxford and Cambridge were concerned, was decided for the next thirty years.

In 1867, Manning apparently evaded any opposition from the other bishops by securing a unanimous agreement on general principles and avoiding divisions over details:

> the Archbishop put forward general principles and a general direction for conduct to which all have committed themselves; some from conviction but some also from mere acquiescence and not perceiving the reach and effect of their consent. The consequence is, he has secured unanimity in the Episcopate up to the furthest point they could be got. Had details, prescribing the precise application of the remedy, been brought forward, there could have resulted a division which would have jeopardized an unanimous agreement in general principles. Nothing could more certainly secure all we want than that the Bishops should unanimously invite the H. See to instruct them as to the duties to be laid upon the clergy ... he has pledged them all to his own principles and they receive unanimously all his details by asking for instructions from the Holy See upon the points which must include them ... Between ourselves, I know of more than one Bishop not unfavourable even to Oxford education, and yet they are now committed to the right side by their signature.[53]

In this letter, Vaughan also outlined the sort of prohibition which, he thought, should be adopted — a command to the clergy who would be forbidden under pain of censure or suspension to encourage Catholics to attend Protestant universities and who would be obliged to teach parents their duty with regard to education. According to Vaughan, a prohibition on the laity would be imprudent at the time. Always apparently ready to identify his own opinions with the guidance of the Holy Spirit, Manning simply became more rigid in his views. In 1883, he wrote to Vaughan who ironically would change his policy:

> How I thank God that neither you nor I have ever wavered! How

easily you might have been deceived, and how easily I might have been blinded and biassed by my love of Oxford and England! But I have been saved in this and in other things by nothing less than the Holy Ghost.[54]

The ultimate issue was at once far wider and more fundamental than Newman returning to Oxford, Catholics attending the university or even the danger to their faith. As Manning himself wrote, 'There is abundant mischief short of losing faith, such as losing humility, modesty, respect for authority, and, in a word, the *sentire cum ecclesia*'.[55] The struggle over higher education was simply another aspect of the struggle between the Ultramontanes and their opponents. This at least seems to be the implication of Manning's fears about the development of an English Catholicism and Vaughan's remarks to the Pope in April, 1867. Vaughan told Pio Nono that there was an immediate danger of 'our losing control of our higher studies' and 'the formation of a liberal and anti-Roman school at Oxford'; Newman being the obvious representative of this liberal and national school of thought.[56] Newman himself believed that the Ultramontanes preferred Catholics:

to remain a distinct caste among the Protestant gentry – and, if inferiority in mind be the necessary consequence or condition of such isolation, well, never mind, it must be accepted by us. It is not that Oxford will corrupt Catholic youths more than Woolwich or London, but that it will improve their intellectual powers, or create a mutual understanding between them and Protestants.[57]

Three days before Vaughan had his audience with the Pope in 1867, E.R. Martin, a convert studying for the priesthood who also acted as Roman correspondent for the Catholic press in England, attacked the plan of allowing Newman to return to Oxford in the *Weekly Register*:

It is almost needless to say – for anyone who knows the prevailing spirit of Rome – that this distinguished man has no longer, in Roman opinion, the high place he once held. It could hardly be otherwise, after the sermon on the temporal power, certain passages of the 'Apologia', and then having allowed his name to be linked with that of one of the bitterest haters of Rome in the dedication of Mr Oxenham's translation of Dr Döllinger's 'First Ages of the Church'. Now, when the Church is tossed about as it is, and when Germanizing is its deadliest danger, the mere shadow of a suspicion of Germanizing, however unfounded, please God, it may really be, could hardly save any man, however great and illustrious as a Catholic,

Cardinal Newman

from having the confidence in him greatly shaken. The decision of the Holy Father does not, however, amount to more than this. Good soldier of the faith as Dr Newman has been, and devoted Catholic as he still doubtless is, a mission of so delicate a nature as that proposed for Oxford could not safely be entrusted to one who had compromised himself in the opinion of Rome by certain statements, and who, though no doubt undeservedly, is leaned upon by the Germanizing school of younger Catholics in England as their strongest staff. Only an Ultramontane without a taint in his fidelty could enter such an arena as that of Oxford life with results to the advantage of the faith in England.[58]

Following this attack on Newman's orthodoxy, the leading Catholic laity presented him with an address of gratitude and appreciation, and a similar address from the clergy was apparently stopped by Manning on the grounds that it would be regarded by the Roman authorities as an attempt to dictate to them. The editor of the *Register* disavowed the opinions of his correspondent and many letters of protest appeared in the Catholic press. Even Manning dissociated himself from the attack; Vaughan feared 'That fool, Martin . . . will have done much mischief'; Talbot denied having seen him for a year and was as disgusted as Vaughan 'at his head-long folly'.[59] But the Rector of the English College told Ullathorne that the 'faction' had been surprised at the support which Newman had received and had then put the blame on Martin:

I think he has been treated very harshly. He knows as well as I know that words more harsh and cruel have been spoken than he has written; he has shaded off rather than exaggerated what, as correspondent, he was bound to relate of the current gossip of the Town. I have told Talbot that neither he nor another personage [Manning] can escape the imputation of having suggested the remarks of the writer's article which exonerate them. Every English ecclesiastic whom I have heard speak on the subject, with the exception of Fr Burke the Dominican, who is eager to defend Dr Newman, have spoken in the same sense as Martin.[60]

Newman himself described Martin's letter as 'the best luck we have had a long time'; 'it has let a cat out of the bag, and a black cat it is'. Newman believed that, in spite of denials, Manning had been 'at the root of the oppositon of my going to Oxford'.[61] McClelland has argued, on the other hand, that Ullathorne was responsible for Propaganda's instruction allowing the establishment of an Oratory at Oxford, while refusing Newman permission to reside there.[62] Ullathorne might well have been in a somewhat ambiguous position; Newman himself felt that although the Bishop was personally kind, he also wished to 'stand well' with the Roman authorities, 'So he is a coward'. Certainly, Ullathorne's later pastoral warning Catholics against attending Protestant universities described the *Syllabus* and its encyclical as 'that great doctrinal instruction ... the precious gift ... a light from heaven to guide us through the intellectual danger of these perilous times'. At the same time, Ullathorne also expressed the opinion that Newman had been 'shamefully misrepresented' by Englishmen in Rome and he sympathized with Newman's decision not to establish an Oratory in Oxford; 'Were I in the same position', he added, 'I should do the same'.[63]

However, Manning was not opposed to all forms of higher education. In 1868, following instructions from Propaganda which were possibly the result of a memorandum written by Vaughan, the English bishops decided to establish a personal university which really amounted to a board examining pupils in the existing Catholic colleges at university level. Even twenty years later, Manning believed that this 'was and always has been' the way to proceed, but others were no doubt grateful that the Vatican Council intervened.[64] Manning also suggested that English Catholics might attend a Roman university, though this should possibly be seen as another example of the devotion to Rome which was so evident at the time, rather than as a realistic attempt to provide a university education for English Catholics. As the Pope himself pointed out, the only objection was that no one would go to it!

In 1872, all the bishops except Brown of Newport believed that the possibility of establishing a Catholic Hall at Oxford had been closed by the decisions of the Roman authorities. Clifford, however, attempted to reopen the question and won the support of five other bishops; seven bishops voted against him. The bishops then unanimously agreed to a compromise, reporting to Propaganda and seeking futher guidance. Manning, Clifford and Ullathorne prepared the draft of a report which was also unanimously approved, but in view of the differences of opinion, the report could not be particularly sympathetic to the establishment of a Catholic Hall at Oxford; as McClelland has commented, '*Propaganda* could be in little doubt as to the answer required'.[65]

By 1872, Newman concluded that English Catholics were in an impossible position as a result of the decisions of their ecclesiastical authorities who would never allow the establishment of a real Catholic university free from clerical control and academically autonomous. Meanwhile, he felt unable to recommend the establishment of a Catholic

College at Oxford because of the scepticism within the university itself and because Catholic theologians were so ill-prepared for apologetic controversies following the decrees of the Vatican Council. Newman was therefore forced to conclude that 'mixed' education was as necessary in England during the nineteenth century as it had been at the time of the early church. The bishops should allow English Catholics to attend the Protestant colleges in Oxford and Cambridge, while establishing a strong mission of competent theologians to protect the faith of the Catholic undergraduates.

Manning on the other hand, apparently hoped that English Catholics would eventually be able to follow the example of Catholics in America, France and Belgium, and establish a Catholic university, an English Louvain or Angers. Such an institution would enable Catholics to make a positive contribution to the development of nineteenth century thought and, by transcending national boundaries, would enrich the life of the country, while uniting English Catholics more firmly with those on the continent. But as Chadwick has pointed out, English Catholics had neither the men nor the money to establish an effective university.[66] This was demonstrated in 1874, when Manning himself made his major attempt to provide higher education for English Catholics by establishing the Kensington University College which Wilfrid Ward was to describe as 'a ludicrous failure'.[67] After only four years, although the College continued with one professor and three or four students, it became associated with St. Charles's College which had also been opened in 1874 in order to provide a middle class and grammar school education for Catholics.

The Kensington scheme soon ran into difficulties. Even members of the staff had their reservations. Mivart accepted his 'post there very reluctantly and only in obedience to the express desire of the Archbishop of Westminster'; he himself had always preferred some other scheme which would have allowed Catholics to go to Oxford or Cambridge rather than London.[68] Some of the bishops, in the meantime, questioned Mivart's orthodoxy and were even prepared to condemn him which Manning prevented by a tactical move. The College's reputation was not enhanced by accusations that its students were exposed to moral dangers, evidence of lax discipline and complaints of immorality. Rumours of the Rector's liaison with a young woman eventually led to his suspension and a long legal battle in Rome. As usually happens in these cases, the number and seriousness of the incidents were probably exaggerated, but the public scandal was real enough.

Financing the establishment, however, proved to be the most serious problem. The small number of students could not possibly pay the money required to provide a sufficient number of suitably qualified Staff. Meanwhile, the Rector, Mgr T.J. Capel, was commissioning elaborate designs for a College chapel, while failing to keep accurate financial records and was soon deep in debt. At one stage, the bishops decided not to reveal the financial position since they felt that this revelation would effectively bring the institution to an end. During 1877 and 1878, Manning spent some £4,000 of his own money in a vain attempt to keep the College solvent.

When Capel was apparently threatened with liquidation, Estcourt declared:

> If Capel had got into his difficulties solely by undertaking the College at the wish of the Bishops; and if he had carried it on in a business like way, and on sound principles, we should be inclined to have more sympathy with him.[69]

Ullathorne himself pointed out that when he had been asked about appointing Capel, 'I expressed an opinion that he might be tried, provided he gave up his own school, and devoted the whole man to the work, which he never did'.[70] However, in order to avoid the scandal of a public trial, the bishops eventually decided to settle Capel's claims for damages; Manning contributed £3,000 and the other bishops, except one, another £1,000. Apart from Manning, the other English bishops had never shown much interest in the College and Ullathorne himself concluded,

> In short I have in all ways kept aloof from it, and have never given a vote on any of its business, although I have been unavoidably present when Mgr Capel read his Annual Report, and I once asked him two questions, simply that the answers might show that the College could not go on.[71]

Wilfrid Ward who was a student at the College complained of the ignorance of some of his contemporaries who did not even know how to spell, though he also reported that there were several capable men and that he himself had enjoyed an intense and stimulating intellectual life during his time there. But far more serious, as Ward himself explained, were some of the other unfortunate consequences of Manning's policy:

> In cutting me and other Catholics off from the Universities – and it was mainly my father's influence on Manning which led to our exclusion from Oxford and Cambridge – the ecclesiastical authorities

cut off in some cases the most natural avenues to healthy ambition. Also they cut off a ready-made groove – a serious drawback to those who though capable of hard work in a recognized profession were not fitted to invent a line of work in some new direction. Danger to faith and morals was the motive assigned against our going to Oxford. I do not deny that such danger existed – it exists everywhere. But the question is whether danger of this kind is not far greater if one's life is put out of joint and many influences are removed which help one to work with an inspiring purpose in life. So far as I can judge of my own case I could not have realized the arguments against the Christian and Catholic faith more keenly than I did had I lived for years at a University and had many agnostics among my friends and teachers. As far as morals went nothing could have been worse than the absence of a congenial and normal career, the sense of having no inspiring object in life.[72]

When Vaughan succeeded Manning in 1892, the new Archbishop was faced with an unenviable situation. An increasing number of Catholics were attending the universities in spite of official discouragements and were deprived of pastoral care because of ecclesiastical policy. It is not clear whether Catholics who wanted to go to Oxford or Cambridge were in fact put off by the official ban. Between 1867 and 1887, about 50 Catholics matriculated at Oxford and over 100 between 1887 and 1894. Individual bishops were prepared to give dispensations and on one occasion, the Pope himself allowed a young man to go to Cambridge and expressed the hope that he would prove a credit to the university; the local bishop was 'absolutely rabid'.[73] Another significant factor might have been that by 1890, it was generally believed that Oxford was less dangerous than it had seemed twenty five years before; both Oxford and Cambridge appeared friendlier to religion between 1885 and 1895 than during the previous twenty years.

In February, 1893, the curator of the archaeological museum in Cambridge, Anatole von Hügel, attended a papal audience dressed in his Cambridge hood and gown; he presented an address and a gift to the Pope from the undergraduates of Cambridge University who, according to the ecclesiastical authorities, were not supposed to exist. Von Hügel then went on to organize a strong petition from the influential and interested Catholic clergy and laity asking that the question should be reopened. Not all the bishops, however, were convinced that the situation had changed and even Vaughan himself seems to have shared their feeling that he was in danger of submitting to a powerful pressure group.[74] The voting was close, but in January, 1895, the bishops decided to ask the Roman authorities to allow Catholics to attend the older universities; several resolutions were drawn up and approved by Leo XIII. In the following year, the bishops announced in accordance with instructions from Propaganda the appointment of Catholic chaplains and the formation of a Universities Board to finance special conferences for the Catholic undergraduates, 'in which Philosophy, History and Religion shall be treated with such amplitude and solidity as to furnish effectual protection against false and erroneous teaching'.[75]

On Manning's death, Anatole's more famous brother, Baron Friedrich von Hügel, complained that the late Cardinal had left English Catholics without any real guidance in dealing with the intellectual problems of the time.[76] The same complaint might equally well have been made against Vaughan who was unfamiliar and did not sympathize with intellectual difficulties. Vaughan's attitude was essentially negative, defensive or simply apologetic. Following the publication of *Providentissimus Deus* and as a result of reading a memorandum from von Hügel, Vaughan advised the Holy Office against issuing any 'Instruction' on the practical implications of the encyclical. Again, when the Holy Office stated that the authenticity of the 'Three Heavenly Witnesses' or the Johannine Comma could not be questioned or safely denied, Vaughan ascertained for practical rather than academic reasons that this decision was not intended to close discussion or to affect the findings of biblical criticism. Nevertheless, Vaughan's faith in ecclesiastical decisions was unquestioning. When it was reported that the Holy Office was about to condemn the theory of evolution, Vaughan apparently told von Hügel that he should be grateful for any light which might be thrown on the subject.[77]

In spite of the difficulties created by earlier theological controversies, some English Catholics in the years before the Modernist crisis were able to respond positively and confidently in dealing with biblical problems. It was still possible to discuss biblical problems in an academic and friendly way, and the solution of technical problems was not necessarily considered to be a manifestation of 'orthodox' or 'heretical' opinions. This can be seen in Bishop Clifford's discussion of the book of Genesis in the *Dublin Review* or in Ryder's correspondence with von Hügel which showed that both men, if in different degrees, accepted the results of scientific and historical criticism, and appreciated the writings of Loisy.[78] In 1892, Gasquet also praised Loisy and compared English Catholic scholars unfavourably with him. Von Hügel succeeded in persuading Vaughan to write to Loisy and the Cardinal later invited him to lecture to the Catholic undergraduates in Cambridge.[79] However it became increasingly difficult to engage in academic scholarship, not only because of scientific or historical developments, but as a result of the attitudes and decisions of the ecclesiastical authorities on the local as well as the universal level. Thus, although Ryder signed the appeal to Vaughan and the bishops of the province opposing Mivart's article 'Happiness in Hell', he did not altogether approve of the subsequent condemnation.[80]

In 1884, a writer in the *Irish Ecclesiastical Record* had denied that an orthodox Catholic could accept the theory of evolution. In the following year, Mivart replied with an article which claimed that a scientist, as in Galileo's case, might have a better understanding of scripture than the ecclesiastical authorities. Having thus reduced the significance of the Roman Congregations without being censured, Mivart turned his attention to reducing the horrors of hell which he did in three further articles also published in the *Nineteenth Century* during 1892 and 1893. These articles, however, were put on the Index, though Mivart immediately submitted on the grounds that the wording did not condemn any of his propositions. The publication of *Providentissimus Deus* in 1893 was a far more significant event from Mivart's point of view; some Catholics who had accepted Mivart's theory of physical as distinct from psychical evolution were forced to retract and Mivart himself came to the conclusion that 'Catholic doctrine and science were fatally at variance'.[81]

When the new edition of the Index published in 1899 still included his articles, Mivart asked which propositions were being questioned and when this information was refused, he withdrew his submission. Mivart also denounced the Roman Congregations and called for some modification in the force of the doctrine of infallibility in view of the obvious 'errors' which the Church had committed in the controversies between science and religion. Finally, Mivart demanded from Vaughan, as owner of the *Tablet*, an apology for certain remarks which had been made about him, but was instead presented with a Profession of Faith which he refused to sign. Mivart continued to demand a suitable apology for the attacks published in the *Tablet*, but Vaughan was primarily concerned with his theological views and so in the course of their correspondence, Mivart turned his attention to some of the issues raised by the Cardinal.

Mivart accused Vaughan of not having read the articles he was prepared to condemn and maintained that he did not question the fact or doctrine, but discussed the mode or nature of the Incarnation and the Resurrection.[82] When Vaughan simply repeated for 'a third and last time' his demand for Mivart's submission, the scientist replied by asking what was the dogmatic force of *Providentissimus Deus* and whether a belief in the divine authorship of the Bible necessarily equated inspiration with inerrancy.[83] Vaughan's personal impatience with intellectual difficulties was reflected in his reply:

> Let me first of all urge you to plant your feet down upon the firm and fundamental principle, which is the ground on which every true Catholic stands; viz. that the Church, being the Divine Teacher established by Christ in the world, rightly claims from her disciples a hearty and intellectual acceptance of all that she authoritatively teaches. This principle, given us by Our Lord — will carry you safely over all objections and difficulties that may spring up along your path. It was applied by St Augustine to his acceptance of the Scripture where he says, 'Ego vero Evangelio non crederem, nisi me Catholicae Ecclesiae commoveret auctoritas'. But if you are going to give the assent of Faith only to such doctrines as present no difficulties beyond the power of your finite intelligence to see through and solve by direct answer, you must put aside at once all the mysteries of faith; and you must frankly turn yourself into a rationalist pure and simple. You then constitute your own ability to solve difficulties, intellectual or scientific, into your test of the doctrines proposed for your acceptance. This is to return to the old protestant system of private judgment, or to open rationalism and unbelief. But you will let me I hope be frank and urge that it is your moral rather than your intellectual nature that needs attention. God gives His grace to the humble, it is 'the clean of heart' who 'shall see God'. Let me press upon you the primary necessity of humility and of preserving prayer for light and grace.[84]

In answer to Mivart's specific questions, Vaughan simply referred to *Providentissimus Deus*, recommended the works of Franzelin and Hummelauer, and suggested that he might have a word with Tyrrell or Clarke. This rather unhelpful approach might explain why in replying, two days later, Mivart again explained his intellectual and religious position at some length. Vaughan's correspondence illustrates the fact that in spite of a genuine sincerity and kindness, which Mivart himself recognized, the Cardinal lacked the ability, or perhaps more significantly the attitude, which might have been able to help.[85] Furthermore, Mivart believed that Vaughan was restricted in his theological approach by the doctrine of infallibility which would 'eat away' the substance of the Church and reduce it to a 'mouldering, repulsive skeleton', if it was not 'explained away by learned and dexterous Catholic theologians'.[86] Vaughan then issued a circular letter in which he claimed that whereas Mivart

> has declared, or at least seemed to declare, that it is permissible for Catholics to hold certain heresies – regarding the virginal birth of Our Lord and the perpetual virginity of the Blessed Virgin; the gospel account of the resurrection and the immunity of the sacred body from corruption; the reality and transmission of original sin; the redemption of a real satisfaction for the sins of men; the everlasting punishment of the wicked; the inspiration and integrity of Holy Scripture; the right of the Catholic church to interpret the sense of Scripture with authority; her perpetual retention of her doctrines in the same sense; not to speak of other false propositions . . .[87]

he was declared suspect of heresy and denied the sacraments until such time as he proved his orthodoxy.

The strongest reactions to these events not unnaturally came from those who would later be involved in the Modernist crisis. At Wilfrid Ward's suggestion, Vaughan had previously advised Mivart to seek Tyrrell's help. After the condemnation, Tyrrell commented, 'How horrid all this about Mivart. It will throw everything back a decade and leave the Ark of God in the hands of the Philistines'. Wilfrid Ward was afraid that the ecclesiastical authorities were not 'alive to the real difficulties of the situation . . . they will inevitably tend to identify one form of liberalism with the other, and meet the situation by sheer intolerance'. Von Hügel thought it was necessary for Vaughan to take some action, but wished that he might

> have been slower in taking the last step; that Mivart could have been given a more general and simpler formulary; and, above all, that the Cardinal could have had official and quasi-official interpretations of a more persuasive and helpful kind to offer for Mivart's assistance, than the 'Providentissimus' Encyclical, and Cardinal Franzelin's treatise.[88]

By this time, the methods of the Holy Office had also aroused a good deal of public criticism. There was a long correspondence in the *Weekly Register* on 'A Plea for Habeas Corpus in the Church' and the Catholic Union of Great Britain protested against the tone of the *Osservatore Romano* when it was dealing with English and other affairs.

Merry del Val reacted strongly:

> The action of the Catholic Union is as foolish as it is deplorable.
> No doubt the utterances quoted from the Osservatore are objection-
> able, but how much more of the same sort of thing has been written
> and said all over Europe and even in England! See a specimen in the
> enclosed number of the Opinione, Rudini's paper, the moderate,
> *liberal-conservative* organ. One could easily quote any number of
> other papers, anti-clerical, that write in the same tone. Yet Steed
> does not say a word of this in the Times, nor does any one dream of
> protesting, here or in England. It is reserved to the Duke of Norfolk
> and to the Catholic Union to accentuate divergent feelings and
> divisions between Catholics, by taking formal action, to the great
> delight of the anti-religious parties here and of Protestants in England.
> The declaration on the last page of the Gazette reveals the spirit
> which is at the bottom of all this. It certainly reads like Lilley and is
> a disgrace to the Union. The arrogance with which they dwell upon
> their superiority is childish and can only call forth contempt. 'They
> dream of restoring a past which is dead and gone and which from the
> nature of things cannot return' (p. 15). Does that mean the temporal
> power, the sovereign independence of the Holy See? If so the sentence
> is worthy of the anti-Catholic papers here, and denotes a strange
> position for the Catholic Union, instituted I believe primarily to
> uphold the rights of the Holy See.[89]

In December, 1900, Cardinal Vaughan and the bishops of the Westminster Province issued a Joint Pastoral Letter on 'The Church and
Liberal Catholicism' – the 'Liberal Catholicism', it would seem, of
Mivart.[90] Both Vaughan and Merry del Val had been concerned at the
extent of the 'liberal' support which Mivart apparently enjoyed:·

> I need hardly say how sadly impressed I am by what you tell me of
> the number of liberal-Catholics, priests and laymen, who would
> refuse to sign the profession of faith you put before Mivart, and
> which as you say contained nothing that is not found in the Creeds,
> etc. I am not surprised for I had suspected the existence of this state
> of things for some time, but it is dreadful to thus see one's worst
> fears confirmed. It is something more than liberal Catholicism,
> though this is bad enough. There is a lot of trouble in store and we
> must be ready to face it bravely. We shall lose a certain number but
> the Church in England will gain by their withdrawal, I am convinced,
> no matter who they are. You do not mention names, but I should
> not be intimidated by anybody in such matters.[91]

The Joint Pastoral now described the nature of ecclesiastical authority in the most extreme and unqualified terms. As God spoke through Christ, He now spoke through the legitimate successors of Saint Peter and the Apostles. The *ecclesia docens* was sharply and clearly distinguished from the *ecclesia discens*. Catholics were not only obliged to accept the truths of faith, but called to an unswerving loyalty and obedience to the non-infallible teaching or ordinary authority of the Church which included the pastoral letters of bishops as well as the decisions of Roman Congregations.

Tyrrell thought that the Pastoral illustrated the bishops' ignorance of contemporary difficulties and he attacked the novel idea of a passive and active body in the Church which would put the Pope above the Church; the Pope would then cease to be considered as part of the Church and would become a partner, a spouse or a Lord 'in a sense proper to Christ alone'.[92] Bishops would be sheared of their proper prerogatives while increasing their power as agents of an infallible pope with unlimited authority. 'The bishops have mounted on metaphors as witches on broomsticks', Tyrrell told von Hügel, 'and have ridden to the devil ... The sheep are brainless, passive; their part is to be led, fed, fleeced and slain for the profit of the shepherd for whose benefit solely they exist'.[93] Tyrrell encouraged Lord Halifax to attack the Joint Pastoral and Wilfrid Ward published an explanation.

According to Ward the Pastoral should be seen in the context of the different functions of the Church and interpreted in the light of the fact that a pastoral teaches Catholic theology rather than contradicts it. There was a distinction between the theologians or doctors of the Church and the bishops who were concerned to defend the faith of the people. But those who needed help in intellectual difficulties were 'more likely to go to the pages of Cardinal Newman than to those of a pastoral, however admirable it may be'.[94] At the same time, Ward himself and some of his correspondents recognized the wider danger that such pastorals might give a false impression to Catholics and non-Catholics alike.

> It is an ungrateful task to be continually protecting those in authority from the consequences of their own utterances — and, after all, *they* do mean what they say, and the average man knows they do, even if he does not accept it as binding upon him to accept it. Worse, I think, is the plan by which their Lordships are induced to put their names to a document with which certainly not all are in perfect accord — this I know to be true of one of the two bishops

whom you name. The fear of giving scandal by refusing to sign leads to the real scandal of signing what one does not *ex animo* accept.

A concern for a narrow uniformity out of a sense of pastoral responsibility or conceived as an apologetic weapon became almost typical of English Catholics as a result of the example of leaders like Vaughan who was rigid and ruthless with himself as well as others and in every sphere of life, intellectual, administrative or devotional. Archbishop Mathew described Vaughan's mind as vigorous and clear rather than complex or original; secure in the application of his principles, he could not circumvent nor, it may be added, could he compromise.[95] Even his sympathetic biographer admitted that he was so disciplined 'that in the end personal claims seemed to forget to assert themselves'. He advised his father during his last illness that he was free to use morphia, though he added, 'if I were you, I should stick to the Cross'. In later life, Vaughan himself used a vicious spiked bracelet on his arm as a means of mortification.[96]

Vaughan's aims were apologetic or pastoral rather than scholarly or philanthropic. In 1868, he had founded the Catholic Truth Society which was successfully revived in 1884 and within four years there were branches in America and Canada, Australia and New Zealand, India and Africa, the West Indies and British Guiana. He was also involved in the work of the Converts Aid Society and associated with the Catholic Evidence apostolate, while his last project was the formation of an apologetic and pastoral society of priests which eventually became the Catholic Missionary Society. Yet it would be unfair to criticize Vaughan too strongly for his narrow apologetic concern. A convinced minority finds it difficult to resist the temptation of unduly indulging in self-justification and this becomes almost impossible when there is a real practical need to do so. Vaughan had to struggle continually with internal difficulties which resulted from the fact that the administrative system remained unsatisfactory and which also gave rise to apologetic considerations because of the danger of scandals and their effect on the Church's public image.

The story of the conflict between the Bishop of Nottingham and his clergy is too long and complicated to be discussed adequately here, but it illustrates the danger of public scandal and the extent to which the ecclesiastical organization of English Catholics was still far from satisfactory even at the end of the century. The death of one of the canons in 1900 had removed the only moderating influence in the diocese and within a month its administration had become intolerable. The Bishop appointed two of his closest supporters to the chapter. One of these had been publicly discredited during a libel case involving the *Catholic Times* over a scandalous collection of alms and the vicar general who had served the diocese with considerable distinction for over twenty years resigned in protest. The Bishop then filled three key positions with two former religious who had been expelled by their superiors and a secular priest expelled from his own diocese. A series of satirical attacks and anonymous pamphlets now appeared and Vaughan referred the situation to Rome.

Vaughan's dossier included information on those uncanonical intruders found in the pages of the *Catholic Directory* at the end of the nineteenth century. One individual who claimed to have converted a certain duke, presented himself to the Bishop, received orders within a week and was subsequently found never to have been baptized! This inquiry, however, failed to bring about an effective reform of the diocese. Some time later, a priest who had also been discredited for fraudulent begging attempted to use funds intended for an elementary school in order to establish an 'Academy for Young Ladies and Gentlemen'. The former vicar general, as one of the trustees, refused to part with these funds; he was suspended by the bishop and then appealed to Rome. On this occasion, the Bishop resigned, though he was left in charge as administrator until his successor was appointed. During this period, Bagshawe obtained prelacies for the two priests whose quest for alms had caused most of his difficulties and although Vaughan succeeded in having the briefs recalled, the diocese was to suffer from the consequences of Bagshawe's actions for the next ten years.[97]

Troubled with pastoral or apologetic conflicts, the effectiveness of Vaughan's rule was further reduced by illness and he died on the 19 June, 1903. If Vaughan was not a great man, and he does not appear so at least in comparison with his predecessors, he showed some remarkable qualities as a devoted pastor and able administrator. In this respect, he might be considered to have set a pattern for later English bishops who often seem more typical of him than of either Wiseman or Manning. And if this is so, it is surely not unfitting that the exemplar of the future English hierarchy should have been an Ultramontane descendant of an Old Catholic family, who had been a devoted and successful, if uncomplicated, pastor of the Irish in Lancashire.

Notes

1. S. Leslie, *Henry Edward Manning* (London, 1921) 181; V.A. McClelland, *Cardinal Manning* (London, 1962) 217; E.S. Purcell, *Life of Cardinal Manning* (London, 1896) II: 20, 71, 74, 269-70;

J.G. Snead-Cox, *The Life of Cardinal Vaughan* (London, 1910) I: 38, 239-40, 454-7; II: 1-2; M. Ward, *The Wilfrid Wards and the transition* (London, 1934) I: 260-1.

2. *Letters of Herbert Cardinal Vaughan to Lady Herbert of Lea*, ed. S. Leslie (London, 1942) 365; see also 360; D. Milburn, *A History of Ushaw College* (Ushaw, 1964) 176.

3. Vaughan, *Lea Letters* 39.

4. Snead-Cox, *Vaughan* I: 464.

5. Snead-Cox, *Vaughan* II: 3-4.

6. Vaughan, *Lea Letters* 405.

7. A. McCormack, *Cardinal Vaughan* (London, 1966) 231-2; Snead-Cox, *Vaughan* II: 15-18, 21-2.

8. Snead-Cox, *Vaughan* II: 452.

9. Vaughan, *Diary* IV: 8, AAW; see also McCormack, *Vaughan* 177-9; Snead-Cox, *Vaughan* I: 377-83.

10. McCormack, *Vaughan* 179-80; Snead-Cox, *Vaughan* I: 401.

11. McCormack, *Vaughan* 157; Purcell, *Manning* II: 508; Snead-Cox, *Vaughan* I: 332-3.

12. C. Butler, *The Life and Times of Bishop Ullathorne* (London, 1926) II: 188-9.

13. Quoted by M. Gaine, 'The Development of Official Roman Catholic Educational Policy in England and Wales' *Religious Education Drift or Decision*, ed. P. Jebb (London, 1967) 160.

14. *The Synods in English: being the text of the four synods of Westminster*, ed. R.E. Guy (Stratford on Avon, 1886) 268; the statistics are taken from the education census of 1851, T. Murphy, *The Position of the Catholic Church in England and Wales* (London, 1892) 66, 71; see also *Recusant History* II (1972) 253-5.

15. M. Conlon, *St Alban's Blackburn* (Chorley, 1973) 51, 68.

16. Murphy, *Position of the Catholic Church* 73-76, 93.

17. T. Burke, *Catholic History of Liverpool* (Liverpool, 1910) 151; see also 184, 187-8, 190-2, 203-4.

18. McClelland, *Manning* 62.

19. Butler, *Ullathorne* II: 246-7; Leslie, *Manning* 175; see also W.O. Chadwick, *The Victorian Church* (London, 1966-70) II: 191, 299, 302-6.

20. Snead-Cox, *Vaughan* II: 87-99; see also G.A. Beck, ed., *The English Catholics* (London, 1950) 373-85; J. Fitzsimons, ed., *Manning: Anglican and Catholic* (London, 1951) 103-10; McClelland, *Manning* 83 claims that Manning founded the Association, whereas Snead-Cox, McCormack, *Vaughan* 170-1, and Beck, *English Catholics* 26, 165, 379 give the credit to Vaughan.

21. Snead-Cox, *Vaughan* II: 105, 126-7.

22. J. Morris, *Catholic England in Modern Times* (London, 1892) 97.

23. Manning to Lawless, 18 February 1889, LCA Ushaw.

24. Snead-Cox, *Vaughan* I: 403-6.
25. Snead-Cox, *Vaughan* I: 407-18.
26. Snead-Cox, *Vaughan* I: 419-27.
27. Snead-Cox, *Vaughan* I: 428-33.
28. McCormack, *Vaughan* 214; see also Snead-Cox, *Vaughan* I: 436-9, 475.
29. Snead-Cox, *Vaughan* I: 482; see also 476-7, 483; McCormack, *Vaughan* 233, 281-5; Vaughan was generous enough to admit in writing of his differences with Manning, that should he appear to criticize his predecessor, he would be passing censure on himself rather than on Manning.
30. Snead-Cox, *Vaughan* I: 178; see also 104-6, 113; Manning's letter quoted by Purcell, *Manning* II: 364 and his later remarks in *Sermons on Ecclesiastical Subjects* (London, 1870-73) II: 344.
31. Vaughan, *Lea Letters* 89.
32. Vaughan, *Lea Letters* 415.
33. Halifax to Vaughan, 29 September 1896, AAW.
34. Snead-Cox, *Vaughan* II: 173.
35. Snead-Cox, *Vaughan* II: 226-7.
36. Snead-Cox, *Vaughan* II: 174-5; see also Moyes to Vaughan, 4 May 1896, and the letters to Vaughan from Bishop Macdonald, Archbishops MacEvilly and Eyre, and Cardinal Logue, AAW.
37. Merry del Val to Vaughan, Christmas [1902?] AAW.
38. Merry del Val to Vaughan, 10, 11, 13 January 1900, AAW.
39. Acton to Stonor, 24 July 1893, AAW.
40. Merry del Val to Vaughan, 15, 22 June 1896, AAW.
41. Merry del Val to Vaughan, 2 June 1896, AAW.
42. Merry del Val to Vaughan, 29 November 1896, AAW.
43. Moyes to Vaughan, 19 June 1896, AAW.
44. Moyes to Vaughan, 23 March 1896, AAW.
45. J.J. Hughes, *Absolutely Null and Utterly Void An account of the Papal Condemnation of Anglican Orders 1896* (London, 1968) 305-6; for Halifax's reply see 'Archbishops of Westminster and the Reunion Movement during the nineteenth century' *One in Christ* VIII (1972) 66-7.
46. Ward, *Wards and Transition* I: 294; see also 289-90, 293-6; M. de la Bedoyere, *The Life of Baron von Hügel* (London, 1951) 91-2, 95-6; Hughes, *Null and Void* 199, 234-7.
47. Snead-Cox, *Vaughan* II: 298.
48. J.B. Gwatkin, *A Study of the Life and Role of Peter Le Page Renouf* (unpublished mss.) 60.
49. H.E. Manning, *Miscellanies* (London, 1877-88) I: 65-6, 71.
50. Ward, *Wards and Transition* I: 265; see also Butler, *Ullathorne* II: 9; W. Ward, *The Life of John Henry Cardinal Newman* (London, 1912) II: 66.

51. Butler, *Ullathorne* II: 304.
52. Purcell, *Manning* II: 208; Butler, *Ullathorne* II: 10-12; V.A. McClelland, *English Roman Catholics and Higher Education* (Oxford, 1973) 210-215.
53. Vaughan to Talbot, 6 May [1867], Archives of the English College Rome, partly quoted by M. Trevor, *Newman Light in Winter* (London, 1962) 426.
54. Snead-Cox, *Vaughan* I: 469; Butler, *Ullathorne* II: 37, 304.
55. Leslie, *Manning* 186.
56. Vaughan to Manning, 10 April 1867, copy BOA; partly quoted by McClelland, *Manning* 99; see also Purcell, *Manning* II: 300-1; Vaughan's claims were apparently accepted in Rome; he distinguished Manning and a few of his friends who looked to the Holy See from the other English Bishops who were weak and timid, though good and devoted to their work; Vaughan also reported that Manning was all powerful at Propaganda and would be granted whatever he asked even though the other English Bishops might oppose it. When the Pope defended Newman as one who was willing to obey, Vaughan referred to his 'unretracted' article in the *Rambler* 'about the sensus fidelium' as proof that he was unreliable; yet Manning had known for years that Newman was under the impression that this issue had been settled; Trevor, *Light in Winter* 400; Ward, *Newman* II: 170.
57. *The Letters and Diaries of John Henry Newman*, ed. C.S. Dessain (London, 1961-) XXIII: 230; see also XXIV: 79.
58. *Letters and Diaries* XXIII: 127. 137; Ward, *Newman* II: 543-4.
59. Vaughan to Manning, 10 April 1867, BOA partly quoted by Trevor, *Light in Winter* 399; see also *Letters and Diaries* XXIII: 139, 202; Butler, *Ullathorne* II: 23-6; Purcell, *Manning* II: 312-14; Ward, *Newman* II: 143-4.
60. Butler, *Ullathorne* II: 26-7.
61. *Letters and Diaries* XXIII: 136-7, 139, 141, 149, 156, 162.
62. McClelland, *Higher Education* 223-4; but see also *Letters and Diaries* XXIII: 390.
63. *Letters and Diaries* XXIII: 296, 312, 357.
64. Purcell, *Manning* II: 303; see also Butler, *Ullathorne* II: 33-4; Leslie, *Manning* 145-6; Milburn, *Ushaw College* 279; W. Ward, *The Life and Times of Cardinal Wiseman* (London, 1900) II: 419; Manning also encouraged the Academia originally established by Wiseman, but even this declined during the 1880s, McClelland, *Manning* 126-8.
65. McClelland, *Higher Education* 175; see also 248-9, 269-75.
66. Chadwick, *Victorian Church* II: 454; McClelland, *Higher Education* 353.

67. Ward, *Newman* II: 198.
68. Mivart to Newman, 12 March 1884, BOA.
69. Estcourt to Ullathorne, 18 January 1879, Archives of the Archbishop of Birmingham (AAB); see also Arnold and Co. to Ullathorne, 26 May 1879, AAB; McClelland, *Manning* 118-23; *Higher Education* 314-16, 319-20.
70. Ullathorne to Estcourt, 17 January 1879, AAB; see also McClelland, *Higher Education* 330.
71. Ullathorne to Estcourt, 17 January 1879, AAB.
72. Ward, *Wards and Transition* I: 76-7; see also 46-8.
73. McClelland, *Higher Education* 379; see also Chadwick, *Victorian Church* II: 457; Snead-Cox, *Vaughan* II: 80-5.
74. McClelland, *Higher Education* 382-4, 407.
75. An Instruction from the Archbishop and Bishops of the Province of Westminster, 1 August 1896.
76. Ward, *Wards and Transition* I: 205.
77. L.F. Barmann, *Baron Friedrich von Hügel and the Modernist Crisis in England* (Cambridge, 1972) 71; Bedoyere, *von Hügel* 76, 79, 120; Snead-Cox, *Vaughan* II: 398-402.
78. von Hügel to Ryder, 23 November, 6, 15, December 1892, BOA.
79. Bedoyere, *von Hügel* 74, 88; but see also 133.
80. Ryder was asked by the Bishop of Birmingham to reply to this article in a letter dated 21 December 1892, BOA; in an undated address on 'Higher Criticism and Catholic Orthodoxy', Ryder criticized one of Mivart's earlier articles and praised Gore in *Lux Mundi* by comparison.
81. J.W. Gruber, *A Conscience in Conflict* (New York, 1960) 189; see also 'Newman and Mivart' *Clergy Review* L (1965) 863-7.
82. Mivart to Vaughan, 14 January 1900, AAW; part of this correspondence was reprinted in the *Times* and this source was used by Gruber.
83. Vaughan to Mivart, 16 January 1900; Mivart to Vaughan, 19 January 1900, AAW.
84. Vaughan to Mivart, 21 January 1900, AAW.
85. See also 'English Catholicism from Wiseman to Bourne' *Clergy Review* LXI (1976) 112-13.
86. Mivart to Vaughan, 27 January 1900, AAW.
87. Gruber, *Conscience in Conflict* 209-10; see also *Tablet* 95 (1900) 5-7, 62, 99, 126.
88. Ward, *Wards and Transition* I: 323-4, 326; see also, 360; Barmann, *von Hügel* 75-7; J. Ratté, *Three Modernists* (London, 1968) 163, 253.
89. Merry del Val to Vaughan, not dated, AAW.
90. *Tablet* 97 (1901) 8-12, 50-52; see also 5-6, 441.

91. Merry del Val to Vaughan, not dated, AAW; see also 'Cardinal Raphael Merry del Val' *Catholic Historical Review* LX (1974) 55-64.
92. Ratté, *Three Modernists* 181.
93. Barmann, *von Hügel* 151.
94. Ward, *Wards and Transition* II: 140, 143.
95. D. Mathew, *Catholicism in England* (London, 1955) 222.
96. Snead-Cox, *Vaughan* I: 370; II: 373, 451.
97. I must again express my gratitude to Canon Sweeney whose researches provide the material for this summary.

Lord Acton

Conclusion: Prospect and retrospect: An English spring?

Criticisms of the attitudes and the policies adopted by English Catholics during the nineteenth century are not new. In 1884, Mivart put forward several reasons to explain why the hopes for the conversion of England expressed at the time of the Restoration of the Hierarchy had not been realized. He pointed to the inevitable tendency of a minority to merge within the majority; to the indiscreet actions of continental Catholics, 'an insolent and aggressive faction' which aroused an intense and widespread opposition; to the rejection of English customs and national characteristics and the adoption of strange and new practices, especially 'Italianisms'; to the lack of an educated clergy and laity, particularly in the fields of history and science; to the absence of laymen who might help the clergy in their difficulties, particularly with their financial problems.[1]

In the early 1890s, Thomas Murphy made some further pertinent criticisms in spite of continuing to profess what must have seemed increasingly dated and curious sentiments.[2] The fundamental mistakes, he claimed, had been to imagine that England would soon be converted and the attempt to establish the normal pattern of institutional ecclesiastical organization in what was still, from the Catholic point of view, a missionary country. One result of this was that cathedrals and churches had sometimes been built in remote hamlets, whereas missionary centres were occasionally lacking even in quite densely populated areas. Many people especially in Wales knew nothing about Catholicism simply because there was no local church which might have been built if the available resources had not been recklessly lavished elsewhere. The expansion of colleges and seminaries was seen as another example of an extravagant use of limited supplies of finance and manpower. Consequently, dioceses and parishes were short of money or in debt, few Catholic chapels or churches were consecrated because of their debts, while Catholics in some towns of considerable size were still unable to go to Mass on Sundays. Murphy proposed that the rural parochial structure which demanded the presence of a priest who was frequently over-worked at week ends and often under-employed during the rest of the week should be replaced by the establishment of communities of priests and missionary catechists.

The point that, from the Roman Catholic point of view, England was essentially a missionary country was accepted by Pope Leo XIII at the end of the nineteenth century when he discussed the practical measures which might help the conversion of the country. He expressed the opinion 'that just as one could not call upon the Eastern missions to help England, so was it unsuitable to expect English Catholics who have millions of heathens and heretics to evangelize, to dedicate their means to religious interests outside the country'.[3] The Pope himself promised to co-operate with all the means in his power and suggested that all ecclesiastical collections for Catholic causes outside England including Peter's Pence, should be reduced or used to provide funds for converts or churches, schools and seminaries. He proposed to encourage religious orders and congregations who might send men and money to establish houses in England and also suggested that greater efforts should be made to provide higher education for the clergy. The shortage of priests imposed restrictions on the time which students spent in study and preparation, while the priests themselves were so over-worked and burdened with financial responsibilities that they had little time for scholarly or apologetic activities.

By the turn of the century, however, some English Catholics were to be found playing their part in public life and were increasingly treated with respect, though Catholics in general were still isolated from the rest of the community and had clearly failed to provide for all their administrative, pastoral and educational needs. When Lord Ripon became a Catholic in 1874, the *Times* declared that his conversion was a renunciation of moral and mental freedom, and evidence of fatal demoralization; a statesman who became a Roman Catholic forfeited the confidence of the English people. Yet when Ripon became Viceroy of India only six years later, the newspapers remained calm. Acton was raised to the peerage in 1869 and Lord Llandaff became the first Catholic cabinet minister in 1886. In May, 1887, Queen Victoria received a papal envoy at her jubilee and in November of the same year, she sent the Duke of Norfolk to assure the Pope of her friendship and respect. Fr Bernard Vaughan became a personal friend of King Edward VII who was the first reigning sovereign to visit the Pope since the Reformation.[4]

Several reasons help to explain why Englishmen were demonstrating increasing respect for the Roman Catholic Church. One of the most important was the social work done by the religious communities, both male and female, which were growing steadily in number. By 1900, there were 33 male and 49 female religious communities in the Archdiocese of Westminster, 22 and 42 respectively in Birmingham, 17 and 14 in Clifton, and 17 and 35 in Hexham. Manning's social and political attitudes had helped to thrust Roman Catholicism into the public life of the nation. Newman's *Apologia* was instrumental in convincing Protestant Englishmen that the Catholic Church cared for truth, that Roman priests might be human, English and large-hearted, and that it was possible to become a Roman Catholic without insulting or condemning the Church of England; when Newman became a Cardinal, the leading journal of the Church of England invited subscriptions for his portrait.[5]

Nevertheless, Roman Catholicism remained unpopular as a result of the activities of Irish nationalists, the continuing prejudice of 'no popery' and an intellectual contempt for Ultramontane developments; Englishmen did not welcome the definition of papal infallibility, the condemnation of Anglican Orders and Modernism, nor did they sympathize with Ultramontane attitudes to devotions and pilgrimages, relics and miracles. For their part not many English Catholics became involved in the political life of the country, except on specifically 'Catholic' issues such as education, while the immigrants tended to concentrate on Irish politics. Even during the twentieth century, assimilation resulted from the breakdown of religious and social isolation, rather than from any conscious or positive action. The forces of anti-Catholicism declined with increasing religious apathy, the general acceptance of Catholic public figures and more recently with the development of the ecumenical movement. Several factors contributed to the greater assimilation of Catholics and the decline of that sense of belonging to a specifically 'Catholic' community which became evident after the second World War. With the acceptance of Irish independence, the only remaining nationalist issue was that of partition, while a period of social and economic prosperity coupled with developments in education helped to create a generation of middle class Catholics who enjoyed increased social mobility, with more frequent intermarriage with other Christians.

The earlier emphasis on Catholic separation or isolation from English society became evident in the attitudes of the ecclesiastical authorities towards Catholic marriages and Catholic education as religious obligations to preserve the faith of Catholic children. Such apologetic and pastoral considerations help to explain the attitude of a bishop in the north of England who by equating attendance at non-Catholic schools with educating Catholic children in a non-Catholic religion, presumed to deny their parents the sacraments. The same bishop was notoriously unwilling to grant Catholics the necessary dispensations to marry non-Catholics — a policy which had unhappy results both for those who obeyed and those who did not. The 'new curate' was previously concerned with establishing a Catholic environment to encourage Catholic friendships with a view to Catholic marriages. His successors, however, are far more concerned with the value or validity of Catholic education and the viability of parochial structures when many Catholics, partly at least as a result of social and economic developments, seem in danger of losing any sense of being a real local community. Furthermore, during the nineteenth century, Catholic priests were immediately and obviously 'relevant' as pastoral and social workers for a religious and immigrant community. The contemporary priest, on the other hand, needs to find another and more theological justification for his role; he is in danger of finding himself no longer the religious and often secular leader of the local Catholic community, and not yet simply the president of the Eucharistic Assembly.

Practical problems, however, cannot be divorced from ideological considerations. Abbot Butler was too optimistic when he concluded in 1925 that Bishop Ullathorne — better than Wiseman, Newman or Manning — represented the progressive form of the old Challoner English Catholicism which had maintained itself and was still predominantly the Catholicism of English Catholics.[6] Historical developments and more specifically Irish immigration and the progress of Ultramontanism ultimately brought about fundamental changes in the character of English Catholicism. Butler was also impressed by the prudence, moderation and justice of the Roman authorities when dealing with English Catholics during the nineteenth century and to some extent this is undoubtedly fair as a few of the points made by Bishop Grant on the restoration of the hierarchy might indicate;

> In this case, then, [the colleges] as in every other, the Holy See wishes us to feel that the future well-being of our Colleges and of our missions and the effectual management and distribution of our resources will rest with ourselves ... It is clear that upon all these points [canonical processes] the Holy See wishes us to consider all our local interests and wants and to provide rules for our peculiar necessities. In the Brief of Erection there is a special promise that the Authority of the Sovereign Pontiff will be afforded to the Bishops in carrying out measures that may be framed in the spirit of the Canons for our special difficulties.

But the underlying Ultramontane trend was reflected by Grant himself on the same occasion when he wrote:

> Canonists ought to be educated in Rome . . . it is in that city that
> the supreme courts of the Church exist . . . Educated in the Roman
> schools and under the shadow of the Apostolic Chair, many learned
> men will arise, whose pupils and followers will shed the light of their
> knowledge upon a future generation.[7]

Although English bishops frequently adopted unhappy policies as a
consequence of instructions from Rome, the Roman authorities cannot
always be held responsible even on some of these occasions. Vaughan,
for example, successfully won Roman approval for reversing his predecessors' policies which, sometimes as a result of English influence,
had previously been approved by Rome. It would seem that 'Rome'
could be used in the nineteenth century in much the same way as it is
today, as an added reason for adopting a policy personally supported
by the bishop or bishops concerned. On the other hand, the attempt to
mould the English, or the French and the German churches on the
pattern of Rome was certainly not discouraged by the Roman authorities.
The Ultramontanes and then the Integrists might not have won every
appeal to Rome, but they were often able to use Roman authority to
the full. Consequently, although English Catholics had their own
peculiar problems as members of an immigrant or missionary community,
the history of the Church in England during the nineteenth century
cannot be isolated from the wider ecclesiastical history of the period
and English Catholicism was dominated by the development of Ultramontane Catholicism throughout the world.

The political attitudes of bishops like Vaughan and especially
members of the Irish hierarchy illustrate the complications which
resulted from the Catholic 'reaction' to liberalism. It became difficult
to campaign effectively for social and political justice in Ireland for
example, while supporting the Pope against the Italian nationalists.
This was a particular problem for Manning who originally opposed
Home Rule and was later criticized for failing to appreciate that those
who supported the disestablishment of the Irish Church belonged to the
irreligious party which opposed Catholic teaching on the union of
Church and State! The *Syllabus of Errors* had condemned some of the
hopes of the Irish bishops and in 1868, the *Dublin Review* was hostile
to the links between Irish Catholics and English Liberals or Dissenters.
The controversy occasioned by Gladstone's attack on the *Vatican
Decrees* helped to confirm Cardinal Cullen in his belief that Irish
Catholicism was incompatible with Gladstonian Liberalism. Roman

policies were apparently more important than the solution of Irish grievances and the Ultramontane cardinal refused to work with the Liberal politician.[8]

Butler also suggested that at the time he was writing, Newman would have been allowed the necessary academic freedom which he was so obviously denied and that his intellectual powers would have been used as he wished in the service of the Church. But Butler ignores the fact that as a result of the 'Modernist crisis', he himself had learned to avoid critical questions and he is also forced to admit that during the nineteenth century English Catholics were concerned with intellectual as well as practical issues, whereas his contemporary coreligionists were chiefly engaged on practical rather than intellectual activities.[9]

It would be impossible to give an adequate account of the development of 'Modernism' in the present context where the point of interest inevitably focuses on the divergent careers of Tyrrell and von Hügel. The 'Modernists' included philosophers and theologians, biblical critics and historians, social and political liberals, and critics of popular Catholicism and the institutional Church. Modernism was not a movement and the Modernists were not a homogeneous group. Several of those involved could more accurately be described as Liberal Catholics, while others were not only moderate, but even scholastically orthodox in their doctrinal beliefs. On the whole, the so-called Modernist movement is probably better seen as a series of distinct attempts, some more successful than others, to reconcile Catholicism with contemporary developments in the social, political and especially the intellectual world.

When the English hierarchy sent a joint letter of loyal submission to the Pope following the publication of *Pascendi* in 1907, Merry del Val commented on:

> one sentence which does not come very opportunely just now, I mean where it is said that there is little or nothing of modernism amongst English Catholics ... though there are not many English Modernists, there is quite a sufficient number of them, of *different grades*, in proportion to the comparatively limited number of English Catholics, clerical or lay, who are in a position to discuss such matters.[10]

Merry del Val's fears and suspicions of English Liberal Catholicism at the turn of the century could easily have been reinforced from other and sometimes rather unexpected sources.

When Newman had died in 1890, the *Weekly Register* published some revealing obituary verses by the poet Francis Thompson:

When our high Church's builders planned
To re-erect within the land
　　The ruined edifice
　　What was the builder's price?

Stern was the toil, the profits slow,
The struggling wall would scantly grow:
　　What way to expedite?
　　Men had of old a rite!

Into the wall that would not thrive
He gave him to be built alive,
　　A human sacrifice —
　　And lo! the walls uprise.[11]

Thompson, himself acquainted with several of the Modernists, complained in a manuscript entitled *An Enemy hath done this*:

> We are too much given to thinking that the Almighty, getting tired of His slow way of teaching, came down suddenly from heaven and finished off the whole of revelation in a neat and complete little compendium, with His Holiness the Pope as perpetual editor, to keep it up to date like an encyclopaedia . . . all was said and completed — needing just a trifling definition from a general council or so: there was nothing more left but for all mankind to get to Heaven as fast as they could, now that the way was entirely surveyed and mapped out for them.

After Tyrrell was dismissed from the Jesuits and suspended from the priesthood, he himself became increasingly disillusioned with what he called 'Vaticanism' or 'Romanism' and he identified his own experience with that of Döllinger at the first Vatican Council. Like Acton, Tyrrell began to feel that the principle of Ultramontanism was un-Christian or immoral. The Ultramontanes seemed to believe that there was no alternative between an ecclesiastical dictatorship or the anarchy of individualism. Tyrrell, for his part, associated himself with Acton, Döllinger and even Newman in supporting the supremacy of the whole Church over popes, bishops and councils; authority was not something external to or above the Church, but derived from the living Church as a whole.

Von Hügel, on the other hand, was opposed to the Liberal Catholicism which he associated with Döllinger and Acton; he expressed his gratitude for the definition of 1870 and preferred to identify himself with

Newman and Ryder whom he described as Ultramontane in the old sense and members of the centre party.[12] Von Hügel was not tempted to revolt from the Church of Rome to which he was so deeply attached, in spite of what he suffered at the time of the Modernist crisis. He remained vividly conscious of the spiritual tradition and sacramental life of Catholicism, and aware of the sanctity within the Church. In due course, von Hügel accepted the condemnation of Modernism and became increasingly critical of those he had previously supported. He later distinguished between the attempt to reform the Church and reinterpret the faith during the first decade of the twentieth century, from the perpetual and continuing need for modernization. The particular attempt by the Modernists failed, according to von Hügel, not only because it was condemned by the ecclesiastical authorities, but also because of the scepticism and anarchy within the movement itself. Some time later, von Hügel explained:

> I have, then, for myself come less and less to believe in any and every Minimistic Catholicism or Diminished Papalism. Not the Nationalistic Councils of Constance and Basle, still less the already largely rampant *solipsism* of a William of Occham, do I believe should be our guides. Even the real devoutness of some of the men I have personally known who more or less regretted the elimination of those nationalistic and individualist movements from out of the Church, did not, in the long run, succeed in winning me to such centrifugal activity. We require, I am deeply convinced, a *High* doctrine and temper, not a Low: a High Church (not a Low Church) Catholicism.[13]

But perhaps Newman put it better, more simply and more judiciously when he wrote:

> There is a depth and a power in the Catholic religion, a fulness of satisfaction in its creed, its theology, its rites, its sacraments, its discipline, a freedom yet a support also ... This is the true secret of the Church's strength, the principle of its indefectibility, and the bond of its indissoluble unity. It is the earnest and the beginning of the repose of Heaven.[14]

Notes

1. 'The Conversion of England' *Dublin Review* XII (1884) 65-86; but see also 358-87 where S.H. Little argues that Mivart exaggerated the 'confident hopes' of Catholics at the time of the Oxford Movement and also complains of the pessimism of the views of Lord Braye who later wrote the preface to Murphy, *Position of the Catholic Church*.
2. Murphy, *Position of the Catholic Church* 5-13, 100-4, 111.
3. Merry del Val to Vaughan, 4 February 1897, AAW.
4. Chadwick, *Victorian Church* II: 405-7.
5. Chadwick, *Victorian Church* II: 409, 415-16, 420, 422.
6. Butler, *Ullathorne* II: 311, 316-17.
7. Notes on the practical consequences of the restoration of the Hierarchy by Thomas Grant, February, 1851, AAW.
8. Norman, *Catholic Church and Ireland* 326, 330, 412-14, 457-60; *Catholic Church and Irish Politics* 29-30.
9. Butler, *Ullathorne* II: 314; Ratté, *Three Modernists* 20.
10. Barmann, *von Hügel* 202.
11. Quoted by B.M. Boardman, 'Francis Thompson: Towards a Reappraisal' *Clergy Review* LXI (1976) 225.
12. M. Nedoncelle, *Baron Friedrich von Hügel* (London, 1936) 136; Ratté, *Three Modernists* 204-10; M. Ward, *William George Ward and the Catholic Revival* (London, 1893) 371.
13. Quoted by T.M. Loome, 'The Enigma of Baron Friedrich von Hügel — as Modernist' *Downside Review* 91 (1973) 223.
14. *Letters and Diaries* XXIV: 25.

Bibliography

Acton, J.E.E.D. *Correspondence of Lord Acton and Richard Simpson.* Edited by Josef L. Atholz, Damian McElrath and James C. Holland. 3 vols (Cambridge, 1971-75).

Essays on Church and State. Edited by Douglas Woodruff (London, 1952).

Essays on Freedom and Power. Edited by Gertrude Himmelfarb (London, 1956).

Ignaz v. Döllinger Briefwechsel mit Lord Acton. Edited by V. Conzemius. 3 vols (Munich, 1963-1970).

Letters from Rome [by 'Quirinus'] (London, 1870).

Lord Acton and His Circle. Edited by Cardinal F.A. Gasquet (London, 1906).

Lord Acton and the first Vatican Council: A. Journal. Edited with an introduction by Edmund Campion (Sydney, 1975).

Selections from the Correspondence of the First Lord Acton. Edited by J.N. Figgis and R.V. Laurence (London, 1917).

Addington, R. (ed) *Faber Poet and Priest Selected Letters by Frederick William Faber* 1833-1863. (Cowbridge and Bridgend, 1974).

Addison, W.G. *Religious Equality in Modern England 1714-1914* (London, 1944)

Allies, M.H. *Thomas William Allies* (London, 1907).

Altholz, J.L. *The Liberal Catholic Movement in England The Rambler and its contributors 1848-1864* (London, 1962).

Amherst, W.J. *The History of Catholic Emancipation and the progress of the Catholic Church in the British Isles (chiefly in England) from 1771 to 1820.* 2 vols (London, 1886).

Anon *Catalogue of the Collection of Relics belonging to St Cuthbert's College, Ushaw.* Preston, 1881.

Anon *The Life of Cornelia Connelly 1809-1879* (London, 1922).

Anon (ed) *Roads to Rome being personal records of some of the more recent converts to the Catholic Faith* (London, 1901).

Anstruther, G.E. *A Hundred Years of Catholic Progress* (London, 1929).

Arnstein, W.L. *The Bradlaugh Case A Study in Late Victorian Opinion and Politics* (Oxford, 1965).

Aspinwall, B. 'Montalembert and Idolatry', *Downside Review,* 89 (1971).

Aveling, J.C.H. *The Handle and the Axe The Catholic Recusants in England from Reformation to Emancipation* (London, 1976).

Aubert, R. *Le Pontificat de Pie IX (1846-1878)* (Paris, 1952).

Barmann, L.F. *Baron Friedrich von Hügel and the Modernist Crisis in England* (Cambridge, 1972).

Beck, G.A. (ed) *The English Catholics 1850-1950* (London, 1950).

Bedoyere, M.de la. *The Life of Baron von Hügel* (London, 1951).

Bellasis, E. *Memorials of Mr Serjeant Ballasis* 1800-1873 (London, 1895).

Berington, J. *Reflections Addressed to the Rev. John Hawkins to which is added an Exposition of Roman Catholic Principles in in Reference to God and the Country* (London, 1785).

Berrington, J. and Kirk, J. *The Faith of Catholics confirmed by Scripture and attested by the Fathers of the five first centuries of the Church* (London, 1813).

    The Faith of Catholics . . . Revised and Greatly Enlarged by James Waterworth. 3 vols (London, 1846).

Best, G. *Mid-Victorian Britain 1851-1875* (London, 1971).

Bettenson, H. (ed) *Documents of the Christian Church* (London, 1944).

Blakiston, N. (ed) *The Roman Question Extracts from the dispatches of Odo Russell from Rome 1858-1870* (London, 1962).

Blehl, V.F. and Connolly, F.X. (ed) *Newman's Apologia: A Classic Reconsidered* (New York, 1964).

Blundell, F.O. *Broughton Catholic Charitable Society. History 1787 to 1922* (Preston, 1923).

Boardman, B.M. 'Francis Thompson: Towards a Reappraisal'. *Clergy Review,* LXI (1976).

Bolster, E. *The Sisters of Mercy in the Crimean War* (Cork, 1964).

Bolton, C.A. *Salford Diocese and its Catholic Past* (Manchester, 1950).

Bossy, J. *The English Catholic Community 1570-1850* (London, 1975).

Bottalla, P. *The Pope and the Church considered in their Mutual Relations Part II The Infallibility of the Pope* (London, 1870).

Bourne, F. (ed) *Catholic Emancipation 1829-1929* (London, 1929).

Bouyer, L. *Newman His Life and Spirituality* (London, 1958).

Bowden, J.W. *The Life and Letters of Frederick William Faber* (London, 1869).

Brady, W. Maziere. *Annals of the Catholic Hierarchy in England and Scotland A.D. 1581-1876* (Rome, 1877).

Briggs, A. *The Age of Improvement 1783-1867* (London, 1960).

Burdett, O. *The Rev. Smith, Sydney* (London, 1934).

Burke, T. *Catholic History of Liverpool* (Liverpool, 1910).

Burtchaell, J.T. *Catholic Theories of Biblical Inspiration since 1810 A Review and Critique* (Cambridge, 1969).

Buscot, W. *The History of Cotton College* (London, 1940).

Butler, C. *The Life and Times of Bishop Ullathorne* 2 vols (London 1926).

The Vatican Council 1869-1870 (London, 1962)

Capes, J.M. *Reasons for returning to the Church of England* (London, 1871).

The Spectre of the Vatican (London, 1876)

To Rome and back (London, 1873).

Carpenter, S.C. *Church and People, 1789-1889* (London, 1933).

Carson, W.R. *Reunion Essays* (London, 1903).

Catchside, P.H. 'Father Gentili and the Restoration of the Hierarchy' *Tablet*, 196 (1950).

Chadwick, W.O. *The Victorian Church.* 2 vols (London, 1966-1970).

Chapman, R. *Father Faber* (London, 1961)

Collingwood, C. *The Catholic Truth Society* (London, 1965).

Conlon, M. *St Alban's, Blackburn 1773-1793 A Study in Two Centuries of Blackburn Catholicism* (Chorley, 1973).

Cross, F.L. *John Henry Newman* (London, 1933).

Culler, A.D. *The Imperial Intellect A Study of Newman's Educational Ideal* (New Haven, 1955).

Cwiekowski, F.J. *The English Bishops and the First Vatican Council* Louvain, 1971).

Dessain, C.S. *John Henry Newman* (London, 1966).

'What Newman Taught in Manning's Church'.

Infallibility in the Church (London, 1968).

Döllinger, J.J. I. Von. *Declarations and Letters on the Vatican Decrees 1869-1887* (Edinburgh, 1891).

The Pope and the Council [by 'Janus'] (London, 1869).

Dupanloup, F.A.P. *The Papal Sovereignty: viewed in its relations to the Catholic Religion and to the Law of Europe* (London, 1860).

Ehler, S.Z. and Morrall, J.B. (ed) *Church and State Through the Centuries A collection of historic documents with commentaries* (London, 1954).

Elliott-Binns, L.E. *Religion in the Victorian Era* (London, 1953).

Ellis, J.T. *American Catholicism* (Chicago, 1955).

Catholics in Colonial America (Baltimore, 1965).

Ensor, R.C.K. *England 1870-1914* (Oxford, 1960).

Faber, F.W. *Devotions to the Pope* (London, 1860).

Hymns (London, 1862).

Faber, F.W. *Notes on Doctrinal and Spiritual Subjects.* 2 vols (London, 1866).

Femiano, S.D. *Infallibility of the Laity The Legacy of Newman* (New York, 1967).

Ferrey, B. *Recollections of A.N. Welby Pugin, and his father, Augustus Pugin: with Notices of their Works* (London, 1861).

Ffoulkes, E.S. *The Roman Index and its late proceedings. A Second Letter to the Most Rev. Archbishop Manning, etc., etc* (London, 1869).

Finlayson, W.F. *Report of the Trial and Preliminary Proceedings in the case of the Queen on the prosecution of G. Achilli v. Dr. Newman* (London, 1852).

Fitzsimons, J., ed. *Manning: Anglican and Catholic* (London, 1951).

Fothergill, B. *Nicholas Wiseman* (London, 1963).

Fowler, J. *Richard Waldo Sibthorp: A Biography, told chiefly in his own correspondence* (London, 1880).

Gaine, M. 'The Development of Official Roman Catholic Educational Policy in England and Wales' *Religious Education Drift or Decision.* Edited by P. Jebb (London, 1967).

George, H. *Progress and Poverty: an inquiry into the cause of industrial depressions, and of increase of want with increase of wealth. The Remedy* (London, 1883).

Gilley, S. 'English Catholic Charity and the Irish Poor in London' *Recusant History*, 11 (1972).

Gillow, J. *A Literary and Biographical History, or Bibliographical Dictionary of the English Catholics.* 5 vols (London, 1885-1903).

Gladstone, W.E. *Correspondence on Church and Religion.* Edited by D.C. Lathbury. 2 vols (London, 1910).
Rome and the newest fashions in religion (London, 1875).

Gorman, W.G. *Converts to Rome a biographical list of the more notable converts to the Catholic Church in the United Kingdom during the last sixty years* (London, 1910).

Gruber, J.W. *A Conscience in Conflict The Life of St George Jackson Mivart* (New York, 1960).

Guitton, J. *The Church and the Laity* (New York, 1964).

Guy, R.E. (ed) *The Synods in English: being the text of the four synods of Westminster, translated into English, and arranged under headings; with numerous documents and references* (Stratford on Avon, 1886).

Gwatkin, J.B. 'Döllinger, the Renoufs and Rome' *Tablet,* 222 (1968).

Gwynn, D.R. *A Hundred Years of Catholic Emancipation 1829-1929* (London, 1929).

Cardinal Wiseman (London, 1929).

Father Dominic Barberi (London, 1947).

Father Luigi Gentili and his mission, 1801-1848 (London, 1951).

Lord Shrewsbury, Pugin and the Catholic Revival (London, 1946).

The Second Spring 1818-1852 (London, 1942).

Haile, M. and Bonney, E. *Life and Letters of John Lingard 1771-1851* (London, n.d.)

Hales, E.E.Y. *Pio Nono A Study in European politics and religion in the nineteenth century* (London, 1956).

Revolution and Papacy 1769-1846 (London, 1960).

The Catholic Church in the Modern World (London, 1958).

Halévy, E. *A History of the English People in the Nineteenth Century.* 6 vols (London, 1949-1952).

Heaney, J.J. *The Modernist Crisis: von Hügel* (London, 1969).

Hemphill, B. *The Early Vicars Apostolic of England 1685-1750* (London, 1953).

Henriques, U. *Religious Toleration in England 1787-1833* (London, 1961).

Heyer, F. *The Catholic Church from 1648 to 1870* (London, 1969).

Hickey, J. *Urban Catholics Urban Catholicism in England and Wales from 1829 to the present day.* (London, 1967).

Hollis, C. *Newman and the Modern World* (London, 1967).

Holmes, J.D. 'Archbishops of Westminster and the Reunion Movement during the nineteenth century'. *One in Christ,* VIII (1972).

'Cardinal Manning's Letters to Father Lawless and Mrs King'. *Downside Review,* 92 (974).

'Cardinal Newman and the Affirmation Bill'. *Historical Magazine of the Protestant Episcopal Church,* XXVI (1967).

'Cardinal Raphael Merry del Val – an uncompromising Ultramontane: gleanings from his correspondence with England'. *Catholic Historical Review,* LX (1974).

'Church Government in England: Past, Present and Future'. *Clergy Review,* LX (1975).

'Conciliarists versus Papalians – the victory of Ultramontanism and the decline of Gallicanism in England illustrated by the controversy over the restoration of the hierarchy'. *Annuarium Historiae Conciliorum,* 3 (1974).

'English Catholicism from Wiseman to Bourne'. *Clergy Review,* LXI (1976).

Holmes, J.D. 'How Newman Blunted the Edge of Ultramontanism'. *Clergy Review*, LIII (1968).

'Liberal Catholicism and Newman's *Letter to the Duke of Norfolk'*. *Clergy Review*, LX (1975).

'Newman and Mivart — Two Attitudes to a Nineteenth century Problem'. *Clergy Review*, L (1965).

'Newman and the Kensington Scheme'. *Month*, 33 (1965).

'Newman's reaction to the definition of papal infallibility'. *Spode House Review occasional papers*, 3 (1976).

'Some English reactions to the publication of *Aeterni Patris'*. *Downside Review*, 93 (1975).

'Some Notes on Liberal Catholicism and Catholic Modernism'. *Irish Theological Quarterly*, XXXVIII (1971).

'Some unpublished passages from Cardinal Wiseman's correspondence'. *Downside Review*, 90 (1972).

'The Lisbon Letter-Books of Edmund Winstanley, 1819-1852'. *Clergy Review*, LX (1975).

'Von Hügel's Letter to Ryder on Biblical Inspiration and Inerrancy'. *Historical Magazine of the Protestant Episcopal Church*, XXXVIII (1969).

Howard, H. *Historical References, in support of the remarks on the erroneous opinions entertained respecting the Catholic Religion: and to prove that its principles are not adverse to civil liberty, and that religious liberty is a civil right* (Carlisle, 1827).

Howard, P. *Address to the Right Reverend the Archbishops and Bishops of England and Ireland* (London, 1801).

Hughes, J.J. *Absolutely Null and Utterly Void An account of the Papal Condemnation of Anglican Orders 1896* (London, 1968).

Hughes, P. *The Catholic Question 1688-1829* (London, 1929).

Husenbeth, F.C. *The Life of the Right Rev. John Milner, D.D.* (Dublin, 1862).

Inglis, K.S. *Churches and the Working Classes in Victorian England* (London, 1963).

Jackson, J.A. *The Irish in Britain* (London, 1963).

Keenan, S. *Controversial Catechism or Protestantism refuted and Catholicism established* (Edinburgh, 1854).

Kenny, T. *The Political Thought of John Henry Newman* (London, 1957).

Kiddle, M. *Caroline Chisholm* (Melbourne, 1950).

Leetham, C.R.H. *Luigi Gentili; a sower for the second spring* (London, 1965).

Leslie, S. *Henry Edward Manning His Life and Labours* (London, 1921).

'Some Birmingham Bygones. Illustrated from the Correspondence of Manning and Ullathorne'. *Dublin Review*. CLXVI (1920).

Leys, M.D.R. *Catholics in England 1559-1829 A Social History* (London, 1961).

Lilley, A.L. *Modernism A Record and Review* (London, 1908).

Lingard, J. *A Review of Certain Anti-Catholic Publications* (London, 1813).

Documents to ascertain the sentiments of British Catholics in former ages, respecting the Power of the Popes (London, 1812).

Observations on the Laws and Ordinances, which Exist in Foreign States (Dublin, 1817).

The History of England. 10 vols (London, 1855).

Linker, R.W. 'The English Roman Catholics and Emancipation: The Politics of Persuasion'. *Journal of Ecclesiastical History*, 27 (1976).

Loome, T.M. 'The Enigma of Baron Friedrich von Hügel – as Modernist'. *Downside Review*. 91 (1973);

Lucas, E. *The Life of Frederick Lucas, M.P.* 2 vols (London, 1887).

Mackenzie, E. *Memoirs of Mrs. Caroline Chisholm, with an account of her philanthropic labours, in India, Australia and England* (London, 1852).

MacDougall, H.A. *The Acton-Newman Relations The Dilemma of Christian Liberalism* (New York, 1962).

Machin, G.I.T. *The Catholic Question in English Politics* (Oxford, 1964).

'The No-Popery Movement in Britain in 1828-1829'. *Historical Journal*, VI (1963).

Manning, H.E. *England and Christendom* (London, 1867).

Essays on Religion and Literature. 3 series (London, 1865, 1867, 1874).

Miscellanies. 3 vols (London, 1877-1888).

Petri Privilegium Three Pastoral Letters to The Clergy of the Diocese (London, 1871).

Religion Viatoria (London, 1888).

Sermons on Ecclesiastical Subjects. 3 vols (London, 1870-1873).

The Eternal Priesthood (London, n.d.).

The Independence of the Holy See (London, 1877).

The Temporal Power of the Vicar of Jesus Christ (London, 1880).

The True Story of the Vatican Council (London, 1877).

Martindale, C.C. *Bernard Vaughan, S.J.* (London, 1923).

   The Life of Monsignor Robert Hugh Benson. 2 vols (London, 1917).

Massy, D. *Dark Deeds of the Papacy contrasted with Bright Lights of the Gospel; also, The Jesuits Unmasked, and Popery Unchangeable* (London, 1851).

Mathew, D. *Catholicism in England. The Portrait of a Minority: its culture and tradition* (London, 1955).

   Lord Acton and His times (London, 1968).

May, J.L. *Father Tyrrell and the Modernist Movement* (London, 1938).

Mayor, S. *The Churches and the Labour Movement* (London, 1967).

McCabe, J. *Twelve Years in a Monastery* (London, 1942).

McClelland, V.A. *Cardinal Manning His Public Life and Influence 1865-1892* (London, 1962).

   English Roman Catholics and Higher Education 1830-1903 (Oxford, 1973).

McCormack, A. *Cardinal Vaughan The Life of the Third Archbishop of Westminster. Founder of St Joseph's Missionary Society, Mill Hill* (London, 1966).

McElrath, D. *The Syllabus of Pius IX Some Reactions in England* (Louvain, 1964).

McGrath, F. *Newman's University Idea and Reality* (Dublin, 1951).

   The Consecration of Learning (Dublin, 1962).

Milburn, D. *A History of Ushaw College* (Ushaw, 1964).

   'Ushaw Papers XVI'. *Ushaw Magazine,* LXX-LXXII (1960-1962).

Mills, A. *The Life of Pope Pius IX* (London, 1877).

Mivart, St. G.J. 'The Conversion of England' *Dublin Review,* XII (1884).

Morley, J. *The Life of William Ewart Gladstone.* 3 vols (London, 1911).

Morris, J. *Catholic England in Modern Times* (London, 1892).

Moyes, J. *Aspects of Anglicanism or some comments on certain events in the 'nineties* (London, 1906).

Murphy, T. *The Position of the Catholic Church in England and Wales during the last two centuries Retrospect and Forecast* (London, 1892.

Nédoncelle, M. *Baron Friedrich von Hügel A Study of his life and thought* (London, 1936).

Newman, J.H. *Addresses to Cardinal Newman with His Replies etc. 1879-1882.* Edited by W.P. Neville (London, 1905).

   Apologia Pro Vita Sua. Edited by M.J. Svaglic (Oxford, 1967).

   Autobiographical Writings. Edited by H. Tristram (London, 1956).

   Certain Difficulties felt by Anglicans in Catholic Teaching. 2 vols. (London, 1901, 1907).

Newman, J.H. *Fifteen Sermons preached before the University of Oxford* (London, 1906).

My Campaign in Ireland, Part I (Aberdeen, 1896).

On Consulting the Faithful in Matters of Doctrine. Edited with an Introduction by John Coulson (London, 1961).

On the Inspiration of Scripture. Edited with an introduction by J. Derek Holmes and Robert Murray, S.J. (London, 1967).

Sermons preached on Various Occasions (London, 1900).

The Idea of a University defined and illustrated (London, 1905).

The Letters and Correspondence of John Henry Newman. Edited by Anne Mozley. 2 vols (London, 1891).

The Letters and Diaries of John Henry Newman. Edited by C.S. Dessain. 21 vols to date (London, 1961-1977).

The Present Position of Catholics in England (London, 1903). Also first edition, 1851.

The Via Media. 2 vols (London, 1901).

Norman, E.R. *Anti-Catholicism in Victorian England* (London, 1968).

The Catholic Church and Ireland in the Age of Rebellion 1859-1873 (London, 1965).

The Catholic Church and Irish Politics in the Eighteen Sixties (Dundalk, 1965).

The Conscience of the State in North America (Cambridge, 1968).

Oliver, G. *Collections, illustrating the History of the Catholic Religion in the counties of Cornwall, Devon, Dorset, Somerset, Wilts., and Gloucester* (London, 1857).

O'Meara, K. ['Grace Ramsay'] *Thomas Grant: First Bishop of Southwark* (London, 1874).

Ornsby, R. *Memoirs of James Robert Hope-Scott of Abbotsford, D.C.L., Q.C.* 2 vols (London, 1884).

Pius, Fr. *Life of Father Ignatius of St Paul. (The Hon. & Rev. George Spencer).* (Dublin, 1866).

Pond, K. 'Letters from Newman and others to Sir Peter Le Page Renouf'. *Dublin Review,* 229 (1955).

Pugin, A.W. *Church and State* (London, 1875).

Purcell, E.S. *Life of Cardinal Manning Archbishop of Westminster* 2 vols (London, 1896).

Life and Letters of Ambrose Phillipps de Lisle 2 vols (London, 1900).

Quinlan, J. *The People's History of Catholic Emancipation* (London, 1929).

Ratté, J. *Three Modernists Alfred Loisy George Tyrrell William L. Sullivan* (London, 1968).

Reilly, S.M.P. *Aubrey de Vere: Victorian Observer* (Dublin, 1956).

Renouf, P. Le Page. *The Condemnation of Pope Honorius* (London, 1868).

Reynolds, E.E. *Three Cardinals: Newman – Wiseman – Manning* (London, 1958).

Riethmüller, C.J. *Frederick Lucas. A Biography* (London, 1862).

Roe, W.G. *Lamennais and England The Reception of Lamennais's Religious Ideas in England in the Nineteenth Century* (Oxford, 1966).

Roskell, M.F. *Memoirs of Francis Kerril Amherst, D.D. Lord Bishop of Northampton* (London, 1903).

Rowlands, M. 'The Staffordshire Clergy, 1688-1803'. *Recusant History*, 9 (1968)

Ryder, H.I.D. *A Letter to William George Ward, Esq., D.Ph., on His Theory of Infallible Instruction* (London, 1868).

Essays (London, 1911).

Idealism in Theology a Review of Dr. Ward's Scheme of Dogmatic Authority (London, 1867).

Postscriptum to Letter to W.G. Ward, Esq., D.Ph. (London, 1868).

The Mosaic Cosmogony. A case of conscience (Oscott, 1874).

Schiefen, R.J. 'Some Aspects of the Controversy between Cardinal Wiseman and the Westminster Chapter'. *Journal of Ecclesiastical History* 21 (1970).

'The English Catholic Reaction to the Tractarian Movement'. *Canadian Catholic Historical Association* (1974).

'The First Provincial Synod of Westminster (1852)'. *Annuarium Historiae Conciliorum*, 3 (1971-1972).

Schoenl, W.J. 'George Tyrrell and the English Liberal Catholic Crisis, 1900-1901'. *Downside Review*, 92 (1974).

Sheppard, L.C. *Lacordaire: A Biographical Essay* (London, 1964).

Smith, S. ['Peter Plymley'] *Letters on the Subject of the Catholics, to my brother Abraham, who lives in the country.* (London, 1807-1808).

Snead-Cox, J.G. *The Life of Cardinal Vaughan.* 2 vols. (London, 1910).

Spencer, P. *Politics of Belief in Nineteenth-Century France* (London, 1954).

St. John E. *Manning's Work for Children A Second Chapter in Catholic Emancipation* (London, 1929).

Strachey, L. *Five Victorians* (London, 1942).

Trappes-Lomax, M. *Pugin A Mediaeval Victorian* (London, 1932).

Trevor, M. *Prophets and Guardians Renewal and Tradition in the Church* (London, 1969).

The Arnolds Thomas Arnold and His Family (New York, 1973).

Newman Light in Winter (London, 1962).

Newman The Pillar of the Cloud (London, 1962).

Tyrrell, G. *Autobiography and Life of George Tyrrell.* Arranged, with supplements, by M.D. Petre. 2 vols (London, 1912).

The Faith of Millions: First Series (London, 1901).

Ullathorne, W.B. *From Cabin-boy to Archbishop The Autobiography of Archbishop Ullathorne* (London, 1941).

Letters of Archbishop Ullathorne (London, 1892)

The Autobiography of Archbishop Ullathorne with selections from his letters (London, 1891).

Vaughan, H. *Letters of Herbert Cardinal Vaughan to Lady Herbert of Lea 1867 to 1903.* Edited by Shane Leslie (London, 1942).

The Year of Preparation for the Vatican Council. Including the Original and English of the Encyclical and Syllabus, and of the Papal Documents Connected with its Convocation (London, 1869).

Vidler, A.R. *A Century of Social Catholicism: 1820-1920* (London, 1964).

A Variety of Catholic Modernists (Cambridge, 1970).

Prophecy and Papacy: A Study of Lamennais, the Church and the Revolution (London, 1954).

The Church in an Age of Revolution (London, 1961).

The Modernist Movement in the Roman Church: Its origins and outcome (Cambridge, 1934).

Wadham, J. *The Case of Cornelia Connelly* (London, 1958).

Ward, B. *History of St. Edmund's College Old Hall,* (London, 1893).

The Dawn of the Catholic Revival in England, 1781-1803. 2 vols (London, 1909).

The Eve of Catholic Emancipation: Being the history of the English Catholics during the first thirty years of the nineteenth century. 3 vols (London, 1911-1912).

The Sequel to Catholic Emancipation The Story of the English Catholics continued down to the reestablishment of their hierarchy in 1850. 2 vols (London, 1915).

Ward, M. *The Wilfrid Wards and the transition.* 2 vols (London, 1934, 1938).

Young Mr Newman (London, 1952).

Ward, W. *Men and Matters* (London, 1914).

Problems and Persons (London, 1903).

Ward, W. *The Life and Times of Cardinal Wiseman.* 2 vols. (London, 1900).

The Life of John Henry Cardinal Newman. 2 vols (London, 1912).

William George Ward and the Catholic Revival (London, 1893).

William George Ward and the Oxford Movement (London, 1890).

Witnesses to the Unseen and other essays (London, 1893).

Ward, W.G. *A Brief Summary of the Recent Controversy on Infallibility: being a Reply to Rev. Father Ryder on his Postscript* (London, 1868).

A Letter to Rev. Father Ryder on his recent Pamphlet (London, 1867).

A Second Letter to the Rev. Father Ryder (London, 1868).

The Authority of Doctrinal Decisions (London, 1866).

Watkin, E.I. *Roman Catholicism in England from the Reformation to/ 1950* (London, 1957).

Wiseman, N. *A Letter on Catholic Unity, addressed to the Right Hon. The Earl of Shrewsbury* (London, 1841).

An Appeal to the reason and good felling of the English People on the subject of the Catholic Hierarchy (London, 1850).

Dr Achilli. Authentic 'Brief Sketch of the Life of Dr Giacinto Achilli', containing a Confutation of the Mis-statements of former narratives. Extracted from the Dublin Review, No. LVI, with additions and corrections (London, n.d.).

Lectures on the Principal Doctrines and Practices of the Catholic Church (London, 1888).

'Letters of Cardinal Wiseman: with a Commentary by Cardinal Gasquet'. *Dublin Review,* CLXIV (1919).

'More Letters of Wiseman and Manning', *Dublin Review,* CLXXII (1923).

Recollections of the last four Popes and of Rome in their times (London, n.d.).

Twelve Lectures on the connexion between Science and Revealed Religion. 2 vols (London, 1849).

'Unpublished Letters of Cardinal Wiseman to Dr. Manning'. *Dublin Review,* CLXIX (1921).

Woodham-Smith, C. *Florence Nightingale* (London, 1952).

Woodward, E.L. *The Age of Reform 1815-1870* (Oxford, 1954).

Wranger, T. 'Emergence of John T. Keane as a Liberal Catholic and Americanist (1878-1887)' *American Ecclesiastical Review.* 166 (1972).

Index

A

Abraham   118
Achilli, G.   44, 82, 88
Acton, Lord J.E.D.   65, 113-16,
    120-3, 125-6, 131-2, 139,
    141, 148-9, 151, 155,
    220-1, 224-5, 243, 250
    255, 258
Addington, R.   105, 150, 258
Altholz, J.L.   149-51, 193, 258
Ambrose, St   67
Amherst, W.J.   51, 258
Andrews, W.E.   39
Antonelli, Cardinal G.   87, 141
Arch, J.   176
Arnold, M.   123
Arnold, T.   57
Arnstein, W.L.   196, 258
Aspinwall, B.   152, 258
Augustine, St   64-5, 236
Augustine of Canterbury, St   126
Aveling, J.C.H.   50, 259

B

Bagnall,   52
Bagshawe, Bishop E.G.   174-5,
    182-3, 196, 240-1
Bailly, L.   170
Baines, Bishop P.A.   62-3, 66,
    104
Barber, B.   159
Barmann, L.F.   245, 246, 257, 259

Barnabo, Cardinal A.   61, 114-5,
    131, 156
Barnardo, T.J.   165, 167
Barry, W.F.   223
Bartolo, S. di   149
Beaumont, Lord   79
Beck, Archbishop G.A.   107-8,
    193, 242, 259
Bedoyère, M. de la   244-5, 259
Benson, Archbishop E.W. of
    Canterbury   218-9
Berington, J.   49, 259
Binning, Lord   34
Bishop, E.   221
Blehl, V.F.   151, 259
Blount, E.   28, 30
Blundell, F.O.   150, 259
Boardman, B.M.   257, 259
Bolster, E.   195, 259
Bonney, E.   52, 105-6, 262
Booth, J.   29
Borromeo, St Charles   71
Bossy, J.   50, 193, 259
Bottalla, P.   148, 259
Bowyer, Sir G.   81
Bradlaugh, C.   186-9
Bramston, Bishop J.Y.   39
Braye, Lord   225, 257
Briggs, Bishop J.   71, 104-5,
    161, 205
Briggs, A.   51, 259
Brown, Bishop J. of Shrewsbury   90
Brown, Bishop T.J. of Newport
    83, 100, 106, 114, 137,
    144, 171, 230

Brownlow, Bishop W.R. 223
Bruce, H.A. 169
Burke, Edmund 19
Burke, Revd. T. 229
Burke, T. 150, 193-5, 242, 259
Butler, Charles 29
Butler, Cuthbert 51, 97-8, 100, 106-8, 150-3, 190, 193, 195-7, 242-4, 252, 254, 257, 260

C

Canterbury, Archbishop of 23, 62, 218-9.
Capecelatro, Cardinal 184
Capel, T.J. 231-2
Capes, J.M. 52, 68, 112-3, 260
Carson, W.R. 223, 260
Casartelli, Bishop L.C. 124, 151
Cavour, C. di 124
Chadwick, Bishop J. 142, 144
Chadwick, W.O. 51, 106, 108, 193, 197, 231, 242, 244-5 257, 260
Challoner, Bishop R. 49, 252
Chapman, R. 105, 260
Chesson, F.W. 196
Chichester, Bishop of 76
Chisholme Anstey, T. 194
Clarendon, Lord 141
Clarke, R.F. 236
Clifford, Bishop W.J. 127, 137, 143-4, 155, 171, 203-4, 226, 230, 234
Coffin, Bishop R.A. 126, 175
Coleridge, H.J. 126, 151
Conlon, M. 52, 242, 260
Connelly, C. 83

Connelly, P. 83
Connolly, F.X. 151, 259
Constantinople, Patriarch of 132
Cornthwaite, Bishop R. 90, 142 144, 171
Cox, E. 171
Cross, Sir R. 210
Cullen, Cardinal P. 180-1, 185 253
Cumberland, Duke of 42
Cwiekowski, F.J. 16, 106-7, 152-3, 193, 260

D

Davis, Jefferson 217
de Augustinis, A.M. 221
de Lisle, A. Phillipps 56, 62, 69, 71, 73, 99, 106
de Llaveneras, C. 221
de Montfort, St L.G. 199
de Mun, A. 184
de Sales, St F. 146
de Vere, A. 126, 151
Derby, Lord 82
Dessain, C.S. 15, 105, 150, 152-3, 193, 244, 260
Digby, K.H. 56, 64
Disraeli, B. 82, 106, 180
Doherty, J. 179
Döllinger, J.J.I. 113, 121, 124-5, 132, 139, 146-7, 170, 192, 227, 255, 260
Douglass, Bishop J. 65
Dublin Archbishop of 219
Duchesne, L. 219, 221
Duggan, J. 223
Dupanloup, Bishop F.A.P. 124, 128-9, 132, 137, 140, 150, 260

E

Edward VII   185, 220-1, 248
Eldon, Lord   29
Errington, Archbishop G.   74,
   83, 91-6, 98, 100, 102,
   143-4, 155, 226
Estcourt, E.E.   232, 245

F

Faber, F.W.   71, 94, 100, 112,
   117-8, 150, 260-1
Fawkes, G.   76
Femiano, S.D.   149-50, 261
Fessler, Bishop J.   144
Ffoulkes, E.S.   68, 261
Figgis, J.N.   153, 258
Finlayson, W.F.   106, 261
Fitzgerald, W.V.   38
Fitzsimons, J.   194-6, 242, 261
Fleming, D.   221-3
Forster, W.E.   208
Fothergill, B.   103-4, 106-8,
   151, 193, 197, 261
Fowler, J.   105, 261
Fox, C.J.   19
Franzelin, Cardinal J.B.   236-7
Froude, R.H.   55

G

Gaine, M.   242, 261
Galileo, 235
Garibaldi, G.   120
Gasparri, P.   221
Gasquet, Cardinal F.A.   104,
   201, 221-3, 234, 258
Gentili, L.   49, 73, 84

George, H.   186, 261
George III   27, 33
George IV   25, 33, 36-9
Gibbons, Cardinal J.   184, 186
Gilley, S.   193, 261
Gillow, J.   170
Gladstone, W.E.   13, 16, 67,
   129, 139, 141, 147-9,
   180-1, 185, 188, 191, 253,
   261
Gore, Bishop C.   245
Gorham, G.C.   74
Goss, Bishop A.   14, 100, 142-4,
   164
Grant, Bishop T.   61, 88, 92, 98
   100-2, 104, 107, 144, 155,
   175, 252, 257
Gregory, St   64
Gregory VII   78
Gregory XVI   59-61, 63
Grey, Earl   180
Griffiths, Bishop T.   52, 60, 62-3
   65, 71, 104
Gruber, J.W.   245, 261
Guy, R.E.   242, 261
Gwatkin, J.B.   15, 104, 152-3,
   243, 261
Gwynn, D.R.   51, 103, 105, 194,
   262

H

Haile, M.   52, 105-6, 262
Hales, E.E.Y.   151, 153, 262
Halifax, Lord   218-9, 222-3, 239,
   243
Hardwicke, Lord   41
Hefele, Bishop K.J.   149
Hemphill, B.   194, 262
Henriques, U.   50-1, 262

Henry VIII   84
Heyer, F.   50, 262
Hickey, J.   194-5, 262
Himmelfarb, G.   151, 258
Holland, J.C.   149, 193, 258
Howard, H.   28, 50
Howard, P.   20, 50, 263
Huddleston family   160
    Huddleston, E.   28
    Huddleston, R.   28
Hughes, J.J.   243, 263
Hummelauer, F. von   236
Huskisson, W.   37
Huxley, T.H.   185

I

Inglis, K.S.   193-6, 263
Innocent III   78
Ivers, H.   105

J

Jackson, J.A.   193-5, 263
Januarius, St   119
Jerome, St   185

K

Keane, Bishop J.J.   186
Kelly, E.   151
Kennedy, J.F.   44
Kenyon, A.   41
Kenyon, Lord   41
Kerry, Bishop of   136
Ketteler, Bishop W.E. von   184
King, H.   196

Kingsley, C.   125
Kinnaird, Lord   167

L

Lacordaire, J.B.H.   55, 57, 98
Lamennais, H.F.R. de   55, 90
Lamy, T.J.   124
Lathbury, D.C.   16, 195, 261
Laurence, R.V.   153, 258
Lawless, W.   168, 194, 242
Leeds, Duchess of   120
Leetham, C.R.H.   106, 263
Lemire, J.   184
Leo XII   55
Leo XIII   184, 191, 200, 219,
    221-2, 225, 233-4, 250
Leslie, S.   108, 150, 152-3,
    193-7, 241-4, 264, 268
Lewis, D.   57, 170
Lilley, A.L.   238, 264
Lingard, J.   25, 29, 49-50, 72,
    84, 89-90, 107, 136, 264
Linker, R.W.   50, 264
Little, S.H.   255
Liverpool, Lord   36
Llandaff, Lord   250
Loisy, A.F.   234-5
London, Bishop of   76, 177
Loome, T.M.   257, 264
Lucas, F.   66, 160, 264

M

MacColl, M.   196
MacDonnell, E.   103
MacDougall, H.A.   150-3, 264
Machin, G.I.T.   50-1, 264
Mahomet   118

Manning, Cardinal H.E. 13-4, 16, 73-4, 78, 81, 91-100, 102, 107-8, 112, 114, 117, 121-2, 126-8, 130-1, 133-7, 139-45, 148-53, *chapter IV passim*, 199-201, 203-4, 208, 210-11, 213, 215-7, 224-7, 229-34, 241-4, 251-3, 264-5
Martin, E.R. 227, 229
Massy, D. 51, 265
Mathew, Archbishop D. 150, 152, 194, 240, 246, 265
Mathew, Fr 168
Mawhood, J. 28
Max Müller, F. 123
Mazzella, Cardinal C. 221-2
McCabe, J. 44, 265
McClelland, V.A. 106, 194-6, 229-30, 241-5, 265
McCormack, A. 152, 195, 242-3, 265
McElrath, D. 149, 151-3, 193, 265
Mermillod, Cardinal G. 184
Merry del Val, Cardinal R. 220-3, 238, 243, 245-6, 254, 257
Meyer, R. 184
Milburn, D. 107, 242, 244, 265
Mildmay, Sir H. 21
Millington, V.A. 120
Milner, Bishop J. 24
Mivart, St G.J. 220, 231, 235-8, 244-5, 249, 257, 265
Möhler, J.A. 57
'Monk, M.' 44
Monsell, W. 129, 137, 265
Montalembert, Comte C.F.R, de 55, 98-9, 113, 124, 128, 134-5, 137, 155

Moran, Archbishop P. 184
Morel, J.J. 21
Morris, J. 51, 194, 242, 265
Mostyn, Bishop F.G. 52, 61
Moyes, J. 221-23, 243, 265
Mozley, A. 104, 266
Mozley, T. 57, 139
Murphy, T. 108, 242, 249, 257, 265

N

Nardi, F. 139
Naville, E. 104
Nédoncelle, M. 257, 265
Neve, F. 171, 194, 229
Neville, W.P. 197, 265
New Orleans, Bishop of 83
Newsham, C. 67, 79, 104-7, 202
Newman, Cardinal J.H. 14, 16, 46, 50-1, 55, 65-6, 68-9, 74, 82-4, 87, 98-100, 102, 104-5, *Chapter III passim*, 155, 170, 187-92, 196-7, 215, 224-5, 227, 229-31, 239, 244-5, 251-2, 254-6, 265-6
Nightingale, F. 176
Norfolk, 14th Duke of 21, 29, 31, 42, 79
Norfolk, 15th Duke of 148, 190-1, 219, 223, 238, 250
Norman, E.R. 51, 181, 195, 257,264
Northcote, J. Spencer 61, 104, 225
Northcote, Sir S. 188
Nugent, J. 179

O

O'Brien, B. 179
O'Callaghan, H. 171

Occam, William of   256
O'Connell, D.   27-8, 30-1, 36, 38, 40, 68-9, 178
O'Connor, F.   179
Oliver, G.   50, 92, 107, 266
O'Meara, K.   107, 266
O'Reilly, Bishop B.   179
Owen, Sir R.   55
Oxenham, H.N.   115, 227
Oxford, Bishop of   62, 76

P

Parnell, C.S.   179, 181-2
Patterson, J. Laird   106-8, 150, 171
Peel, Sir R.   37-9, 42
Peter, St   71, 89, 96, 133, 140, 199, 222, 239,
Petre, Lord   29, 31, 190
Philomena, St   67
Pitt, W.   27
Pius VII   27
Pius VIII   55
Pius IX   73-4, 76, 81-2, 90, 92, 94-7, 105, 107, 111, 115-20, 124-5, 128-30, 132, 134, 137, 140, 142-3, 146, 149, 155, 157, 160, 170, 185, 216, 227, 229-30, 253
Pius X   254
Pole, Cardinal R.   87
Portal, E.F.   218-9, 221-2
Poynter, Bishop W.   28, 50, 160
Pugin, A.W.   56, 69-70, 266
Purcell, E.S.   52, 100, 104-8, 150-3, 193-6, 241-4, 266
Pusey, E.B.   66, 127

R

Rampolla del Tindoro, Cardinal M.   219
Ratisbon, Bishop Senestrey of   140
Ratté, J.   245-6, 257, 264
Redmond, J.   182
Renouf, P. le Page   64-5, 137, 139, 142, 146, 224-5, 267
Riddell, Bishop W.   60, 104, 161
Ripon, Lord   190, 248
Rochester, Bishop of   21
Rock, D.   85-6
Roe, W.G.   107, 265
Rudini, O.   238
Russell, Lord J.   37, 77, 106
Russell, O.   129
Ryder, H.I.D.   130-1, 144-5, 170, 234-5, 245, 256, 267
Rymer, F.   95-6, 171-2, 194

S

Salisbury, Lord   211
Sandwich, Lord   29
San Francisco, Archbishop of   216
Scannell, T.B.   221
Schiefen, R.J.   104-5, 267
Seddon, T.   165, 167
Sheil, R.L.   30
Shrewsbury, Earl of   21, 47, 51, 60, 62-3, 67, 104-6, 159, 193
Sibthorp, R.W.   68
Simpson, R.   113-6, 121, 123, 125, 129
Smith, Al.   44

Smith, J. 103
Smith, S. 26, 34, 265
Smith, Bishop T. 24, 50
Snead-Cox, J.G. 107-8, 151-2, 181, 193-5, 201, 220, 240-6, 267
Spencer, G.I. 56, 62, 64
Spencer, P. 152, 267
Steed, F. 238
Stephenson, G. 22
Stephenson, R. 22
St John, A. 115
St John, E. 194, 267
Stourton, Lord 27
Strachey, L. 195, 267
Sussex, Duke of 160
Svaglic, M.J. 104, 151, 265
Sweeney, G.D. 15, 174, 195, 246

T

Talbot, G. 67, 73-4, 90, 92, 94-100, 102, 106-8, 114-5, 118-9, 122, 126-7, 129, 150, 155, 158, 171, 194, 229, 244
Teebay, C. 151
Temple, Lord 29
Tennyson, Lord 13
Thompson, F. 254-5
Thompson, J. 126, 151, 197
Tierney, M.A. 75, 79, 86, 89-90, 106-7,
Tillett, B. 179
Toledo, Archbishop of 219
Toomey, J. 179
Trappes-Lomax, M. 105, 267
Trevor, M. 197, 244, 268
Tristram, H. 151, 265

Turner, Bishop W. 48, 144, 172, 201
Tyrrell, G. 220, 223, 236-7, 239, 254-5, 268

U

Ullathorne, Archbishop W.B. 48, 51, 59, 73-5, 87, 97, 100-4 107, 115, 127, 139, 141, 143-4, 148, 155, 170-1, 180, 190-1, 194, 203-4, 208, 229-30, 232, 244-5, 252, 268

V

Vaughan, B. 248
Vaughan, Cardinal H.A. 14, 96-7, 99-100, 124, 126, 132-7, 152, 155-6, 167, 172-3, 175, 181-2, 184, 191-2, 197, *Chapter V passim*, 253, 255, 268
Vaughan, Bishop W. 101, 144
Vavasour, Sir. E. 31
Veuillot, L. 113, 129
Victoria, Queen 76-7, 250
von Hügel, A. 233-4
Von Hügel, Baron F. 223-4, 237, 239, 245, 254-6

W

Walker, J. 107, 136
Walsh, Archbishop of Dublin 181
Walsh, Bishop T. 47, 51, 60-1, 63-4, 66-7, 71, 104-5, 193

Ward, B.   41, 50-1, 69, 87,
    103-7, 131, 194, 268
Ward, M.   152, 157, 193, 196,
    242-3, 246, 257, 268
Ward, W.   89, 99, 102-8, 116,
    124, 131, 150-2, 155, 193,
    197, 220, 231-2, 237, 239,
    243-5, 268-9
Ward, W.G.   92-3, 100, 112, 116,
    121, 123, 126-7, 129-31,
    133-6, 144-7, 149, 155-6
    170-1, 190, 224, 232, 269
Weathers, W.   194
Weld, E.   29
Wellington, Lord   37-9, 41-2, 103
Whitty, M.J.   120

Winchilsea, Earl of   41, 76
Winstanley, E.   64, 66, 71, 79,
    104-6
Wiseman, Cardinal N.P.   14, 48,
    50-2, *Chapter II passim*,
    112, 114-6, 120-1, 123-4,
    155-7, 162, 171, 175, 194,
    201, 216, 226, 241, 252,
    269
Woodham-Smith, C.   195, 269
Woodruff, D.   151, 258
Wrangler, T.   196, 269

Y

York, Archbishop of   76